BIRTH SCHOOL METALLICA DEATH, 1983–1991

Paul Brannigan and Ian Winwood are two of the UK's foremost music writers. A former *Kerrang!* editor, Brannigan is the author of the *Sunday Times* Bestseller *This Is A Call: The Life And Times Of Dave Grohl* while Winwood has written for *Rolling Stone*, the *Guardian*, *Mojo*, *Kerrang!*, *NME* and the BBC.

Further praise for *Birth School Metallica Death, 1983–1991*:

'The Metallica story has been told many times before, but seldom as entertainingly or as smartly as this . . . Ian Winwood and Paul Brannigan's vivid prose makes this well-worn saga seem somehow fresh and fascinating again. The second volume promises to be an absolute belter.' *Metal Hammer*

'A well-researched look at everything from frontman James Hetfield's initial crippling shyness to Lars Ulrich's bolshie arrogance and all points in between. Brannigan and Winwood are seasoned rock journalists and have interviewed the band dozens of times over the years, as well as just about everyone else who's ever had dealings with them, and what emerges is a refreshingly honest look at the ups and downs of life in the juggernaut of a heavy metal band.' Doug Johnstone, *Big Issue*

'Paul Brannigan and Ian Winwood have worked closely with the band over the years, and it shows, both in the access they've gained, the anecdotes they witnessed first-hand and the warmth they afford their subjects. No stone is left unturned as the band's insane life is metic⋯ ⋯vo will pick up the ⋯ ⋯evidence, it'll be v⋯

'Brannigan and Winwood have done a fine job of chronicling the golden age – in studio, on stage and among the crowd – taking us up to 1991 and eve of the *Black Album*'s release. Even for those who know the story inside out, it's a pacy and punchy read, going from chapter to chapter at roughly the same speed as the riff from *Battery* and with plenty of nuggets along the way.' *RTE 10* online

'Though by no means authorised, it's hard to imagine the tale of San Francisco metal behemoths Metallica being told any more authoritatively than it is here . . . Given that the authors rarely flinch from the group's shortcomings, the second volume . . . should make for similarly gripping reading.' Stevie Chick, *Mojo*

'It is big, and impressive and, like its subject, irresistible.' Robert Collins, *Sunday Times*

'The first part of the band's story is so definitive that, when it comes to the topic of the band's early days, nothing else matters.' James Hickie, *Kerrang!*

BIRTH

†

SCHOOL

†

METALLICA

†

DEATH

1983–1991

PAUL BRANNIGAN & IAN WINWOOD

FABER & FABER

First published in Great Britain in 2013
by Faber and Faber Limited
Bloomsbury House
74–77 Great Russell Street
London WC1B 3DA

This paperback edition first published in 2014

Typeset by Palindrome
Printed in the UK by CPI Group (UK) Ltd, Croydon, CR0 4YY

A CIP record for this book
is available from the British Library

ISBN 978–0–571–29415–2

CONTENTS

THE ECSTASY OF GOLD

On June 5, 1993, Metallica drew a crowd of 60,000 rock fans to Milton Keynes Bowl for their first open-air headline show in the United Kingdom. While this deliberately recalled such grand occasions as Led Zeppelin's historic two-night stand at Knebworth House in the summer of 1979, the quartet's appearance at the verdant man-made arena on that overcast June evening represented a very singular triumph, a triumph of determination and talent over compromise and equivocation. This was a group that had begun their journey not so much on a road less travelled as on a thoroughfare entirely of their own making. In the nine years that had elapsed since the San Franciscan band first played live on British soil, an appearance before just four hundred people at the Marquee club in central London, they had plotted their course to the stages of the world's largest venues with a ferocity of purpose that was always determined, and sometimes plain perverse. For the longest time, Metallica had resisted playing the standard music industry games, yet despite this – actually, *because* of this – the group had acquired millions of fans.

With their 1983 debut album, *Kill 'Em All*, Metallica staked their claim to be the fastest, heaviest metal band on the planet. Three years later their pivotal *Master of Puppets* album sold one million copies worldwide without a single, a promotional video or any support from mainstream radio or television, establishing the Bay Area quartet as the most compelling band of that decade. With the 1991 release of their self-titled fifth album – universally known as 'The Black Album' – this most uncompromising and defiantly independent collective became international superstars.

But even as Metallica shifted the tectonic plates upon which mainstream music stood, their audience affixed themselves to the group with a devotion that was remarkable even by the standards of modern metal. In acknowledgement of this fiercely obsessive fan-base, the band chose the occasion of their European tour in summer 1993 to deliver a most brazen statement. This they issued on the back of a black T-shirt displayed on boards erected behind and above the heads of the merchandise sellers exchanging soft clothing for hard currency at 'The Bowl' on June 5. On its front the faces of the four members of the visiting band were featured, each man's forearms positioned in a manner that resembled the crossbones on the flag of a pirate ship. It was, though, the words emblazoned on the reverse side of this garment that truly kidnapped the imagination:

'Birth. School. Metallica. Death.'

One might drive oneself mad attempting to replace the third of this quartet of words with the name of a different band. The field occupied by those that might make the claim that life can be distilled down to just four components, only one of which is nominated by choice, is vanishingly small. The Clash, perhaps; Nirvana, probably; the Grateful Dead, certainly. The difference is, of course, that each of these groups exists only in the past, their reputation burnished and buffed by the soft touch of nostalgia. But Metallica made this claim not only in the present tense but at the very first point at which they would not appear foolish. In doing so, the band exalted their own position without seeming to demean that of their audience. Rather than appearing arrogant, Metallica were simply being emphatic. It was a statement of chutzpah and brio entirely typical of the band. Two decades on, this is a group still equipped to make such a claim. And this is the story of their most extraordinary union.

†

What a long strange trip it has been. Formed in Los Angeles in 1981 by James Hetfield and Lars Ulrich, and fuelled by the influence of Motörhead, the New Wave of British Heavy Metal (NWOBHM) and nihilistic American punk rock, Metallica began life as front-runners of the nascent American thrash metal scene, an underground community powered by fanzines, the trading of badly dubbed cassette tapes and a peer-to-peer buzz gradually amplified from a whisper to a scream. But in the three decades that have elapsed since the release of their debut album, the band have effectively developed into two separate groups. One of these is a crowd-pleasing operation that rolls into motion each summer as the quartet convene in foreign fields and stadia to play songs – most of which are more than twenty years old – for tens of thousands of people in exchange for appearance fees in excess of a million pounds each night. It would be wrong, however, to suggest that these days Metallica spends its entire time in the pasture. Because for the 'other' Metallica, a group that constantly seeks to stand in opposition to the established order, the fear of becoming creatively irrelevant is a demon that never sleeps. This anxiety has led the quartet to act with a sense of creative and artistic derring-do the fearlessness of which borders on the reckless, as evidenced by their collaboration with Lou Reed on 2011's brutally uncommercial *Lulu* album.

Occasionally Metallica as brand and Metallica as band coalesce as one. This was the case on the weekend of June 23 and 24, 2012, when the group staged the inaugural Orion Music + More event, their own bespoke, self-curated music festival. The gathering was staged at Bader Field, an abandoned airstrip in Atlantic City, New Jersey, and featured appearances from groups as diverse as Modest Mouse, the Arctic Monkeys, Best Coast, Roky Erickson and Fucked Up. The event also featured installations such as a showcase of James Hetfield's classic cars and a display of guitarist Kirk Hammett's collection of vintage horror movie memorabilia.

Elsewhere a talk was given by music journalist Brian Lew, one of the authors of *Murder in the Front Row*, a fabulous coffee-table book chronicling the Bay Area thrash metal scene that first gave Metallica life. Indeed such was the scope of the lovingly compiled festival that Lars Ulrich was even moved to joke that Orion Music + More would feature Metallica toilet paper, with each patron afforded the choice of which band member's face to despoil.

While at pains to point out that Orion was emphatically *not* a 'metal' festival – 'Because we're doing it, it gets branded as a particular thing,' Lars Ulrich noted. 'If Radiohead does it, it's cool. If we do it, it's not.' – inevitably and fittingly, Metallica themselves headlined their own event. On the first of the two evenings, the group performed their 1984 album *Ride the Lightning* in its entirety for the first time, while night two saw 'The Black Album' profiled in full. As has been their tradition, the quartet called time on their set both evenings with 'Seek & Destroy', one of the highlights on their debut album. Introducing the song on June 24, James Hetfield addressed the mass of people gathered in the darkness before him at Bader Field.

'We've had the spotlights on us all night,' he said. '[Now] we want to turn it on the fifth member of Metallica . . . [you] the Metallica family.'

Hetfield's belief, some might say obsession, that Metallica and their audience together comprise a family is strong and sincere. For their part the feeling of the people that have provided his band with wealth beyond their dreams and sometimes pressures beyond their nightmares is mutual. But while this union may be familial, it is not democratic. Metallica's first responsibility has always been to please themselves, it is just that in doing so they have managed to delight millions of people.

†

This book is the first of a two-volume biography. It spans the period from the childhoods of James Hetfield and Lars Ulrich to the point at which Metallica stood ready to secure the title deeds to the planet with the release of 'The Black Album'. For the authors it has been an excursion into the world of a 'family' that at times resembles a mafia organisation, occasionally a cult, and often the coolest gang in the world. In pursuit of the story we have attempted to retrace the journey made by our subjects. These endeavours have taken us from the front door of the erstwhile 'Metallica Mansion', the bungalow in which James Hetfield and Lars Ulrich roomed together upon relocating to San Francisco's Bay Area, to the building that once housed Sweet Silence Studios in Copenhagen, where both *Ride the Lightning* and *Master of Puppets* were recorded, to stage left at various stops on the quartet's most recent world tour. Combined with this are insights gained from interviewing Metallica on scores of occasions. As teenage rock fans we stood in the front rows of Metallica concerts in the United Kingdom and United States; as working journalists we have flown on the band's private jet and sat in dressing rooms from Cowboys Stadium in Dallas to the BBC Television Centre in London's White City. We have seen the band perform with an orchestra in Berlin and on the back of a lorry, in front of an audience of just two people, in Istanbul. Theirs is a remarkable story, one embracing community, self-belief, the pursuit of dreams and the continued dominance of a musical form they have made entirely their own. Volume two of *Birth School Metallica Death*, set for publication in the autumn of 2014, will document the band's journey into a future as yet unwritten, their status as the Led Zeppelin of their generation assured. No rock band will ever again come to equal their success.

The game's over: Metallica won.

1 – NO LIFE 'TIL LEATHER

On the bathroom wall of Metallica's headquarters in San Rafael, California, there can be seen a photograph of the band as they appeared in 1982. Shot in the dressing room of one of the insalubrious San Francisco nightclubs where they served their apprenticeship, it captures four young men in the aftermath of a live show, stripped to the waist and bristling with attitude as they leer into the camera lens. Drenched with sweat, adrenaline and testosterone, it is a snapshot of teenage machismo so studied and gauche as to appear almost charming.

Today the image holds bitter-sweet memories for James Hetfield. When Metallica's front man appraises the image, he can see beyond his band's two-dimensional posturing and recall, with genuine warmth, a more innocent time, a time of youthful excitement, camaraderie and shared dreams. But, inevitably, his eyes are drawn to the centre of the frame, to the acne-scarred face of a sad, damaged teenager, ill at ease with the world and furiously unhappy with his place within it. And blacker memories are quick to surface, recollections of betrayal, abandonment and loss. It was, says Hetfield, a difficult time.

When it comes to telling stories, musicians are not always the most reliable of narrators. Beyond its blue-chip corporation boardrooms, the music business is run from offices full of the trickery provided by smoke and mirrors, where perception and reality rarely share desk space. In the battle to transform artists into brands, truth is often an early casualty, and musicians' back stories are carefully manipulated, manicured and managed. But when James Hetfield rolls out one of the rock 'n' roll industry's favourite clichés, telling you that without music, without Metallica, he'd be 'dead, dead or in jail', he does so without a flicker of a smile, without a trace of self-doubt. That boy in the photograph, he'll tell you, was a 'really sad kid' who had imploded with his own anger. Music, he says, 'cracked the shell' he'd pulled around himself since early childhood, and became his 'escape and therapy and saviour'.

In the mid-Nineties Metallica's front man commissioned the renowned Californian tattoo artist Jack Rudy to ink on his left forearm an image of an angel delivering a single musical note through tongues of flame into his outstretched hands. Within the piece, an image signifying struggle and salvation, are the Latin words *Donum Dei* – 'A gift from God'. And if the welter of motivational mantras tattooed elsewhere on James Hetfield's upper body – *Live To Win Dare To Fail*, *Carpe Diem Baby*, *Lead Us Not Into Temptation, Faith* – are designed to act as road markings for his journey ahead, that one simple tribute serves to signal his gratitude for paths not taken.

'A gift from God' was the phrase that Virgil and Cynthia Hetfield employed when informing family and friends of the birth of their first-born son, James Alan, on August 3, 1963. Faith had brought the couple together as the decade of peace and love dawned. A truck driver by trade, with a modest haulage company of his own, Virgil Hetfield spent his Sunday mornings doing God's work, preaching the gospel of Jesus Christ to the children of his adopted home town, Downey, California. Cynthia Hale (née Nourse) had initially accompanied her sons Christopher and David to Sunday School classes from a sense of parental obligation, but in the wake of the dissolution of her first marriage, Virgil Hetfield's calm, thoughtful meditations on suffering and strength in adversity began to chime within her with a profound resonance. Romance soon blossomed. When the couple married in Nevada on July 8, 1961, Cynthia thanked her Lord and Saviour for delivering unto her a second chance of happiness.

On the face of it, the newly-weds were very different people. California-born Cynthia was vivacious, creative and liberal-minded, a thirty-one-year-old artist and graphic designer with a love of light opera and musical theatre; five years her senior, Virgil was taciturn, reserved and conservative, a broad-shouldered Nebraska-born grafter whose sole indulgence of frippery came in the form of his meticulously maintained goatee beard. But the couple shared an adherence to the Christian Science belief system, a curious blend of olde worlde Puritanism and superstitious mumbo-jumbo relying heavily upon faith in the healing power of Christ. They viewed their union as being part of God's preordained plan.

Situated fifteen miles south-east of Hollywood, Downey at the dawn of the 1960s was, as now, a wholly unremarkable little town, devoid of glamour or intrigue, which suited Virgil and Cynthia just fine. But in the year of President John F. Kennedy's assassination, with civil unrest spreading from state to state as the nascent civil rights movement gathered momentum, few American citizens were immune to escalating national tensions. From the moment baby James left hospital, then, his doting parents sought to cocoon him in cotton wool, as if their blue-eyed angel was made of fine bone china and Downey's quiet suburban streets were under threat of invasion by barbarians wielding hammers. Where other truck drivers took their offspring on drives across state lines, bonding over AM radio songs as the asphalt rolled beneath their wheels, Virgil Hetfield determined that his son's world should be safe, sheltered and snow-globe small. Each morning Cynthia clutched James to her side for the three-minute walk to Rio San Gabriel Elementary School; each afternoon she would be in place at its gates as classes discharged, shepherding her boy away from his classmates for the short walk home, lest a single misdirected strand of school yard badinage might despoil her child's innocence.

Rio San Gabriel's curriculum presented an early test to the family's religious convictions. As Christian Scientists Cynthia and Virgil were duty bound to forswear health education, as their faith contends that the human body is merely the vessel that houses the soul of the believer: consequently, James's teachers were informed that their son would not be permitted to attend health class, the school's introductory science course. In place of this, each afternoon the youngster would be required to stand alone in the school hallway, or outside the principal's office, drawing unwanted attention as passing students wondered aloud as to the nature of the actions that had resulted in this punishment. Word soon got around that young Hetfield was 'different', a tag no child welcomes.

'That alienated me from a lot of the kids at school,' Hetfield recalled. 'Like when I wanted to get involved with something like football. You needed a physical from a doctor, and I would be like, "I don't believe in this, I have this little waiver saying I don't need this." In a way, it was going against the rules, which I kinda like. But as a child, it really fucked with me as far as being different from other kids. You wanna be part of the gang, you wanna do the things they do.'

Virgil and Cynthia were largely too preoccupied to notice James's growing isolation from his peers and the attendant anxiety this engendered. With the arrival of their first daughter, Deanna, in the summer of 1966 the couple now had four mouths to feed from a single income. As much as the head of the family assured his wife that God would provide, the Almighty wasn't prepared to clock in at 6 a.m. each morning in order to drive an eighteen-wheel rig for minimum wage, so Virgil's stints on the road expanded from days at a time into weeks. With her eldest boys having descended into the hormonal clusterfuck of adolescence, and her infant daughter reacting to Virgil's prolonged absences with ever more rebellious behaviour, Cynthia considered her sensitive youngest son's sullen silences the least of her worries. But in a bid to bond with the boy, and draw him out of his black moods, she suggested to James that he might enjoy piano lessons, just as she herself had as a child. If three years of tuition proved to be an utterly joyless experience for Hetfield – 'I hated it,' he has stated baldly on more than one occasion – nonetheless in later years he was gracious enough to concede that it was not time entirely wasted, admitting, 'I am so glad it was somewhat forced upon me, because the act of left and right hand doing different things, and also singing at the same time, it gave me some inkling of what I do now.'

With his interest in music piqued, the child began experimenting with some of the other instruments lying around the family home. His half-brother David played drums in a rock 'n' roll covers band called the Bitter End, while Christopher Hale, much taken by the developing singer-songwriter scene developing in the Los Angeles Canyons, flirted with acoustic guitar: neither instrument initially made much sense to James's young ears, though the obvious irritation his exploratory noise-making caused other family members secretly delighted the youngster and served as some incentive to persevere. But it was the discovery of David Hale's record collection that truly brought the power of music into focus for James. David had warned his half-brother countless times that the vinyl in the corner of their shared bedroom was off-limits to him, instructions which only served to inflame the younger boy's curiosity. And so, one afternoon while David was at his accountancy class, nine-year-old James plucked up the courage to rummage through the dog-eared sleeves. He was drawn, 'like a magnet to metal', to one album cover in particular, the artwork for which featured a mysterious, unsmiling black-garbed woman standing outside an old watermill in a woodland clearing. He placed the black vinyl within on David's record-player turntable, and dropped the stylus on its outermost groove. The sound of rainfall, thunder and a single, solemn, tolling church bell crept from the stereo's battered speakers. And in that moment everything changed for James Hetfield, changed utterly.

Released on Friday February 13, 1970, Black Sabbath's self-titled debut album stands as a death knell for the idealistic hippie dreams of the Sixties. Inspired by horror movies, bad dreams, drug come-downs and the terminal grind of the factory floor, it was designed to unnerve and unsettle – 'Everybody has sung about all the good things,' reasoned bassist Geezer Butler. 'Nobody ever sings about what's frightening and evil.' – and succeeded in offending the sensibilities of every notable music critic of the era. But in Ozzy Osbourne's baleful vocals and guitarist Tony Iommi's dread-laden, down-tuned riffs, young James heard the sound of liberation. 'This was more than just *music*,' he recalled, '[this was] a powerful, loud, heavy sound that moved [my] soul.'

'Sabbath was the band that put "heavy" in my head,' he said. 'That first Sabbath album I would sneak out of my brother's record collection and play on the forbidden record player. I wasn't supposed to touch any of that stuff, but I did, and the first Sabbath album got in my head. That initial song, "Black Sabbath", was the one [where] when you'd put your headphones on and sit in the dark and get scared to death. Then the Devil's riff comes in, and it got you!'

For Hetfield the *Black Sabbath* album served as a portal into an alternative universe. Each forbidden excavation into his half-brother's record stacks brought forth new delights – Led Zeppelin, Blue Oyster Cult, Alice Cooper, the Amboy Dukes – a succession of lank-haired libertines channelling the raw, ragged howl of the blues into monolithic proto-metal. When Hetfield placed his headphones over his ears and twisted the volume control on David's record player hard right, the world outside his bedroom seemed to fade away.

'Music was a way to get away from my screwed-up family,' he explained. 'I liked being alone, I liked being able to close off the world and music helped with that a lot. I'd put on the headphones and just listen . . . Music would speak my voice and, man, it connected on so many levels.'

Perhaps if he had been a little less immersed in his elder sibling's vinyl treasure trove, James might have been a little more aware of the escalating rumble of domestic discord at home. As it was, he remembers nothing special about the day in 1976 on which his father walked out on his family. There were no cross words exchanged that morning, no lingering hugs on the doorstep; no tear-moistened note of farewell was found resting on the mantelpiece as Virgil hit the road. In point of fact, months would pass before Cynthia Hetfield gathered James and Deanna to her side and informed them that this time their father would not be coming home from his travels. The children were hurt, angry and confused, scarcely able to comprehend their mother's words. When Cynthia told James that he must be strong, that with David and Christopher now living their own lives under their own roofs, he was now the man of the house, the teenager was terrified. He withdrew further into himself, raging against his father for his selfishness, despising him for not even saying goodbye. 'It devastated me,' he admitted.

To block out the constant hiss of white noise in his head, James attempted to drown himself in sound. Pocket money previously spent on candy and Topps trading cards was now deflected towards the acquisition of a record collection of his own, with Lynyrd Skynyrd's 'Sweet Home Alabama' single and Aerosmith's *Toys in the Attic* album the teenager's first two purchases. Inspired by a poster of Aerosmith guitarist Joe Perry adorning his bedroom wall, he began picking out chords and melodies on Christopher's guitar, slowing down his favourite songs on David's turntable from 45 rpm to 33 rpm so that he could play along.

'My ear was developed quite a bit from the piano playing so I knew what was in tune, what was not in tune, what sounded right and what didn't,' he says. 'I was always into the big, fat riffs. I was drawn to the rhythm and percussion bit because I had messed around on drums as well. The rhythm style came from percussion as well, hitting the guitar as hard as you would a drum.'

In September 1977 Hetfield enrolled as a freshman at Downey High School on Brookshire Avenue. He instantly hated the place, with its cliques and clubs and insider codes. When he trialled for the school football team, the Vikings, Coach Cummings informed him that he had a choice to make: he could lose his long hair and join the team, or keep his locks and forfeit his shot at gridiron glory. Despite nurturing pipe dreams of a starting position with the Oakland Raiders, Hetfield turned on his heels, knowing full well that he was condemning himself to pariah status within the school echelons.

'I was a misfit,' he says. 'Didn't fit in, didn't want to fit in. I hid as much as possible in my music . . . I did not feel like I identified with anyone . . . Basically, instead of hanging out at school, I went home and practised guitar.'

By the school lockers one morning Hetfield ran into Ron McGovney, a former classmate from Downey's East Middle School. McGovney's parents owned a vehicle repair shop directly across the street from Virgil Hetfield's trucking company, but the boys had never been close: McGovney only remembered the younger boy because Hetfield was the one student in music class who could play guitar, while Hetfield did not recall McGovney at all. But cast adrift from their status-obsessed peers, each recognised a certain loneliness in the other. Drawn together by a common obsession with music, their friendship developed cautiously – McGovney's first clumsy attempt at bonding saw him scribble the word 'Fag' across a photo of Aerosmith's Steven Tyler on Hetfield's homework folder, while Hetfield taunted his new buddy by mocking the recent passing of McGovney's musical idol Elvis Presley – but soon settled into an easy rhythm. When James purchased a 1969 Gibson SG from the guitarist in the school jazz band, Ron began taking acoustic guitar lessons, keen not to be left behind. Later that year when Hetfield joined his first band, Obsession, the older teenager offered to act as his buddy's guitar tech.

As with most high-school bands the world over, Obsession were little more than a vehicle in which small boys put on big boys' trousers and lived out their rock 'n' roll fantasies. A quartet comprising Hetfield, fellow guitarist Jim Arnold and brothers Ron and Rich Veloz on bass and drums respectively, the group would convene in the garage of the Veloz family home on Eastbrook Avenue each Friday and Saturday to chew through vaguely recognisable versions of classic rock staples – Black Sabbath's 'Never Say Die', Led Zeppelin's 'Communication Breakdown', Jimi Hendrix's 'Purple Haze' and Deep Purple's 'Highway Star' among them – taking turns at the mic as they played at being rock stars. That their audience at this point consisted solely of Ron McGovney and his friend Dave Marrs was immaterial: when the garage door was thrown open, in their collective imaginations Obsession were holding captive a sold-out Hollywood Bowl with their high-voltage soundtrack. For one young man, however, this was not enough. On July 12, 1978, a few weeks before his fifteenth birthday, Hetfield was given the opportunity to see Aerosmith (supported by AC/DC) play the 13,500-seat Long Beach Arena. Cynthia Hetfield had previously decorated her son's bedroom with life-size painted portraits of Steven Tyler and Joe Perry, but seeing the 'Toxic Twins' strut and swagger across the stage of a packed arena was an overwhelming experience for James. Inspired, he returned to the Velozs' garage with a clutch of self-penned riffs he hoped the band could develop into their first original song. Instead of this, his band mates listened politely then duly went back to practising UFO licks. It was the signal for Hetfield to move on. With his confidence dented, he temporarily shelved the notion of performing his own material, and instead started Syrinx, a Rush tribute act who took their name from movement two of *2112*'s epic title track. Fleshed out by Jim Arnold and his drummer brother Chris, Syrinx were, by all accounts, a powerful live proposition, but the union lasted only marginally longer than a Neil Peart drum solo, and Hetfield was soon alone in his bedroom once more.

One afternoon as he sat practising scales at home, James glanced through his bedroom window to see a familiar figure standing outside on the driveway. More than a year after abandoning his family, Virgil Hetfield was back in Downey, with a new haircut, a new wardrobe and a brand-new Corvette Stingray. He brought with him armfuls of expensive gifts and stories of international travel, and he spoke of being reborn and at peace once more following the most turbulent, confusing year of his life. He had made mistakes, he conceded, but he hoped that his children might find it in their hearts to forgive him for his abrupt exit. Daddy's girl Deanna immediately flung herself into her father's arms, but James kept his distance, eyeing up the virtual stranger in his home with calm, detached fury. When he finally spoke, his words were cold and blunt.

'Dude,' he said, 'you screwed us over . . .'

'It was like "Who's this guy?" ' he recalled. 'My sister instantly accepted him back, but I was not having it. It was never resolved.'

†

As the winter of 1980 nudged its way inexorably towards spring, Ron McGovney arrived at school one morning to find Hetfield clearing out the locker next to his own. Bemused, McGovney asked his friend what he was doing. Hetfield replied that his mother had just passed away and so he and his sister needed to leave Downey to take up residence with David Hale and his wife Lorraine in Brea, sixteen miles east.

Cynthia Hetfield's health had been slowly deteriorating for years. But, forbidden by her Christian Scientist faith to seek medical attention, she refused to countenance diagnosis or treatment. On February 19, 1980, one month shy of her fiftieth birthday, Cynthia passed away. In keeping with Christian Science tradition, there was to be no funeral, nor any grieving period for her children to process their loss.

'We watched my mom wither away,' says Hetfield. 'I attribute it to a lot of the discomfort with the divorce and the turmoil there. It was very traumatic. Dad took the business; she didn't have the money and had to support us. My sister and I would look at each other and we couldn't really say anything. It was that whole catch-22 about acknowledging the illness, then of course you are going to be sick. We were imprisoned, trapped with this. We couldn't say any thing. My brothers, finally – they were old enough to understand this – said, "Something's really wrong, let's get her some help." At that point it was much too late.'

'We had no idea,' McGovney admitted. 'He was gone for like ten days and we had thought he went on vacation. When he told us that his mom had just died, we were stunned.'

McGovney remained in touch as Hetfield recommenced his senior year at Brea Olinda High School. He soon received word that his friend had started a new band, Phantom Lord, with drummer classmate Jim Mulligan and a junior named Hugh Tanner, whom Hetfield first began speaking to when the younger boy brought a Flying V guitar to school to renovate in woodwork class. In truth Phantom Lord existed more as a concept than an actual band – the trio never played a show, and practised only sporadically – but in Tanner's bedroom they plotted out strategies for nothing less than a new rock revolution. The success of Van Halen's dazzlingly cocksure 1978 debut album had overnight rendered much of America's hard rock establishment yesterday's news, and Phantom Lord were confident they could further the cause of the new order by combining the Pasadena band's sass and swagger with the heavier, darker sound of European bands such as Judas Priest, Accept and Scorpions. First, though, they needed a bassist, and Hetfield identified McGovney as the solution to that particular problem, despite the fact that his friend neither owned, nor could play, bass. An instrument was duly procured from the Downey Music Centre, and each weekend Hetfield would take on the role of tutor in McGovney's bedroom, before the duo would hook up with Tanner and Dave Marrs for field trips to Sunset Boulevard nightspots such as the Whisky a Go Go, the Starwood and the Troubadour in order to evaluate bands the bedroom rockers perceived as their peers.

The Hollywood rock scene circa 1980 was a circus informed by theatre and spectacle, sparkle and glitz. Descended from the mid-Seventies 'glitter rock' scene and incubated in Sunset Strip clubs such as Rodney Bingenheimer's English Disco, where artists such as the Runaways and Zolar X swapped make-up tips and Quaaludes with drag-queen hustlers and jailbait Valley girls, its shtick was loud, gaudy and shameless, a flamboyant *demi-monde* utterly convinced of its own fabulousness. It both terrified and repulsed Hetfield and his teenage consorts, who would return to the suburbs convinced that the likes of Dante Fox, White Sister and Satyr would present little obstacle to their own plans for world domination. As Hetfield graduated from Brea Olinda High, he laid out his future plans clearly in the school yearbook: 'Play Music, Get Rich.' When he reappeared at the institution some weeks later as Brea Olinda's new janitor, fellow staff members were kind enough to keep their thoughts to themselves.

That same summer, buoyed by his new-found financial independence, Hetfield moved out of David and Lorraine Hale's house. McGovney's parents owned three rental properties in Norwalk in an area designated for demolition by the California Transportation Commission ahead of the construction of freeway 105, and an invitation was extended to James and Ron to move into one of the vacant properties rent-free, until such time as the state bulldozers rolled in. The teenagers did not need to be asked twice. The walls of 13004 Curtis and King Road were promptly decorated with Aerosmith, Judas Priest and Michael Schenker posters. The pair then set about renovating and sound-proofing the adjoining garage for use as Phantom Lord's new rehearsal space. But with the paint yet to dry upon the facility's walls, Hetfield unveiled a radical new blueprint for the band. Temporarily dazzled by the scene on Sunset, or perhaps simply high on paint fumes, he declared Phantom Lord no more, and announced that the collective were to be reconstituted as Leather Charm, LA's newest rock 'n' roll renegades.

It is surely for the best that Leather Charm's oeuvre has been lost to history. One can only speculate as to the raw sexuality a teenage James Hetfield might have poured into the chorus of 'Hades Ladies', or what hysteria the libidinous throb of 'Handsome Ransom' and 'Let's Go Rock 'n' Roll' may have unleashed among West Hollywood's teenage rock queens. But when first Hugh Tanner and then Jim Mulligan informed their band leader that his vision for the outfit did not concur with their own, Leather Charm tumbled off their stacked heels.

Somewhat guilty after torpedoing his friend's rock 'n' roll dreams, Tanner vowed to assist Hetfield in assembling a new vehicle for his talents. In the first week of May 1981, he produced a copy of the Los Angeles listings magazine *The Recycler*, in which he had circled an advert in the 'Musicians Wanted' section. 'Drummer looking for other metal musicians to jam with', it read.

'Influences: Tygers of Pan Tang, Diamond Head, Iron Maiden.' The ad featured a Newport Beach area code phone number and advised interested parties to ask for Lars. Tanner placed the call and scheduled a rehearsal session at a Fullerton recording facility for the following week.

There is a special chemistry that occurs when certain musicians meet for the first time, an instinctive identification that transcends the simple appreciation of shared talents and aspirations. When the fifteen-year-old Paul McCartney met John Lennon, one year his senior, at Woolton Parish Church's garden fete on the afternoon of July 6, 1957, both boys were struck by one another's charm and musicianship, and McCartney was cajoled into joining Lennon's band the Quarrymen two weeks later. When Jimmy Page invited John Paul Jones, Robert Plant and John Bonham to convene in a basement rehearsal studio in London's Gerrard Street on the afternoon of August 12, 1968, each man understood that theirs was a most formidable union long before the group reached the end of the first song they performed together, 'Train Kept A-Rollin'. Song-writing sessions for Led Zeppelin's debut album began the following week.

There was, however, none of that intangible magic present when James Hetfield first encountered Lars Ulrich. By any measure, the session booked by Hugh Tanner was a disaster, the blame for which lay at the drumsticks of Ulrich. Baldly put, the kid couldn't play. He could certainly talk – yap, yap, yapping constantly in a sing-song accent which seemed to traverse the Atlantic Ocean without ever dropping anchor – but the task of holding down even the most rudimentary 4/4 beat seemed hopelessly beyond him. Lost in the music, with his eyes closed at his microphone stand, time and again Hetfield would be jolted back into the room as the session came juddering to a premature halt. Opening his eyes, the Californian would see the young drummer's cymbals or snare drum tumble to the floor beneath his wildly enthusiastic flailing. It was with a certain amount of embarrassment that Tanner called a halt to the session before the trio's allotted time at the facility had expired. Ulrich, however, appeared utterly unfazed. As he packed away his kit into the back of his mother's AMC Pacer car, the drummer enthused, 'We should do this again.' Hetfield and Tanner smiled politely and made noises of assent. Never a man overly concerned with looking in life's rear-view mirror, as he pulled away from the studio for the thirty-minute drive back towards Newport Beach that afternoon, Lars Ulrich wouldn't have noticed his two new friends exchange smiles that then dissolved into laughter.

✝

Twenty years on from that first ill-fated jam session, in May 2001 Hetfield and Ulrich once again found themselves struggling to make a connection in a Californian recording facility. Sessions for their band's eighth studio album were proving fractured and unproductive, only this time Hetfield was singularly failing to find humour in the situation. As spring evenings lengthened into summer, Metallica's front man announced his intention to step away from the process in order to find the space and time in which he might weigh up matters in his life both professional and personal. He gave no guarantees as to when, or even if, he might return.

Early the following day, Ulrich chose to return to Presidio, the former army barracks in which Metallica were stationed, with his father, Torben, in tow. Still stunned by his friend's abrupt exit, it was Ulrich's intention to play his father rough mixes of the material the band had committed to tape thus far, as much to convince himself of the validity and vibrancy of the project as to garner his father's opinions on the recordings.

The drummer decided to begin his playback session with a track recorded when the Presidio sessions were at their most harmonious. In the small hours of May 3 Hetfield, Ulrich, Metallica's lead guitarist Kirk Hammett and producer Bob Rock had entered the studio's live room on a high after attending a concert by the Icelandic rock band Sigur Rós at San Francisco's legendary Fillmore auditorium. The music they were inspired to make that morning, with its reverb-rich guitar drones and off-beat drums, was both heavily indebted to the Reykjavik quartet, and a grand departure from anything previously recorded under the Metallica name. Always obsessive in his desire to push his band into territories new, Ulrich was inordinately proud of the piece. As the song flowed through the studio's state-of-the-art speakers, the drummer made infinitesimal tweaks to the recording's EQ levels on an SSL 4000 console, while his seventy-three-year-old father looked on impassively from the control room's black leather couch.

'Comments on that one?' Lars enquired brightly as the song faded out.

Torben sank back into the sofa and stroked his long grey beard as he weighed up his response.

'If you said, "If you were our advisor what would you say?"' he answered slowly, 'then I would say, "Delete that."'

There followed a split-second silence, during which the air seemed to be sucked from the room. And then Lars Ulrich, a man hitherto wholly unacquainted with the concept of being lost for words, gave a nervous, anxious laugh. With his face communicating a mixture of petulance, exasperation and embarrassment, he began a stammering defence of the track. His father's verdict was 'interesting', he noted, but out of step with feedback the band had received elsewhere. He pointed out that Metallica's co-manager Cliff Burnstein was so taken by the wordless piece that he had ventured the opinion that it might serve as the opening track on the new album.

'Yeah?' said Torben. 'That could well be, but I'm pretty sure that . . . I really don't think so. I *really* don't think so.'

The exchange (captured by film-makers Joe Berlinger and Bruce Sinofsky as they amassed fly-on-the-wall footage for what would become the 2004 documentary *Some Kind of Monster)* was revealing, shining a light on a side of Lars Ulrich rarely seen. Abandoned by his friend and musical soulmate, and understandably emotionally raw as a consequence, in this briefest of moments the years appeared to roll back for Ulrich. Stripped of his usual bullish self-confidence, he stood in front of his father once more as a gauche adolescent, eager to please and craving approval. As a glimpse into the intrinsic motivations which willed Metallica into existence in the first place, the moment is priceless.

†

Lars Ulrich was born on December 26, 1963, in the municipality of Gentofte, in eastern Denmark, a late Christmas present for his parents, Torben and Lone. Transformed from an agricultural community into an affluent industrial society in the post-war years, the nation into which Ulrich was born was progressive, liberal and aspirant, a fully functioning social democracy growing in confidence and ambition. Well-heeled and well-connected, the Ulrich family were considered part of Copenhagen's cosmopolitan elite. Torben was a professional tennis player – like his father, Einar, before him, Denmark's number one – and a celebrated polymath, with a range of cultural interests that stretched far beyond the baselines of the outside courts at Wimbledon or Flushing Meadows. A regular columnist for the Danish daily newspapers *Politiken* and *BT*, by the time of his son's birth Torben had also co-edited a literary magazine, presented on Danish radio, co-founded a Copenhagen jazz club and played clarinet and tenor saxophone with a number of the capital's best-regarded jazz ensembles. A 1969 *Sports Illustrated* profile hailed him as the tennis circuit's 'most fascinating, most captivating figure'.

'He is a sort of gargoyle in a pretty game played and watched by pretty people,' wrote journalist Mark Kram. 'As tennis now slowly and desperately tries to lure the masses, Ulrich is invaluable . . . Win or lose, he provokes reaction and constant comment, the one indispensable vitamin for all sports.'

Torben's free-thinking, philosophical attitude to life was shaped by events in his formative years. In October 1943, at the age of fifteen, the boy and his younger brother, Jorgen, were encouraged to flee Nazi-occupied Denmark with their Jewish mother, Ulla, as concerns for their future welfare intensified. Their intention was to travel across the Oresund strait to Sweden, but the fishing boat commandeered for their flight was spotted by the German army while still in Danish waters, and when the Germans sprayed the vessel with arcs of machine-gun fire, all aboard surrendered. The Ulrich family were sent to a Danish concentration camp, and threatened with a transfer to Auschwitz or Theresienstadt. Two weeks later, however, they were released, the German authorities having apparently decided their Jewish heritage was not sufficiently 'pure' to warrant their deportation. Upon returning to high school in Copenhagen, Torben apologised for his prolonged absence from class, explaining to his teacher that his family had been imprisoned by the Germans. Thinking he was being mocked, the teacher cuffed the youngster around the ears. As his classmates looked on in shock, Torben calmly packed up his books, shouldered his bag and walked out of the school, never to return. His distrust of authority did not waver from that day.

At the time of their son's birth, Lone and Torben lived in a beautiful four-storey house in Hellerup, an affluent upper-middle-class district on the north-eastern side of the Danish capital. The family shared the building's upper floor while Lone's parents, who owned the house, occupied the floors below. Throughout Lars's childhood the property at Lundevangsvej 12 served as a cultural hub for the district, an open house for Hellerup's bohemian set: artists, musicians, film-makers and writers dropped by daily to talk art, politics and philosophy with the urbane tennis pro and his family. American jazz men Dexter Gordon, Don Cherry and Stan Getz were neighbours and close family friends – indeed tenor saxophonist Gordon took on the mantle of Lars's godfather early in 1964 – and their regular visits ensured that the Ulrich family home was always ablaze with music, laughter and conversation long after the house lights of neighbouring apartments had been extinguished. Young Lars was never excluded from the gatherings, never made to feel like an interloper in adult company, and in this fecund, nurturing environment, he developed into a happy, inquisitive and somewhat precocious youth.

'I grew up pretty quick,' he recalls. 'I didn't have any siblings so I was around a lot of adults all the time. I found myself spending more time in the adult world than the adults spent in the child world. There was a very progressive scene [in Copenhagen], a lot of music and a lot of experimenting with thoughts and ideas. My dad was very much at the edge of that with music and writing and with poetry and film and so on. I grew up in that environment.'

'My dad had a room opposite mine that was his music room and there was nothing in there other than records and a big fuck-off stereo . . . A lot of times when I woke up in the morning he would just be finishing in there, and I could hear the music through the walls. He'd be playing the Doors, Hendrix, the Velvet Underground, a lot of jazz stuff, [John] Coltrane, Miles [Davis], Dexter Gordon, Sonny Rollins, Ornette Coleman, that kind of stuff. Those are the earliest musical memories I have.'

The home comforts of the Danish capital were accessible to the Ulrich family, however, only for part of the year, as Torben's professional career necessitated the adoption of an itinerant lifestyle. The family's calendar was broadly dictated by the tennis circuit's four Grand Slam tournaments: January would see Torben,

Lone, Lars and his nanny board long-haul flights to Melbourne, the host city for the Australian Open, while the months of May and June would see the tour relocate to Paris for the French Open. The final week of June brought the circuit to London and the grass courts of Wimbledon, after which the family could be found in the New York borough of Queens as Torben prepared for the late August opening rounds of the US Open. Elsewhere the template expanded to accommodate exhibition games and tournaments in Fiji, Tahiti, South Africa, India . . . wherever on the globe the International Tennis Federation could sell the game. Young Lars took it all in his stride, developing, by his own admission, 'a pretty adventurous mind'.

'I probably travelled an average of four to six school weeks a year, which was quite a lot, especially in the later years,' he recalled. 'So, I mean, of course in some ways it was somewhat unconventional but it wasn't really until I came to America that I started hearing those words. I never heard those words when I was growing up . . . you know, "abnormal" or "unconventional". It was what seemed to be the energy around not just my dad but my mom, the household in general, going back generations. All the artists and that whole scene. And it seemed like I was just a product of a scene.

'I think part of the strength, part of the real positive thing of my early years, was that there was a lot of freedom to experience a lot of things on my own, to seek a lot of answers on my own, to not have anything handed to me, to not have particular ways of thinking, ideologies or whatever, forced upon me. I did a lot of soul-searching. I did a lot of sniffing around, I did a lot of kind of checking into things. Checking into things myself with a kind of a juvenile curiosity.'

In the dog days of the summer of 1969 that curiosity led Lars Ulrich into one of London's most exclusive quarters for a gathering which would secure him bragging rights for years to come.

While his father practised his ground strokes in SW19, young Lars's interest was piqued by a photograph of a group of louche, long-haired young men in a national newspaper; his mother informed him that the gentlemen in question were a rock 'n' roll band who that same week would be staging a free concert in one of London's royal parks. Lars demanded that he be taken along. And so on July 5, 1969, mother and son joined Torben, his South African colleague Ray Moore and approximately 500,000 other music fans in London's Hyde Park for the first live Rolling Stones concert in over two years. On a balmy summer evening, England's most celebrated rock 'n' roll collective turned in a historic performance which sealed their reputation as one of the form's most supple and dexterous live turns.

It would, however, be another English rock band that Lars Ulrich would ultimately credit with setting his life in the direction it would follow to the present day. On February 10, 1973, Deep Purple closed out the first leg of their *Who Do We Think We Are* European tour with a date at the K.B. Hallen in Copenhagen. In the stalls that evening, alongside his father and Moore, was the nine-year-old Lars.

'There was a tennis tournament there – all tennis tournaments start on Monday so on the Sunday all the players were invited to see Deep Purple,' Ulrich recalls. 'So my father and a couple of the other guys went. It was pretty fucking cool. I was just infatuated, not just with the music but the event. The people, the volume, the reverberation, the light show, the whole thing. Ritchie Blackmore – I didn't even know his name – I remember him rubbing his guitar on his ass. That was so cool. The next day I went into the local record store and the only Deep Purple record they had was *Fireball* so I started with that and didn't look back.'

In the aftermath of Deep Purple's Copenhagen bow, Lars set his heart upon learning to play guitar, cajoling his cousin Stein into parting with his own electric guitar in exchange for an album by Danish singer/songwriter John Mogensen. Six months of lessons with the music teachers at Maglegårdsskolen ensued, but the boy had little aptitude for the instrument, and it was soon cast aside, with Lars finding greater entertainment in strumming a tennis racquet in front of his bedroom mirror. His commitment to this 'instrument' was nonetheless impressive: on one occasion he, Stein and a couple of local boys air-racqueted their way through both sides of Status Quo's *Live!* album without a pause, replicating the intensity of Glasgow's Apollo Theatre circa 1976 by turning the heating in his playroom on to full power so that they were dripping with sweat before the first of its twelve tracks reached its end. Such dedication was mirrored in the lengths the youngster would go to in order to see his favourite bands. In spring 1976 Kiss announced a show at Copenhagen's Falkoner Theatre as part of their first ever European tour, news which thrilled Lars Ulrich until he realised that the date fell smack in the middle of a school trip to North Jutland, meaning that he would be almost 450 kilometres away when the Demon, Starchild, Space Ace and Catman first planted their stack heels on a Danish stage. Crestfallen, he explained his predicament to his parents, who promised to have a word with his teachers. And so on May 29, 1976, the twelve-year-old Lars undertook the six-hour train journey from Fjerritslev in North Jutland to Copenhagen's Central Station unaccompanied, so that he and Stein could be stage front when Gene Simmons first drooled fake blood on to the faces of the Danish chapter of the Kiss Army. As dawn broke, the boy was heading north by train to rejoin his classmates.

As 1976 drew to a close, Ulrich acquired his first drum kit. A gift from his grandmother Gudrun, the kit had the same specifications as that used by Deep Purple's Ian Paice, and the teenager would spend long hours in the playroom at Lundevangsvej 12 pounding along to Purple's *Made in Japan* live album. Soon enough Ulrich found a musical mentor to encourage his fanaticism. Ken Anthony worked in the basement of the Bristol Music Centre, a three-storey record shop in central Copenhagen, curating the store's hard rock/heavy metal section. 'Heavy Metal Ken' took great pride in his ability to source the most obscure and rare releases for the delectation of Denmark's headbanging fraternity, filling the basement of the BMC with curios from Bow Wow and Bang, Black Axe and Sledgehammer, Buffalo, Lucifer's Friend and a thousand more unheralded international artistes. Ulrich regarded the shop like a church, and would make pilgrimages to it up to four times a week. Once inside he would stand enraptured by the counter as Anthony spun black circles, filling his young acolyte's head with the names of new bands and introducing him to what Anthony himself considered the most thrilling music scene in the world, the rising New Wave of British Heavy Metal.

In December 1976, the year of *The Song Remains the Same*, *Hotel California*, *2112* and *Frampton Comes Alive!*, a UK music fanzine named *Sideburns* dedicated a full page to a guide for aspiring guitarists. Beneath the headline 'PLAY' IN [*sic*] IN THE BAND . . . FIRST AND LAST IN A SERIES . . .' were printed three crude sketches of a guitar fretboard, revealing the fingering required to play the major chords A, E and G. 'This is a chord, this is another, this is a third,' ran the accompanying text. 'Now form a band.' The message was simple, direct and wholly liberating for a section of suburban teenagers bored with the musical status quo. Yet, the global success of working-class hard-rock musicians from towns disregarded by London's insular music journalists as provincial backwaters could be equally inspirational for music-obsessed young Britons. In the inky pages of the four main English music weeklies – *Melody Maker, Record Mirror, New Musical Express* and *Sounds* – rock fans from Barnsley to Belfast could see Robert Plant from Wolverhampton preening and screaming in front of 90,000 people at the 1977 Day on the Green festival at Oakland–Alameda County Coliseum or read about Deep Purple's

David Coverdale, a former shoe salesman from Saltburn-by-the-Sea, conducting a 200,000 strong choir at the 1974 California Jam. At a time when the media labelled superstar rock acts 'dinosaurs', the notion of aspiring to such heights may have been considered vulgar by the popular music press, but this judgemental attitude held little sway with ambitious young men such as Iron Maiden bassist Steve Harris and Def Leppard front man Joe Elliott, who desired nothing less than that their bands would become numbered among the most successful musical acts in the world. Even as the punk movement gathered momentum in 1976, abetted by an elitist music industry's voyeuristic fascination with violence and teenage rebellion, an underground metal community began to develop along lines parallel to those drawn by punk.

On May 8, 1979, three of the movement's emerging bands – Angel Witch, Samson and Iron Maiden – united for a gig at the 1,400-capacity Music Machine in Camden, north London. Also present that evening, at the invitation of heavy metal DJ turned promoter Neal Kay, was twenty-four-year-old Geoff Barton, a freelance contributor to *Sounds* magazine.

At the tail end of the previous summer Barton had accepted one of Kay's regular entreaties to visit him at his weekly rock club, the Bandwagon Heavy Metal Soundhouse at the Prince of Wales pub at Kingsbury Circle. Here, to his great astonishment, the young writer discovered that the capital's heavy metal scene, commonly held to have been decimated by punk, was flourishing.

'I expected some sort of time warp populated by scruffy longhairs, a place where head-shaking, imaginary-guitar playing, peace-sign flashing and above all blood and thunder reigned supreme,' Barton wrote in the edition of *Sounds* for August 19, 1978. 'And that was all true apart from the fact that the Bandwagon *ain't no time warp*.'

Nine months on from this back-handed compliment, Kay staged the show at the Music Machine as a coming-of-age party for the home-grown heavy metal movement. It was at the point when the scene would graduate in triumph from the back rooms of east London and Essex pubs to the capital's grand theatres. It was an ambitious undertaking, and a less excitable promoter might have blanched at receiving word of the evening's distinctly underwhelming ticket sales figures. But Kay was not to be deterred. 'Welcome to the heavy metal crusade!' the DJ screamed down the microphone as he cued up his first record of the evening. On the edge of the beautiful old theatre's dance floor, a handful of long-haired Bandwagon regulars broke into muted cheers. Expecting frenzy and chaos, Geoff Barton could not help feeling slightly cheated. Nonetheless, the copy the young writer filed for *Sounds* on May 19, 1979, was exuberant, passionate and effusive in tone. Beneath the headline 'If you want blood (and flashbombs and dry ice and confetti) you've got it', he tagged the scene as the 'New Wave of British Heavy Metal' for the first time, and hailed the night as a year zero for this visceral and vital movement. In the basement of the Bristol Music Centre the review was passed around as if it were a sacred text.

'Once *Sounds* showed up in your life on a weekly basis that was sort of the Bible,' Lars Ulrich explains. 'Geoff Barton was the gateway; you would see what was on Geoff Barton's play list and he would write all these articles. Who could ever forget Barton's quote about Angel Witch sounding like Black Sabbath played through a cement mixer? That's one of the all-time great quotes. Angel Witch is not something I listen to a lot these days, but they were certainly one of the greatest named bands of the time, and that counted for a lot when you're sixteen.'

Just as this new musical world opened up for the teenager, Ulrich was packed off to the New World to follow what was considered to be his destiny. If he had been born with a silver spoon in his mouth, then that privilege originated with the tennis racquets his grandfather and father previously held in their hands for decades. It was expected that Lars would learn the family trade. By the time the boy reached puberty, he was ranked among the top ten junior tennis players in Denmark, and in the summer of 1979 the family decided that he should attend a newly opened tennis school in Florida, so that he might develop both the racquet skills and mental strength required to graduate on to the professional circuit.

The Nick Bollettieri Tennis Academy, a forty-acre site located fifty miles south of Tampa, was the first of its kind, a boarding school where students would spend hours each day on the courts in a fiercely competitive, hot-house environment designed to identify and develop future champions. A hard-nosed New Yorker, Bollettieri had never been a professional tennis player, but he brought other skills to the courts: a relentless work ethic, brusque motivational skills and iron discipline. Tennis, he argued, had a reputation as a 'sissy game', a reputation his academy would change. The thinking was revolutionary, the results extraordinary: Andre Agassi, Maria Sharapova, Venus and Serena Williams and Jim Courier are just a handful of the school's alumni. Reflecting upon his own time at the Academy, however, Lars Ulrich likened it to a 'prison'.

'All through the Seventies, as a teenager, I wanted to become a professional tennis player like my father; music was the passion, tennis was the day job,' he recalls. '[At that Academy] I ended up playing tennis every day for six months. That was probably what turned me off.'

'Where I grew up, tennis was something that was about having fun . . . All the players down at the club they would play and then afterwards they would drink beers and smoke cigarettes, it was kinda like a very social endeavour. In America at that time, in the wake of [John] McEnroe and [Jimmy] Connors, every middle-class parent in the United States sent their kids into these tennis factories to try to have the kids be their meal tickets.'

'I'd been there for two or three months and couldn't stand it any more . . . I was one of the worst troublemakers because I didn't do well with all those rules after growing up in Copenhagen with all that freedom. We began to sneak out of school and go down to the local 7/11 store where we'd try to get some beers. One evening we even got some weed. So we smoked weed in the school after all the good upper-class American talent had gone to bed. And then they busted us. They called a meeting with the teachers and the fifty to sixty youngsters. Someone said, "Somebody's been bad" and "We don't tolerate this here" . . .'

In April 1980 Ulrich downed his tennis racquet and quit the Academy. Deciding against returning to Copenhagen immediately (perhaps to allow his parents time to absorb the news that the $20,000 they'd stumped up for his tuition fees might have been better spent on making wishes at the fountains in Rosenborg Castle Gardens), the teenager opted to fly out to the West Coast to see family friends in San Francisco. It was here, while browsing through the heavy metal imports section of a local record shop, he chanced upon the self-titled debut album by New Wave of British Heavy Metal hopefuls Iron Maiden, released that same month in the United Kingdom.

'Nobody in America was talking about NWOBHM as such,' he recalls, 'and I didn't know anything about them, but I picked up the cover and I saw the Eddie monster on the front and then these super next-level live pictures of these guys. There was smoke and hair and fans and energy and chaos and I said, "This has to be great," so I bought the record.'

As the family with whom Ulrich was lodging did not own a record player, this latest addition to his vinyl collection would go unheard until the teenager returned home to Lundevangsvej 12. When he finally did get the opportunity to listen to *Iron Maiden*, Ulrich was mesmerised by its energy, aggression and speed. Back at the Bristol Music Centre, Ken Anthony dutifully began filling in his young friend on the changing face of heavy metal.

'I'd been in America for the better part of the last year and there was a lot of great stuff happening in America on the radio,' Lars recalls. 'Judas Priest and AC/DC were getting some airplay and bands like Pat Travers and Molly Hatchet and so on, so there was obviously heavy rock happening. But when I came back to Europe and back to Denmark it sort of became known to me that there was a bunch of stuff coming out of England that was much harder, much heavier and much more energetic and really, ultimately, much more about a lifestyle. A lot of the stuff in America at that time – it was just hard rock and people were into it, but the stuff that was coming out of England was really about a total commitment and a lifestyle choice.'

That same summer the Ulrich family had their own lifestyle choices to make. With the emergence of younger players such as Jimmy Connors, Bjorn Borg and John McEnroe, the professional tennis circuit was no longer an arena for gentlemen philosophers, and so Torben Ulrich had switched to the rather more edifying Tennis Grand Masters tour, a competition established for players aged forty-five and over. The demands of the tour meant that Ulrich was spending increasing amounts of time in the United States, to the point where the idea of his family permanently relocating to America seemed sensible. And so in August 1980 the family sold their beautiful Copenhagen town house and purchased a three-bedroom condominium at 2600 Park Newport in Newport Beach, California.

Today in one of Newport Beach's public parks there stands a $50,000 bronze statue of former President Ronald Reagan, a bold display of the neighbourhood's political outlook. A WASP-ish enclave which made middle-class, multicultural Hellerup look like Compton, Newport Beach was (and remains) one of America's wealthiest, and most conservative, communities. Just weeks after the family's arrival, Lars was locked up in a police cell for six hours following his arrest for drinking a beer while walking along the beach front. Liberal, laidback Copenhagen must have seemed like a distant memory.

'Because of my last name, I was king shit [in Copenhagen],' Lars recalled. 'And then [we] went to LA and I was king dogshit. Nobody gave a shit about us.'

The teenager enrolled for eleventh grade at Corona Del Mar High School, an institution with an excellent reputation for both academic and sporting pursuits. By his own admission, the new boy was 'pretty geeky' and 'quite the loner', his penchant for garish Iron Maiden and Saxon T-shirts bemusing his preppy, Lacoste polo shirt-wearing classmates.

'They just looked at me like I was from another fucking planet,' he laughs.

Corona Del Mar's number one tennis player was Anthony Emerson, the son of Australia's multiple Grand Slam winner Roy Emerson. The Emerson and Ulrich families were long-time friends, and it was broadly assumed that Lars would slot into the school tennis team as Anthony's number two. However, when a trial was arranged for the boy, the young European prodigy didn't even rank among the school's top seven players. It quickly dawned on him and his disappointed parents that he was never going to make the grade as a professional. Almost immediately, Lars switched to plan B: he informed his father that he was going to get a drum kit, teach himself how to play – within ten days, no less – and then start a rock band. As soon as he had finished laughing, Torben gave his son permission to rent a kit from a music shop in nearby Santa Ana. This done, Lars set about immersing himself in the Hollywood rock scene.

'The first show I went to in Hollywood was Y&T at the Starwood,' he recalls. 'There was a couple of hundred people there, but everybody was having a great fucking time. There was drinking, there were chicks – and this was when you didn't have

to go to the bathroom to do drugs – it was great. Y&T looked
as if they were playing to a stadium of 50,000 people and I was
thinking maybe this would be a lot more fun than standing trying
to hit forehands down the line for hours at a time. I didn't have
any aspirations to forming a band to become Deep Purple, but I
just thought if I could have this sort of fun in a jam band playing
clubs in LA every couple of weeks that would be great.'

On the week of his seventeenth birthday, Ulrich discovered
that former UFO guitarist Michael Schenker had booked a show
at the Country Club in Reseda. Standing in the parking lot after
the gig on December 22 he was approached by another teenager,
who pointed at his Saxon T-shirt and demanded to know where
he had acquired the item. Ulrich informed his interrogator that
he had recently moved to California from Europe, where the
New Wave of British Heavy Metal was a rather bigger deal than
in the United States.

'You need to meet my friend Brian,' the boy responded.

Brian Slagel and John Kornarens were two heavy metal
obsessed teenagers from Woodland Hills and Studio City
respectively, who, like Ulrich, had discovered the NWOBHM
via Geoff Barton's writing in the pages of *Sounds*. At the point
when they met Ulrich, the two were convinced that they were
the only two people in America who had heard of Iron Maiden,
Angel Witch, Saxon and their contemporaries. Meeting the
young Dane then would prove to be quite the education.

'With the few people I knew who listened to Iron Maiden,
talking to them about music was like going to primary school,'
recalls Kornarens, 'but with Lars it was like going to college: it
was definitely a much higher level. Lars really understood the
music and really was passionate about things like I was, like a
certain riff leading into a lead break, just the little details. He
understood why it was such an exciting genre. When it came
to finding out new music, he was like Indiana Jones. I told him

I'd just got the new Angel Witch single and I think his head exploded. He was incredibly passionate about the music, high energy, borderline annoying.'

'In 1980 I was still living at home with my mom, I was going to college, I was working at Sears, I was obsessed with this whole musical thing and I was just about to start a fanzine,' recalls Brian Slagel. 'I used to tape and record live concerts and tape trade with people all around the world and that's how I was indoctrinated into the New Wave of British Heavy Metal, because a guy I was trading with in Sweden sent me an AC/DC live show and said, "Oh, and here's this band Iron Maiden that you might like . . ." Once you get into that world someone will say, "Hey, you should meet this guy," and so your network starts to expand.'

Kornarens, Slagel and Ulrich bonded instantly. Each week, the trio would meet up to tour Southern California's import record shops in search of new New Wave of British Heavy Metal releases they had seen flagged up in the pages of *Sounds*. That Ulrich already had a standing-order subscription with Wigan-based record shop Bullit Records, who would deliver regular shipments of vinyl to 2600 Park Newport every few weeks, did nothing to quell his competitive instincts, as Slagel recalls.

'We became friends because he had a lot of records that I didn't have, and I had all the records that he didn't have, and we both knew the whole scene,' says Slagel. 'So then there was me, Lars and John Kornarens driving hundreds of miles trying to find an Angel Witch seven-inch or something, and having a fight over it because there was only one in the shop! We'd get to the store and Lars would literally be out of the car before we'd even shut off the key, because he knew there'd only be one or two copies.'

One weekend in January 1981 Ulrich's ever-evolving vinyl obsession led him to take a solo road trip to San Francisco, to check out independent record shops in Haight-Ashbury and Berkeley. While shopping on Berkeley's Telegraph Avenue, the young

Dane was approached by a local metal fan named Rich Burch, who complimented him upon the fine selection of New Wave of British Heavy Metal badges on his denim jacket and invited him to a party at the summit of Strawberry Hill, on an island in Stow Lake in Golden Gate Park. Arriving later that evening, Ulrich was met with the sight of twenty or thirty local youths sitting around ghetto blasters, enthusiastically headbanging to Motörhead and Budgie. These teenagers, Burch excitedly explained, were the 'Trues', the Bay Area's most devoted metalheads, defenders of the faith. He introduced Ulrich to his friend Ron Quintana, and the three sat talking about the European metal scene until dawn. Upon hearing that Ulrich played drums, Quintana mentioned that his friends in a local band named Metal Church were on the lookout for a new member, and he offered to pass Ulrich's number on to guitarist Kurdt Vanderhoof. Ulrich politely demurred, saying he already had some band plans back in Los Angeles. That same month, he placed his first 'Musicians Wanted' advert in *The Recycler*.

'It wasn't about "Let's start a band to get laid" like everyone else in LA, my aspirations weren't even that high!' Ulrich laughs. 'I just wanted to start a band to play all my favourite New Wave of British Heavy Metal songs.'

One of the first people to respond to Ulrich's advert was a young guitarist named Patrick Scott, the son of a Huntington Beach doctor. Scott drove over to Ulrich's house in early February, but never got as far as removing his guitar from its case, so distracted was he by the older teenager's record collection.

'I was into bands that a lot of people were into – Kiss and Aerosmith and Black Sabbath and all that kinda stuff – and I knew there was something out there that was further out,' says Scott. 'Then I started seeing Judas Priest records and I looked at the pictures on them and I knew that this had to be what I was looking for . . . so then I just started buying records based on the covers themselves. I used to go to a record store in Costa Mesa, California, which was kinda between Huntington Beach and Newport Beach and we'd go to this store called Music Market and they'd have a bunch of imports there. And then we started seeing Neat Record releases and I found the *Lead Weight* tape that had Raven and Venom and Bitches Sin and all that stuff on it, and that was taking it a little further. And it kinda went from there.

'But it's a funny thing that Lars and I never jammed. I was a beginning guitar player, and I didn't want to go out until I could really play. Lars was [starting out as] a drummer at that point, but he just wanted to play. He didn't care that he wasn't really up to a certain standard of proficiency as a drummer, he didn't care, he just wanted to go out there and play. And you know, he did the right thing.'

'People would come over to talk to me about Van Halen or whoever,' says Ulrich, 'and I'd be like "No, no, no, we gotta learn how to play [songs by] Trespass or that Witchfinder General song or Silverwing's 'Rock 'n' Roll Are Four Letter Words'. I have recordings of me jamming those songs with other people, but they never got it. Hetfield was the only other person who got psyched about those bands . . .'

Frustrated with the lack of progress, in the summer of 1981 Ulrich decided to take his New Wave of British Heavy Metal obsession to its logical conclusion by undertaking a road trip to England. On the evening of Friday, July 10, 1981 the seventeen-year-old pitched up outside the Woolwich Odeon in south London and handed over £3 in exchange for a ticket in the stalls to see his new favourite band. He would subsequently describe the evening as 'life-changing'.

When the hype around the New Wave of British Heavy Metal first began to build, Stourbridge quartet Diamond Head were billed as the scene's equivalent to Led Zeppelin. Built around the high-pitched vocals and matinee idol looks of front man Sean

Harris and the muscular riffing of guitarist Brian Tatler, the band's
independently released debut seven-inch single 'Shoot Out the
Lights' attracted the attention of the United Kingdom's major
label A&R fraternity. All approaches, however, were rebuffed by
manager Linda Harris, Sean's mother, who wanted to build the
band's profile to a point where, like Zeppelin before them, they
could dictate their career on their own terms. By the time the
quartet released their debut album *Lightning to the Nations* on
their own Happy Face records, Ulrich was a confirmed fan.

'I'd heard the single "Shoot Out the Lights"/ "Helpless" and
it was good, but it didn't particularly stand out from all the other
stuff coming out in 1980,' Ulrich admitted. 'But then I heard
"It's Electric" on a compilation called *Brute Force*, and it blew my
fucking head off. Diamond Head had a vibe and an attitude no
other band could match.'

After the show, displaying the kind of breezy nonchalance
that was fast becoming his trademark, Ulrich knocked on the
stage door and asked to speak to Linda, with whom he had
been corresponding by letter while awaiting delivery of his mail-
order copy of *Lightning to the Nations* that spring. Astonished
that a seventeen-year-old boy had flown across the Atlantic
to see her son's band, Harris immediately ushered the sweat-
drenched teenager into Diamond Head's dressing room. When
Tatler enquired as to where Ulrich was staying, the young Dane
shrugged and said, 'I don't know, I've just come straight from
the airport.' Given the lateness of the hour, and the fact that
parts of south London had been on fire just one week earlier as
racial discord spilled over into street riots, the guitarist offered
to let the precocious tourist crash out at his parents' house in
Stourbridge. Within the hour Ulrich was sandwiched in the back
of Sean Harris's Austin Allegro bound for the West Midlands. 'I
think I was just pretty tenacious back then,' he laughs.

The drummer slept at the foot of Tatler's bed for the next week, before relocating to Harris's couch for another month. During his time, Ulrich accompanied Diamond Head to gigs in Hereford and Leeds, blagged Tatler and himself into the Heavy Metal Holocaust festival co-headlined by Motörhead and Ozzy Osbourne in Stoke on August 1, spent a small fortune on vinyl and passed many a night getting drunk on pints of snakebite in Stourbridge pubs. But not once did Ulrich mention to his friends the fact that he himself was a drummer with dreams of starting a band.

'I was just some fucking snot-nosed Danish kid who was really excited about their music and, I don't mean this disrespectfully, but I think they were psyched about having a guy around who was as passionate about their music as they were,' Ulrich later recalled. '[I enjoyed] being around them and watching them write and, watching them play, watching them interact with each other, watching their relationship with the music around them, you know, in terms of Zeppelin and stuff that was inspiring them and so on. I was just interested then in how bands worked.'

In mid-August Ulrich said farewell to his new friends and travelled south to London ahead of his flight to Copenhagen. He had one final mission in mind.

In the summer of 1981, when their ferocious, feral live album *No Sleep 'Til Hammersmith* debuted atop the UK album chart, Motörhead could justifiably lay claim to being not only the noisiest rock band in the United Kingdom, but also the most popular. In the wake of their headline bow at the Heavy Metal Holocaust festival, the trio's redoubtable leader Ian 'Lemmy' Kilmister decided to capitalise on his band's momentum by booking a room at Nomis studios in west London for the purpose of writing material for what would be their fifth studio album. To Lemmy, the unscheduled appearance of a slight Danish teenager at the rehearsal room door one August afternoon would prove to be only a minor distraction; for Lars Ulrich the experience was nothing less than 'a mindfuck'.

'Motörhead were obviously among my two or three favourite bands,' says Ulrich. 'I'd met Motörhead when they were opening for Ozzy in June 1981. That was their first kind of big tour of America so I followed them around California – San Diego, LA, San Francisco – I even drove behind the tour bus at one point. They were very easy-going, friendly people and invited me in. A month or two later, I found out they were rehearsing at Nomis [so I] rang the doorbell and within thirty minutes I was sitting in [their] rehearsal room.'

As Ulrich sat in the corner of the room watching Lemmy, guitarist 'Fast' Eddie Clarke and drummer Phil 'Philthy Animal' Taylor piece together riffs that would soon enough be unveiled to the world as the deathless 'Iron Fist', he found his excitement temporarily overwhelmed by a sense of envy. *This* was what he wanted for himself, this noise, this fury, this power.

Eight weeks later Ulrich was back in Los Angeles. Never tired of the sound of his own voice, the teenager spent much of his first week at home in Newport Beach spinning tales of his adventures to his fellow metal nerds. The new Motörhead material sounded awesome, he assured them. Diamond Head were cool guys, just like us, he shrugged. And yeah, seeing Iron Maiden's final gig with vocalist Paul Di'Anno in Copenhagen in September was kinda neat, but it was a bummer that the guy was so drunk when he and Stein tried to talk to him backstage. Listening enrapt, Brian Slagel almost forgot to tell his friend that he had some news of his own: he and John Kornarens had decided to put out a compilation album of their favourite unsigned LA bands.

'So, hey, can my band be on the record?' Ulrich asked.

Slagel gently reminded his friend that he didn't have a band.

'I'm putting one together,' the drummer insisted. 'Save a space for me.'

Slagel laughed and agreed that he'd reserve a place for Lars's imaginary band, not believing for a moment that his friend was serious.

'I remember specifically being in his house once listening to records and he had a drum set in the corner, stacked up, and he was like, "I'm going to start a band,"' Slagel recalled. 'And I was like, "Sure you are Lars, I'm going to start a band too." Because there was no way that that was going to happen.'

That same evening though Ulrich placed a phone call to 13004 Curtis and King Road in Norwalk. When James Hetfield answered, the accented voice on the other end of the line asked if he wanted to be on a record. Sure, said Hetfield, sure. When the singer replaced the receiver, Ulrich immediately dialled another number. His second conversation of the day with Slagel was much shorter than the first.

'I have a band,' he said simply.

2 – HIT THE LIGHTS

The chairman and chief executive officer of Metal Blade Records is on his hands and knees in a storage cupboard at his company's headquarters in Agoura Hills in Los Angeles County, rifling through a stack of dust-covered twelve-inch record sleeves.

'It's amazing how a bunch of kids hanging out in LA became this gigantic thing,' he says. 'I mean, look, I was in the right place at the right time. I'm just happy to have helped. It's just weird how the whole thing has played out.'

With a triumphant yelp, Brian Slagel emerges from the closet clutching a copy of his record label's first ever release, catalogue number MBR 1001. The album's crudely designed artwork, featuring a set of human skulls suspended in a cloud above the Californian coastline, is macabre but striking: above it the words *The New Heavy Metal Revue presents Metal Massacre* are picked out in stark silver type. Flipping the sleeve, Slagel points to the fifth and final band name listed on the album's second side: Mettallica.

'We spelt their name wrong,' he laughs. 'I don't think it held them back.'

It is a beautiful afternoon in Conejo Valley in Los Angeles, and in his black shorts, black trainers and black T-shirt emblazoned with the logo of Swedish occult metallers Ghost, Slagel is dressed for the skate park rather than the boardroom. A cheerful, convivial character, with a shaven head, black-rimmed spectacles and a neatly trimmed auburn goatee beard, Slagel could pass for a Silverlake bartender as easily as a LA record company mogul. But the silver and gold discs that hang from the walls of his sunlit office offer testament to his significance within the world of heavy metal. Over the years Metal Blade has brought uncompromising acts such as Slayer, Armored Saint, Behemoth and Cannibal Corpse to international prominence, and one month shy of his label's thirtieth anniversary of operation, the fifty-one-year-old's passion for uncovering and encouraging new bands remains undiminished.

Slagel's inspiration for the *Metal Massacre* compilation came, somewhat inevitably, directly from the New Wave of British Heavy Metal, specifically the Iron Maiden-fronted *Metal for Muthas* New Wave of British Heavy Metal compilation, a collection overseen by Neal Kay and released by EMI Records in February 1980. As 1981 neared its end Slagel was working as a buyer for Oz Records in Woodland Hills. By night he ran his own metal fanzine *The New Heavy Metal Revue*, which he would print and sell at local concerts. Looking at the bands featured in the pages of his own publication, Slagel wondered why emerging metal acts from Los Angeles could not be showcased on a compilation similar to that masterminded by Kay. After receiving assurances from distributors that such a product would be marketable, he began contacting his favourite local bands to see if they might care to contribute to the project. Slagel then began the process of scraping together the funds necessary to make this vision a reality. By the spring of 1982 the twenty-one-year-old had amassed nine tracks and sufficient funds to commission a 2,500 unit press-run for the album. Just one thing was missing: the song promised to him by Lars Ulrich.

A decade ago James Hetfield was asked by one of this book's authors if it was true that he would never have formed a band with Ulrich had the drummer not dangled before him the offer of a track on *Metal Massacre* in October 1981. Metallica's front man laughed long and hard before delivering his answer.

'Well, every day there are things that can change the course of history,' he said, deftly deflecting the question. Ulrich's offer was 'pretty interesting', he said, not least because his one previous meeting with the young Danish drummer had 'no vibe'.

'At that time in my life I wanted to play music,' Hetfield reflected, 'I didn't want to work.'

'We certainly didn't hit it off,' admits Ulrich, looking back upon the pair's first meeting in May 1981. 'I had a drum kit that looked as if it had fallen out of a cereal packet and James likes to tell people that it fell over every time I hit a cymbal. He also likes to tell people that he thought I smelled bad, because of course Europeans don't wash. Musically though I could tell that he was more gifted than Hugh Tanner, and after we were done playing and we knew we hadn't clicked we actually hung out and had a pretty good time. It's like when you take a girl on a date and you know that there's no fucking chance you're going to get laid, it takes some of the tension out.'

After reconnecting with Hetfield in the autumn of 1981, Ulrich set about drawing the older teenager closer with a cautious yet determined attentiveness. At the time, both young men had day jobs – Ulrich delivered copies of the *Los Angeles Times* (a position for which he was paid a monthly stipend of $400), while Hetfield made stickers for pharmaceuticals for the Steven Label Corporation in Santa Fe Springs – but each evening the pair would convene in Ulrich's bedroom or at Ron McGovney's house to swap cassettes, pore over the latest editions of *Sounds* and listen to records into the night's smallest hours. Slowly, brick by brick, the defensive wall Hetfield had built around himself throughout adolescence began to crumble.

'At that time Hetfield was the shyest person I'd ever seen in my life,' Ulrich recalls. 'He could barely utter the word "Hello" and he certainly couldn't make eye contact. He was incredibly shy and uncomfortable around people. I remember him meeting my parents; it was almost like hiding, pulling back. I'd just never been around people who were that uncomfortable around adults.

But I instantly felt that there was a connection there. I could tell that he was passionate about music, and there was an attraction to him because he was gifted but he was very reserved. I just remember that we were a perfect match because I thought that I could help pull some of that stuff out of him; he made up for some of my lack of talent. I felt I could do something with his gifts. It was like a yin and yang kind of thing. I felt it instantly. I felt it from the get go.'

'We shared a "let's fucking do something" attitude,' says Hetfield. 'I knew he had a lot of connections and loads of drive. I'd jammed with other guys before, and told them to fuck off because they weren't good enough. With Lars it kinda felt different.

'When I hooked up with Lars, I still didn't really trust anyone. But at least we enjoyed the same kind of music.'

Having committed to making music together, one of the duo's most pressing tasks was to decide upon a name for their new union. Naturally, Lars Ulrich had no shortage of suggestions. No stranger to choosing terrible band names himself, James Hetfield was nonetheless less than impressed as he regarded Ulrich's initial list. The drummer's ideas included Deathwish, Death Threat and Death Chamber. From this starting point, somehow it got worse: Nixon. Dumb Fuck. Bigmouth and Friends. Execution. Exterminator. Helldriver. Napalm. Vietnam. Thunderfuck.

The singer wondered aloud whether his new friend might have any alternatives that were a bit less . . . shit.

'Metallica?' Ulrich suggested.

The fact that this name was not the drummer's to offer was not a matter that detained him. Inspired by the launch of *Sounds* magazine off-shoot *Kerrang!* – the world's first dedicated hard rock/heavy metal periodical, titled in onomatopoeic tribute to the noise made when an over-amplified electric guitar is struck with force – in the summer of 1981, Ron Quintana, Ulrich's friend from San Francisco, had determined to start his own heavy metal fanzine: the word 'Metallica' was among a list of possible titles he drew up for consideration. When Quintana sought Ulrich's counsel on the matter, the opportunist Dane made a mental note of the name and suggested that his buddy might like to go with the title *Metal Mania*. With Motörhead's Lemmy now glowering from the xeroxed front cover of *Metal Mania* issue number one, Ulrich surmised that Quintana would have no further use for the alternative titles on his list. An approving James Hetfield immediately set to work on creating a band logo.

Even as Hetfield and Ulrich edged closer to a creative union, Brian Slagel grew increasingly fretful over their participation in his planned compilation album. Eventually he placed a phone call to Ulrich to inform him that he and John Kornarens had booked a mastering session for the album at Bijou Studios in Hollywood. If Lars's band missed the studio deadline, he was told, they would miss the cut. The drummer asked for the date and time of the mastering session and promised he would deliver. True to his word, at around 3 p.m. on the appointed day, he arrived at Bijou with a cassette tape in his hand. Mastering engineer Joe Borja placed the cassette on the console and asked the drummer if he also had $50 to cover the cost of transferring the track to two-inch audio tape. The colour drained from Ulrich's face. Panicked, and potless, the drummer begged Slagel and Kornarens for help. As Slagel shrugged apologetically, Kornarens opened his wallet to display $52 in cash, which the Dane gratefully snatched from his hands. Borja took the money, inserted the cassette into a tape deck, and pressed 'Record' on the studio's reel-to-reel machine, as Slagel and Kornarens sat back to listen to their friend's band for the very first time.

'Wow,' said Slagel, 'this is actually not bad.'

'Hit the Lights' had its origins in an unfinished Leather Charm song written by Hetfield and Hugh Tanner. Despite a title cribbed from Diamond Head's 'Shoot Out the Lights', and a key and tempo on loan from Motörhead, in Hetfield and Ulrich's hands its presentation and delivery was nonetheless thrilling. It begins, as all significant things should, with chaos: a swell of guitars building in heft, volume and density, a rattle of tom-toms and then a single guitar thrusting forward with an irresistibly propulsive riff. 'No life 'til leather, we are gonna kick some ass tonight' squeals James Hetfield, introducing a lyric as dumb as a sack of spanners but sweetly engaging in its naivety. Appropriately, given that the composition was pieced together in Ulrich's Park Newport bedroom, the song is a bedroom fantasy with its foundations in the duo's own gig-going experiences: at the time, of course, Metallica had no fans, 'screaming', 'insane' or otherwise. But, as a manifesto of intent, the track is quite startling in its clarity and ambition.

'I knew it was going to be heavy,' says Kornarens, 'because when Brian and I were setting up in which order the bands appeared on the record I was talking to Lars and I said, "Lars, it's going to be heavy, right?" And so I said, "I'll put you last on the album because we want to go out strong." So when I heard it I thought, "Well, it's definitely got energy and intensity." The production sounded pretty bad and James's singing was kinda streaky, but who cares? It had the energy and the explosion at the very end was the perfect way for the album to end.'

Only in subsequent weeks did Lars Ulrich admit to his friends exactly how close *Metal Massacre* came to being a nine- rather than ten-track showcase of the Los Angeles underground metal community. He and Hetfield had committed the song to cassette on a borrowed TEAC four-track recorder only the day prior to the album's mastering date. And though Hetfield had supplied both rhythm and bass guitar tracks for the recording, come the morning of deadline day 'Hit the Lights' had yet to be furnished with lead guitar breaks. In desperation, Ulrich called upon a gifted Jamaican guitarist named Lloyd Grant, with whom he had jammed earlier in the year (Grant having responded to one of the drummer's ads in *The Recycler*) to supply lead guitar flourishes. As Slagel and Kornarens sat in Bijou Studios overseeing the first stages of the mastering process, Ulrich and Hetfield were still sitting in Grant's front room, watching the guitarist nail his solo in just one take. 'He was a cool guy with a great attitude,' Hetfield recalled, 'and he could really shred. But he could not play rhythm guitar, which was really strange. So on the way to dropping our tape in to Brian, we stopped off at his house, he threw down a solo and off we went. And that was it for him.'

Though it would be early June before Metallica would receive the initial pressings of their vinyl debut from Brian Slagel, Hetfield and Ulrich now at least had a professional demo tape to play to interested parties. They did not, however, have a band worthy of the name. While Hetfield could adequately cover for the absence of both a guitar player and bassist in a studio environment, he and Ulrich recognised that in order to take their fledgling union beyond the realms of recorded music and out on to the Sunset Strip and beyond, Metallica would require an injection of new blood. To secure a bass player, Hetfield cast his net in the smallest possible arc, leaning on Ron McGovney to help out once again, despite his friend's repeated protestations that he really wasn't interested, having decided instead to pursue a career in photography. The quest for a guitar player, meanwhile, sent Ulrich back to the 'Musicians Wanted' section of the by now invaluable *The Recycler*. This time his advert specified that interested parties should be a fan of Iron Maiden, Motörhead and Welsh power trio Budgie. It was the mention of the last band which led a young guitarist from the recently dissolved Orange County group Panic to pick up the phone and introduce himself to McGovney as 'the best guitar player you've ever heard'.

†

David Scott Mustaine was born on September 13, 1961, in La Mesa, San Diego County, the fourth child, and first son, of parents John and Emily. John was the West Coast branch manager for Bank of America and an alcoholic, an affliction that exacerbated the breakdown of his marriage in 1965, when Dave was just four. The boy's childhood was unsettled and unhappy: post-divorce, John determined to make his former wife's life a living hell, and so Emily and her children were forced to adopt an itinerant lifestyle, moving all over California in order to stay one step ahead of her vengeful ex-husband. 'For the most part,' recalled Mustaine, 'we were a family on the run.'

This fractured lifestyle did little for Mustaine's schooling, but the perennial new kid learned to make friends quickly and had a talent for sports and music. Upon graduation from elementary school, he was rewarded with a gift of an acoustic guitar from his mother, a thoughtful and generous gesture at a time when the family were subsisting on food stamps and Emily's meagre earnings as a domestic maid. He dutifully set about teaching himself the basic chord shapes.

At the age of fourteen Mustaine joined his first band, teaming up with his brother-in-law Mark Balli and guitarist John Vorhees to play Bowie, Kiss and Zeppelin covers at backyard parties and barbecues. Soon enough, to his delight, he discovered that his chosen instrument made him popular with females other than those to whom he was related.

'I knew this cute girl who was going out with a friend of a friend, and as soon as she knew I played guitar she dumped him and became my girlfriend,' he recalled. 'I thought, "This is great. You mean I get laid just because I can play this thing? Cool."'

Having discovered sex and rock 'n' roll, it was perhaps inevitable that Mustaine would soon secure access to the third vital component of a typical Seventies Californian adolescence: drugs. The guitarist was just thirteen when he first got high, by fifteen he was dealing marijuana out of his family's Huntington Beach apartment. The trade earned Mustaine money, new friends and a reputation: for the first time in his life he felt important and valued.

'I was a rock 'n' roll rebel,' he later recalled in his best-selling autobiography *Mustaine: A Life in Metal*. 'I had a guitar strung across my back, I had a knife in my belt, and I had a sneer on my face. And that was it. That was enough.'

'My first impression of him was, "He's a conceited asshole,"' recalled Ron McGovney. It was McGovney who answered the phone to Mustaine when the guitarist answered Lars Ulrich's *Recycler* ad: the bassist stuck his head into the garage where Hetfield and Ulrich were jamming and said, 'Which one of you wants to get this telephone call, because this guy's head will not fit through the door if he ever shows up over here.'

'The first time I met Lars I went to his house in Newport Beach and we listened to the "Hit the Lights" demo that Lloyd Grant had played on,' says Mustaine. 'I remember telling Lars that it needed more guitar solos. A little later I got a call to come down and jam with James and Ron. I was warming up and they just walked off into the other room, which I thought was pretty rude. I said "Are we going to audition or what?" and James said, "No, you've got the job."'

'Things are happening a bit over here now,' wrote Ulrich in a year-end letter to Diamond Head's Brian Tatler. 'This geezer in LA is doing a compilation album of ten new, young LA HM bands and our band are on it with a track called "Hit the Lights". Good break . . . Anyway, our band is called Metallica and I'll send you a copy when it comes out. The lead guitarist is pretty fast. I think you'll like him . . . We rehearse six nights a week so we are getting pretty tight and we are (tryin' to) writing some pretty good songs, where we try and stay away from the norms and be a bit different, so at least we won't be slacked [*sic*] off as being too predictable and stuff like that. Let's see what happens.'

†

There is a story told about the Los Angeles rock scene circa 1982, which has long since passed into Metallica lore. According to legend, Lars Ulrich found himself at the famous Troubadour nightclub on Melrose Avenue one summer evening when Metallica's candy-floss-haired nemeses Mötley Crüe strode into the bar with their entourage. The story has it that the Crüe party were intoxicated, obnoxious and in high spirits, having freshly inked a lucrative major label deal with Elektra Records; Ulrich, meanwhile, was said to have been drinking alone to numb his growing frustration over his own band's failure to detonate a bomb under the Strip. The sight of Crüe bandleader, songwriter and bassist Nikki Sixx, and his coterie holding court in the club that night then served only to inflame the drummer's sense of injustice. Drawing himself to his full height, the five-foot-eight-inch Dane allegedly approached Mötley Crüe's table and informed the group's towering bassist that his band 'sucked', at which point, to howls of laughter, Sixx grabbed the impertinent critic by his lapels and threw him halfway across the room.

It is an amusing anecdote, one which feeds nicely into the received wisdom that at this time Metallica were fearless lone wolves who prowled the hair metal jungle in search of a kill. In truth, however, the incident never happened. The reality of the story is rather more prosaic. As James Hetfield remembers it, Metallica did indeed cross paths with the Crüe one night at the Troubadour, but their encounter was made on uneven terms.

'We were outside a club, sitting on a parked car, pissed off and drunk,' Hetfield recalled. 'We didn't even have enough money to get into the show, so we were sitting outside trying to weasel our way in somehow, meet someone, you know? Then those guys

[Mötley Crüe] come walking out with high heels and grandma's jewellery on. They walked by, and we yelled, "You guys suck!" They turned around like tough guys and just stood there. They looked like fucking giants 'cause they've got their Elton John heels on. Meanwhile, we're standing there in our fucking tennis shoes going, "Huh?" They flicked a cigarette on us and walked away.'

At this time Mötley Crüe were a band of unhinged delinquents as unlikely to back down from a fight as they were to decline a line of cocaine deposited in the cleavage of a stripper. That they chose not to crack Metallica's skulls against the Melrose Avenue sidewalk that evening said everything about the two acts' respective fortunes in the summer of 1982. The Crüe, to borrow a title from their first seven-inch single, were the toast of the town: LA natives whose self-financed, independently released 1981 debut album *Too Fast for Love* had already sold more than 20,000 copies on their own Leathur Records imprint. Metallica, by contrast, were a glorified covers band with a singer who could barely look an audience in the eyes, a drummer who could not keep time, a self-obsessed, damaged guitarist and a bassist who didn't even want to be in the group. As Ulrich has often insisted, Metallica may well have defined themselves as the 'anti-Mötley Crüe', but in the haziest days of 1982 the chasm between the two parties was so vast that the more established group were barely aware of their snotty brethren's existence. To Mötley Crüe, Metallica were invisible men, a life form unworthy of even the most common of Sunset Strip courtesies: contempt.

In truth, one could easily view this casual humiliation as representative of Metallica's status across the Hollywood rock scene as a whole. For while James Hetfield would once describe Los Angeles as being a place that 'didn't show [his group] a lot of love', neither did the city show them any measure of discernible hatred. Instead, the group were met with the most galling of receptions, one of indifference.

'In those days no one was even paying attention,' Hetfield admitted. 'We were playing, and people would just have this lost look on their faces,' he said. 'We'd go, "Man, what the fuck is the matter with you? Give me the finger, spit on me, yell, smile, do something" . . . That made us angry.'

Metallica's first concert took place on March 14, 1982, at Radio City, an unprepossessing, 150-capacity club situated at 945 S. Knott Ave in Anaheim. On the afternoon of the show, Hetfield, Mustaine, McGovney and Ulrich assembled in the garage of 13004 Curtis and King Road, pressed down the 'Record' button on a boombox, and ran through a nine-song set featuring 'Hit the Lights', a new Mustaine-penned composition titled 'Jump in the Fire' and seven New Wave of British Heavy Metal cover versions, including no fewer than four Diamond Head tracks – 'Helpless', 'Sucking My Love', 'Am I Evil?' and 'The Prince'. After listening to their cassette, which also featured versions of 'Blitzkrieg' by Leicester quintet Blitzkrieg, 'Let it Loose' by Mansfield's Savage and 'Killing Time' by Northern Irish metallers Sweet Savage, the satisfied quartet began breaking down their backline for the twenty-minute drive to Orange County.

Practice, of course, can only take a band so far: the acid test of a group's character comes when their songs are presented in front of a paying audience. In this regard Metallica did not get off to the strongest of starts.

'I was really nervous and a little uncomfortable without a guitar,' Hetfield recalls, 'and then during the first song Dave broke a string. It seemed to take him an eternity to change it and I was standing there really embarrassed. We were really disappointed afterwards. But there were never as many people at the following shows as there were at that first one.'

'The crowd didn't get into them,' is the considered verdict of Patrick Scott, who drove the band's drummer to the show. 'But it was still a cool thing to see, just to see somebody playing Sweet

Savage songs and Blitzkrieg songs in LA, because there was none of that going on.'

'I went there with Pat,' says Bob Nalbandian, who at the time edited *Headbanger* fanzine from his parent's Huntington Beach home. 'It wasn't a great show by any means, but it was something different in Orange County, because you never saw bands play like that before.'

For his part Lars Ulrich considered that his band 'went down pretty good'. Recording the details of the gig in his diary, as he would for every future Metallica show that year, the meticulous drummer estimated that the crowd numbered seventy-five people and noted that the quartet were paid $15 for the engagement. 'Very nervous' he admitted. 'Played so-so.'

Ironically, given Ulrich's stated antipathy towards the group, he would have Mötley Crüe to thank for his band's next significant live outings, a pair of performances which would see Metallica share a stage with one of their New Wave of British Heavy Metal heroes, Saxon.

'We had heard that Saxon was gonna be playing the Whisky [a Go Go] in Hollywood,' is Ron McGovney's recollection. 'So I went over to the club with our demo, and as I was walking up, I run into Tommy Lee and Vince Neil from Mötley Crüe (who I was taking pictures for at the time). They said, "Hey Ron, what's up?" I told them that Saxon was doing a gig at the Whisky and I wanted to try to get my band to open up for them. They said, "Yeah, we were gonna open up for them but we're getting too big to open. Come on in and I'll introduce you to the chick that does the booking." So I dropped off the tape and she called me back the very next day, I remember her telling me, "You guys are pretty good . . . you remind me of this local band called Black 'N Blue." Anyway, she said, "Saxon is scheduled to play two nights; we're gonna have Ratt open for them the first night and your band can open the second night."'

For Lars Ulrich this booking – which comprised two opening performances, as Saxon were to play two headline sets each night – amounted to a very big deal. The teenager had discovered the Barnsley quintet's *Wheels of Steel* album in the summer of 1980, and he considered Biff Byford's band to be one of *the* essential New Wave of British Heavy Metal collectives. The shows would prove to be a lesson in the ways of the music industry for the young drummer. Turning up at the Whisky in the middle of the afternoon on March 27, Metallica were immediately advised by Saxon's road crew that they would not be afforded time to sound check for the evening's first sold-out show. Nor would they be provided with dressing room access for the night as Saxon were to be receiving VIP guests, including Mötley Crüe and Ozzy Osbourne and his manager and fiancée Sharon Arden. When Ulrich asked if perhaps his band might be allowed to use an onstage fan to keep their gear from overheating, he was informed that the fan was solely for the use of Mr Byford. So far so "Fuck you".

Such intransigence was never likely to do more than scratch the surface of Ulrich's Teflon-coated ebullience however. At 9 p.m. the drummer walked onstage in front of a 400-strong crowd and launched into the opening rolls of 'Hit the Lights'. Allotted just twenty minutes for their six-song set, Metallica dispensed with stage banter or song introductions and simply attacked. The group did, however, find time to debut another new track, 'Metal Militia'. Analysing his band's earliest songwriting efforts, James Hetfield once observed that 'the epic feel is definitely from Diamond Head, while the simplicity came from Motörhead', and 'Metal Militia' was the clearest example yet of this fusion. Here Hetfield sings of his band in militaristic terms, 'fighting for one cause' in uniforms of 'leather and metal', and encourages those listening to fall in line behind the quartet in their crusade 'to take on the world with our heavy metal.' Offering a rallying call to arms reminiscent of Saxon's own 'Denim and Leather', the new song was met with roars of approval from the Yorkshire band's Californian fans.

Already installed as Metallica's harshest critic, Ulrich was less impressed. The drummer would later write that his group were plagued by 'awful' sound on their first show of the night, adding, 'The band as a whole sucked.' (Amusingly, however, Ulrich noted that he himself 'played great'.) Afforded one extra song for their second show of the night, the four-piece bolstered their set with a third Brian Tatler/Sean Harris composition, 'Sucking My Love'. As was his habit, James Hetfield declined to introduce the song as a cover version, which led Saxon's watching soundman Paul Owen to enquire sarcastically whether the young group were familiar with an English band called Diamond Head. Their faces duly flushed with embarrassment.

'Had a good time,' Ulrich concluded in his diary, 'but never met Saxon.'

Ulrich was not the only person in the room critiquing the band's performance that night. The *LA Times* commissioned their arts correspondent Terry Atkinson to file his own review, which duly appeared in the March 29 edition of the newspaper.

'Saxon could also use a fast, hot guitar player of the Eddie Van Halen ilk,' Atkinson opined. 'Opening quartet Metallica had one, but little else. The local group needs considerable development to overcome a pervasive awkwardness.'

Ulrich's frank assessments of his colleagues' performances on March 27 were an early indication both of his own exacting standards and of the tensions that were already starting to surface in his new band. By his own admission, Dave Mustaine was 'rarely sober and always stoned' during his first six months in Metallica, and the guitarist's constant desire to be the centre of attention grated with Ron McGovney who concluded that his new band mate was less interested in Metallica's music than in 'the kicks, the parties, the fame'. For his part, Mustaine was (justifiably) concerned that as musicians his colleagues simply were not capable enough to share a stage with him: 'There were times when James and I wanted to kick Lars out,' he admitted, 'and times Lars and I talked about letting James go.' Hetfield, meanwhile, was having his own crises of faith. Painfully self-conscious and cripplingly insecure, the singer was concerned that he possessed neither the voice, the looks or the charisma to front the group.

'I was open for *anybody* doing it,' he later confessed. 'I thought that the band wouldn't make it without a front man. I thought that singing and playing guitar didn't look right, and the singer couldn't be focused enough.' Entreaties were made to several of the area's star front men – John Bush from Armored Saint and Sammy Dijon from Ruthless among them – but no firm connections were established.

A decision was reached instead to recruit a second lead guitar player, so that Hetfield might be freed up to focus solely on singing once again. On April 23, the band made their debut as a five-piece at the Concert Factory in Costa Mesa, with one Brad Parker, aka Damian C. Phillips, in their line-up. It would prove to be a short-lived union. No sooner had the words 'And coming up next . . . Metallica' fallen from the MC's lips than Parker appeared onstage on his own, treating the crowd to his finest Eddie Van Halen impressions, as his bemused colleagues looked on aghast from the dressing room. When the band convened in Ron McGovney's garage later that same week for the purpose of recording their first 'proper' demo tape, Parker was not invited to attend.

Untitled, but often erroneously referred to as the 'Power Metal' demo, the four-track demo tape was split between two Mustaine compositions – 'Jump in the Fire' and 'The Mechanix' – and two re-worked Leather Charm originals – 'Hit the Lights' and 'Motorbreath'. Crudely recorded, while the four songs manage to capture the young band's raw energy, the collection is more notable for featuring some of the worst singing and most excruciating lyrics ever committed to tape. In fairness to Hetfield, he had already voiced his own concerns about his singing ability months prior to the recording. But from the moment he delivers the opening line of 'Hit the Lights' here, with his keening vocals lathered in reverb, the singer's discomfiture is as palpable as it is painful to hear. That said, this awkwardness is easy to understand when one considers the nature of the lyrics submitted for him to sing by Mustaine. Already hamstrung by one of the most lumpen riffs in Metallica's catalogue, the earliest recorded version of 'Jump in the Fire' is further besmirched by Mustaine's priapic adolescent poetry that sees the narrator talk of 'Movin' [his] hips in a circular way' and confessing his desire to 'Pull your body to my waist, feel how good it fits'. This, though, was poetry comparable to the finest works of Sylvia Plath when placed alongside the overripe masturbatory fantasy that is 'The Mechanix'.

'You say you wanna get your order filled,' sings Hetfield, 'Made me shiver when I put it in, Pumping just won't do ya know . . . luckily for you.' There then follows a chorus which, with its references to bulging pistons and cranked drive shafts, reads like J. G. Ballard might were the author to turn his hand to writing the letters page for a top-shelf magazine.

Despite this emphatic lack of grace, the band's momentum continued to gather pace. A pair of gigs were booked for May, a further two in June and four in July, while August saw no fewer than seven shows pencilled into Ulrich's diary. It was at the first of these, an August 2 headline appearance at the Troubadour that James Hetfield punched his drummer for the first time.

Ironically, that evening's concert was one of Metallica's best performances to date. At the conclusion of their nine-song set, the audience inside Doug Weston's storied venue called the quartet back to the stage for an encore. The problem, however, lay in the fact that the band had not rehearsed for such an eventuality, and consequently had nothing prepared. During a hastily convened backstage discussion, Hetfield suggested that the band might re-emerge to play 'Blitzkrieg' while Ulrich put forward Diamond Head's 'Helpless' as his preferred choice. After a show of hands 'Blitzkrieg' was nominated and the band trooped back onstage to warm applause. But as Hetfield approached his mic stand, Ulrich, in clear defiance of the principles of democracy, began beating out the intro to 'Helpless' instead. Thrown completely off-guard, the world's most acutely self-conscious front man stuttered and stumbled through the lyrics, his face ablaze with embarrassment. When the song ground painfully to its conclusion, Hetfield walked to the back of the stage, hurled his guitar straight at Ulrich and slugged the shell-shocked drummer hard in the stomach.

'You fucker!' he raged. 'Don't you *ever* do that again.'

Elsewhere, though, matters were progressing in a rather more pleasing manner for the occasionally fractious quartet. Three weeks on from the release of Brian Slagel's *Metal Massacre* compilation, a collection which served to highlight in the starkest terms the gaping chasm in attitude and tone between Metallica and contemporaries such as Ratt, Bitch and Malice, the quartet found themselves in a recording studio once more, this time at the behest of local punk rock impresario Kenny Kane. Kane told Ulrich that he'd been given his own label imprint by the fast-rising Anaheim record label Rocshire Records and that he wanted to make Metallica his first signing. The drummer duly booked the band into a small Orange County recording studio called Chateau East on July 6, where they cut versions of the seven original tracks they had written to date: 'Hit the Lights', 'The Mechanix', 'Motorbreath', 'Seek & Destroy', 'Metal Militia', 'Jump in the Fire' and 'Phantom Lord'. A significant improvement on the uneven 'Power Metal' demo, the recordings were crisp, sharp and aggressive, the work of a band beginning to find their own voice and range. Ulrich duly amended his band's upcoming gig posters with the information that the *Metallica* EP would be released on September 1. When Kenny Kane took possession of the master tapes however, he phoned Ulrich in a rage, claiming that Metallica had duped him. The songs, he claimed were 'too heavy metal'. Why, he demanded to know, had Metallica not recorded the punkish songs he had heard them play live? Ulrich had to calmly explain that those songs were, in fact, cover versions. Kane said he could take the tapes back and do with them as he wished.

In the weeks that followed, Lars Ulrich and his friend Patrick Scott dubbed literally hundreds of cassettes from this master tape, now titled *No Life 'Til Leather*, in tribute to both the opening line of the tape's opening track and the title of Motörhead's 1981 live album, and posted them to every fanzine writer, every tape trader, every record store owner and every gig promoter in their address books. In a matter of weeks, the tape was *everywhere*.

'Kornarens had got a copy of the demo at the record store and he said "Hey, I wanna play you something, but I'm not going to tell you who it is," ' recalls Brian Slagel. 'So he played the tape and I thought it was really good. I thought it was some new English metal band, because he didn't tell me who it was. I said, "This is pretty good, what is this?" and he said, "You don't want to guess?" I said, "No, I have no idea." He said, "This is Metallica." I said, "Wow, this is Metallica? Wow, they've really gone so far!" Because it was *incredible*.'

In the weeks that followed, Lars Ulrich was inundated with requests for interviews from fanzines located all over America. Among these were Ron Quintana's *Metal Mania*, Bob Muldowney's *Kick Ass Monthly*, K. J. Doughton's *Northwest Metal* and John Strednansky's *Metal Rendezvous*. From his booth in a Chevron filling station at which he was now employed, the young Dane spoke passionately about his band's desire to initiate a new age for metal. When Quintana asked Patrick Scott to conduct an interview with Ulrich for *Metal Mania*, the two friends sat giggling in Ulrich's Park Newport bedroom as they composed the notice, which concluded that Metallica had 'the potential to become US metal gods'.

'We were just laughing at the stuff we were talking about,' says Scott now. 'It just seemed so far-fetched at that point.'

But as Metallica's fortunes were falling into place, the band's members were falling out with one another. This discord began with an argument over a dog which descended into a fist fight the aftermath of which saw Hetfield tell Mustaine that he was sacked from the band.

'At the time I was dealing drugs to survive,' explains Mustaine, 'and, whenever Metallica were playing concerts, people knew I was gone so they'd break into my apartment to steal my dope. So I figured I'd get a couple of pit bulls to guard the place. I took one of them to rehearsal one day and it put its paws on the bass player's car. I guess James thought she was going to scratch it, so he pushed her off with his foot. We started arguing. And then I hit him.'

As Hetfield wiped blood and phlegm from his face, Ron McGovney tried to intervene to protect his friend. Mustaine deflected the bassist's attack and flipped him over his hip, sending McGovney crashing down on to an entertainment centre in the corner of the room. As a stunned Ulrich looked on in disbelief, Hetfield screamed at Mustaine to get out of his friend's house.

'You're out of the band!' Hetfield roared. 'Get the fuck out of here!'

'Fuck you!' Mustaine retorted. 'I quit.'

The break-up lasted all of twenty-four hours. The following day, the guitarist sheepishly tendered his apologies to Hetfield and McGovney, and was reinstated in the group. But the events of that afternoon would not quickly be forgotten.

'That,' the guitarist reflected some twenty years on, 'was definitely the beginning of the end for me.'

✝

At the start of October 1982 James Hetfield was moved to write Metallica's first love song. The words he penned in his notebook, however, were not inspired by a girlfriend, but rather by a city situated almost 400 miles north of his home town. An unabashed love letter to San Francisco and its fanatical heavy metal community, the members of which gathered nightly 'to maim and kill', 'Whiplash' contained the singer's most direct and affecting lyrics to date.

Metallica's first invitation to play the city by the Bay came courtesy of Brian Slagel, who had spent the weeks since the release of *Metal Massacre* putting plans in place for an LA metal showcase at the Stone nightclub on Broadway. The band were actually a last-minute addition to the September 18 gig, with Slagel only calling on his friends after Cirith Ungol were forced to drop off the bill, but Ulrich deemed the opportunity to reconnect with old friends in Northern California worthy of the five-hour drive up Interstate 5.

The metal scene in San Francisco had taken on an irresistible momentum since the launch of *Metal Mania* fanzine in August 1981. The city got its own specialist hard rock/heavy metal shop with the opening of the Record Vault on Polk Street at the beginning of 1982. That March, Ron Quintana and his friends Ian Kallen and Howie Klein were granted their own Saturday night metal show, *Rampage Radio*, on the University of San Francisco's KUSF college radio station; the following month city-centre nightclub the Old Waldorf on 444 Battery Street announced the launch of a new weekly metal night, Metal Mondays. In the weeks that followed, Iron Maiden, Motörhead, Scorpions and Saxon made stops in the city and the number of denim-and-leather-clad adolescents on Broadway began to multiply. It was into this fecund environment that Metallica came on September 18. They arrived at The Stone to find local glam-rockers Hans Naughty onstage . . . and more than half the audience sitting on the floor with their backs to the band.

San Francisco's 'Trues' had an unambiguous attitude to live shows in their parish. The message for both audiences and local bands such as Exodus, Violation and Blind Illusion alike was simple: go hard or go home. Gigs were violent, chaotic affairs, punctuated by vicious acts of aggression visited upon those whose commitment to the scene was considered by 'Trues' such as Rich Burch and Toby Rage to be less than total.

'A lot of those shows were patrolled by people who were in – for want of a better word – gangs,' reveals Machine Head front man, and life-long Bay Area resident, Robb Flynn. 'Exodus had the STB, which stood for Slay Team Berkeley. These were the guys that would walk over people's heads. They would line up stools at the back of the pit and use these to launch themselves on to the stage. They would run from the back of the room and end up taking out half of the band. Honestly, some of the shows were absolutely crazy. They were terrifying.'

Having been arrested that afternoon on Broadway for drinking alcohol out of open containers, the members of Metallica had a little frustration of their own to work off as they walked on to the stage of The Stone at 10.30 p.m. that evening. But nothing in their short career had prepared the band for the reaction that would greet their set-opener 'Hit the Lights'. Instantly the room erupted into frenzy, with fans screaming every word of Hetfield's escapist anthem back into the singer's face.

'The sheer intensity was incredible!' wrote Brian Lew in his review for *Northwest Metal*. 'Fusing the pile-driving madness of Motörhead and Venom with their own insanity, the band devastated with a non-stop, fast and ultra-furious set of heavy metal.'

'It was our first encounter with real fans,' said Hetfield. 'It was like, these people are here for us, and they like us, and they hate the other bands – and we like that 'cause we hate 'em too.'

'As soon as we went up there we noticed [that] people [were] there for the music, not for the chicks that were hanging out, not for the scene, not for the bar, it was for the music! They weren't hanging out at the bar they were at the edge of the stage waiting, for Metallica.'

'Everyone in San Francisco was wearing Motörhead and Iron Maiden T-shirts,' recalls Ulrich, 'where in LA it was about hair and posing. So that was exciting to us. We had maybe 300 kids there, where in LA we couldn't *give* 300 tickets away.'

'First real great gig,' the drummer noted in his diary. 'Real bangers, real fans, real encores. Had a great fuckin' weekend.'

Exactly one month later, Metallica returned to San Francisco for a Metal Monday show at the Old Waldorf. Also in the city that evening was English music journalist Xavier Russell, in town to file an article for *Kerrang!* on Mötley Crüe, who were supporting local heroes Y&T at the Concord Pavilion. Russell had stopped off at the Record Vault earlier in the week and had fallen into conversation with Ron Quintana, who had handed him a copy of Metallica's *No Life 'Til Leather* demo.

'That night, in a drunken haze, I played the tape over and over again, my Sony Walkman literally shaking with my excitement,' Russell recalls. 'My first reaction was total shock – this was new; it was like crossing Ted Nugent with Motörhead and then putting it through a blender at 120 mph.'

As Russell arrived at the Old Waldorf on October 18 he was met by Ulrich, who recognised the writer from his byline photograph in the pages of *Kerrang!* As Metallica's stage time neared, Russell asked his new friend what the gig would be like.

'Wait and see,' the Dane replied with a laugh.

'They were in the middle of the bill, a band called Laaz Rockit was headlining, and a band called Overdrive was opening, and they were *fantastic*,' Russell recalls. 'Mustaine and Hetfield were like two brothers that didn't get on, each pushing the other out of the way, but it was so exciting. There's certain bands where the minute you see them, you just know they're going to go all the way.'

In the early hours of October 19, Russell placed a phone call to his bosses at *Kerrang!*

'In ten years' time,' he told them, 'this will be the biggest band on the planet.'

†

At the tail end of November, Metallica journeyed up Interstate 5 for their third and fourth Bay Area shows. When they left Los Angeles on the afternoon of November 29, none of the four knew that the weekend would mark the final appearances of their original line-up.

The catalyst for change had been dropped into their already volatile mix one month earlier. Emboldened by the success of his debut *Metal Massacre* show in San Francisco, Brian Slagel had decided to return the compliment by staging a San Francisco metal night in his home town. James Hetfield and Lars Ulrich's decision to show their faces at the Whisky a Go Go at midnight that evening stemmed purely from a wish to say hello to their old friend. The pair arrived as the band Violation were packing away their gear, and an act named Trauma were positioning their own backline on the stage. Within half an hour, one member of this band had made such an impression upon Hetfield and Ulrich, that the pair agreed that Ron McGovney's days as Metallica's four-stringer were numbered

'We heard this wild solo going on,' Hetfield recalled, 'and thought, "I don't see any guitar player up there." It turned out it was the bass player . . . with a wah-wah pedal and this mop of hair . . . We met him after the show. We said, "We're in this band,

and we're looking for a bass player, and we think you'd really fit in. Because you're a big psycho." '

'It literally was one of those Kodak moments where we both looked at one another and said, "Dude, we have to get this guy in Metallica," ' recalls Ulrich. 'I'd never seen anybody like him – his look, his mannerisms, his whole vibe. After we'd swapped numbers I started going to work on him immediately.'

†

Clifford Lee Burton was born in Castro Valley, a region of 60,000 people located in the inland Alameda County some twenty-five miles from the bridges and skyscrapers of San Francisco. The third and final child of Jan and Ray Burton – respectively a Californian-born school teacher and a highway engineer born in the state of Tennessee – the youngest member of the Burton family joined first child Scott and only daughter Connie at 21:30 hours on February 10, 1962.

As a child Cliff attended Earl Warren Junior High, the school at which his mother Jan taught children with special needs. Jan Burton recalls her youngest child as 'always [being] his own person, even when he was an little bitty kid'.

'I used to say, "All the kids playing outside, why aren't you out there playing with them?" And he would say, "They're not playing, they're just sitting around talking – that's boring." Then he'd go in the house and read his books and put on his own music. Even when he was a tiny little kid he would [prefer to] listen to his own music and read." Indeed, such was the young Burton's affinity with the printed word that when tested in the third grade the schoolboy registered a reading ability commensurate with students eight years his elder.

With time, however, it would be music that would emerge as the foremost passion in the life of the young Cliff Burton. Initially inspired by his parents' collection of classical music, soon enough, like countless young men from Castro Valley to Cape Cod, Burton was held enraptured by the hard rock of Lynyrd Skynrd, Blue Oyster Cult, Ted Nugent and Aerosmith. In this, his formative years in the anonymous suburban sprawl of Northern California were entirely normal.

However, the Burtons' pleasant if entirely quotidian suburban lives were soon to be punctured by tragedy. On May 19, 1975, Scott Burton was the victim of a cerebral aneurysm; the sixteen-year-old was taken to hospital but later died. Needless to say, the effect on the family unit was both searing and immediate; friends of Cliff, the insular and quietly defiant remaining son, observed that although the death of his elder brother affected him in a profound manner, this loss was something about which he rarely spoke. Instead, it seems that the enigmatic thirteen-year-old opted to give voice to his grief in the form of actions; actions which, as befits the cliché, spoke louder than words he chose rarely to utter.

Although Burton had begun playing bass guitar – and prior to that piano – before the tragedy that befell his family, it seems that the loss of a sibling served to focus his mind on the task at his fingers. He studied not only the popular bass players of the day – musicians such as Rush's Geddy Lee and Black Sabbath's Geezer Butler – but also the scales and musical notations heard in Bach and Beethoven, as well as the disciplines of baroque music. As his talents grew, the young player would practise for up to six hours a day, his abilities sufficient to outgrow the tutelage of more than one music teacher.

'Cliff didn't take music lessons until he was thirteen, after his brother died,' recalled his mother. 'He said to a couple of people, "I'm going to be the best bassist [I can be] for my brother." We didn't think he had too much talent at all. We had no idea! We just thought he'd plunk, plunk along, which he did at [the beginning]. It really was not easy for him at first . . . [but] about six months in to the lessons, it started to come together. I thought, "This kid's got real potential." And I was totally amazed, because none of the kids in our family had any musical talent.'

As with all fledgling musicians, the point is soon reached when the young player wishes to develop his talents with others. Burton's first band was named EZ Street, a union which also featured drummer Dave Donato and guitarist Jim Martin. Occasionally the drum stool was manned by Mike 'Puffy' Bordin, who alongside Martin would go on to find success with pioneering Bay Area oddballs Faith No More. EZ Street would practise in the hills of Northern California, discovering their sound through the playing of elongated instrumental pieces that owed more to the powerful and hypnotic rhythms of the English cult band Hawkwind than the snappy pop-played-loud anthems beloved of US stadium-botherers Kiss. Away from their instruments, the young musicians dabbled with experimental drugs such as LSD, while Burton himself savoured the flavour of marijuana. But despite such chemically enhanced excursions, elsewhere Burton remained a dependable American adolescent. If his band mates in EZ Street gathered to listen to music in the Burton family home, they did so at a volume considerate of Cliff's sleeping family. As Jim Martin later recalled, 'We'd rock out, but real quietly.' At other times the group would return to the Burton family home from fishing trips at four in the morning, whereupon Cliff would prepare for the party a huge cooking pot of Mexican food, chiding Donato for a loud voice which occasionally rose to a pitch capable of waking the house's sleeping residents.

As with many first bands, EZ Street did not so much disband as dissolve. The group, though, did afford Burton his first public appearances at such estimable gatherings as a church gala, local talent contests and, inevitably, numerous backyard parties beloved of Californian teenagers. The band could even lay claim to one performance for which they were paid, this being an appearance at the International Café in Berkeley, an establishment run by Greek Americans who were quite happy to have the band play and their friends arrive to watch and to drink the bar dry.

From the ashes of EZ Street Burton and Martin formed Agents of Misfortune, another short-lived, free-form, experimental trio, inspired by Rush, the Velvet Underground, Pink Floyd and Black Sabbath. Interviewed in 1980, after a local Battle of the Bands competition, the bassist was asked to outline his group's future ambitions: his answer was both succinct and lyrical: 'To show [people] what's on the other side of the fence.'

By the spring of 1980 music had positioned itself as the key component in the life of Cliff Burton. This was the season that he graduated from Castro Valley High School, and after he secured his High School Diploma he decided to continue his studies at Chabot College, a community institution in Hayward, California, which features among its alumni such figures as actor Tom Hanks, author Bruce Henderson, as well as Major League Baseball players such as Mark Davis and Ned Yost. Yet as Burton's first semester at the college approached, the prospective student was already certain in his own mind that the vocation he desired for his life was that of a professional musician. But while the back stories of many young people who desire to embark upon a musical path they hope will lead to a destination of fame and glory – or even merely a living – come replete with a chorus from unhappy parents urging their offspring to concentrate on activities that loosely correlate under the banner of 'proper jobs', in the case of the Burton family the response to their son's declaration was more supportive. Both Ray and Jan Burton had noted not only their son's love of music, but also his willingness to apply himself to the business of *playing* music. In light of this, the parents struck a deal with their youngest child.

As Jan recalled, 'We said, "Okay, we'll give you four years. We'll pay for your rent and your food. But after that four years is over, if we don't see some slow progress or moderate progress, if you're just not going any place and it's obvious that you're not going to make a living from it, then you're going to have to get a job and do something else. That's as far as we're going to support you. It should be known by then whether or not you're going to make it." So he said, "Fine." '

In order to begin making good on his end of this bargain, the next group Burton joined was Trauma. Then a regular presence on the Bay Area's live club circuit, at the time of Burton's arrival the group were propelled by singer Donny Hillier and guitarist Mike Overton and played a rather odd combination of straight-ahead power metal combined with the kind of glam-metal stylings that had begun to dominate the boulevards of West Hollywood. The band, though, did possess a solid work ethic, something that was no doubt attractive to a bass player whose own work ethic had afforded him the support of his mother and father. The insertion into Trauma's ranks of a new member dressed in flared jeans and denim jacket – an ensemble often derided as 'a Canadian tuxedo' – only added to the band's sense of musical and stylistic uncertainty. Critical opinion among those who covered the underground metal scene of both Northern and Southern California was mixed. By combining a traditional power rock sensibility with the whiff of a glam rock aesthetic – without fully committing to either – the group's appeal stood some way behind the teeth of those chomping at metal's increasingly jagged cutting edge. After witnessing a performance at The Stone club, writing in *Metal Mania* Ron Quintana observed, 'The guitarists had funny matching outfits, so they stood out more – whereas Cliff looked more like a regular guy.' Hardly the kind of fulsome soundbite a band might choose to place on flyers and posters advertising future live performances.

A more positive recollection is held by Steve 'Zetro' Souza, the one-time singer with early day San Francisco thrashers the

Legacy – who later became Testament – and after that front man for local heroes Exodus. Souza recalls seeing Trauma play when he was a high-school student, and hearing voices in the Northern Californian metal scene declaring, 'Those guys are [gonna be] the next big thing.' Asked to identify an outstanding feature of Trauma's sound, Souza is quick to nominate the playing of Cliff Burton. 'His style was just so awesome,' he says, 'so radical . . . I think people thought he was just too much for [that band] maybe.'

Despite this, Burton did realise a number of achievements with Trauma. In March 1982 the band supported Saxon at the Keystone Club in Palo Alto, the final date of the English group's US tour in support of their defiantly dodgy *Denim & Leather* album. The San Francisco band also contributed the track 'Such a Shame' to Brian Slagel's *Metal Massacre II* – with the group's management desiring as well that the group sign to Slagel's Metal Blade label, despite an acute lack of funds on the part of company. In the same year, Trauma travelled south on Interstate 5 in order to play three concerts in Los Angeles.

It has often been reported that James Hetfield and Lars Ulrich first encountered Cliff Burton at the Troubadour, at the third of the band's three LA showcases. In truth, they already met and spoken to the man who would soon enough come to be known as 'the Windmill', at both that earlier appearance at the Whisky, as well as at a video shoot for the Trauma song 'I Am the Warlock', where they were introduced by Ulrich's friend Patrick Scott.

'Trauma's manager – his name was Tony [Van Lit] – had contacted me through K. J. Doughton to come and watch them shoot a video,' Scott recalls. 'So they came down to Santa Ana, which is by Los Angeles, to shoot a video in a professional studio. I didn't know much about the band other than hearing a tape of them, and I knew I'd be sitting there all day long by myself, so I called Lars just as a friendly thing to come and watch. He was excited about it and I wasn't sure why, and he brought James with him, which I didn't think much about then – it was something to do – and Lars and James were talking to Cliff a lot, the whole time. I didn't really know where they were going with it at that time, but soon after that Lars told me, "Remember that guy, that bass player?" and I said, "Of course," and he told me the whole thing about them trying to get him.'

Dave Mustaine recalls Burton being what he describes as a 'star bass player', before adding 'that term alone – "star bass player" – should tell you something, because bass players are typically the bottom of the rock 'n' roll food chain. Guitar players and singers are at the top, drummers in the middle, bass players at the bottom. I was once quoted as saying, "Playing bass is one step up from playing the kazoo," which certainly pissed off a lot of bass players, but it's essentially true. Of course, there are exceptions to every rule, and Cliff was certainly not a glorified kazoo player. He was brilliant. The first time I saw him play, I knew he was something special, and so did Lars and James, which is why they began surreptitiously courting Cliff while Ron McGovney was still in the band.'

While history has tended to portray the union between Cliff Burton and the Metallica camp as being one weighted heavily in favour of the Bay Area bassist, the truth is that Ulrich's entreaties came at a time when Burton was beginning to feel in need of some kind of exit strategy from Trauma. Mike Overton also confirmed the presence of Ulrich and Hetfield at his band's video shoot, describing the pair as being 'cool to talk to'. Rather touchingly the guitarist also adds that he 'did at the time wonder why they talked to Cliff for [so] long'. Overton admits that 'Cliff was frustrated, Don Hillier and I both knew this. Cliff had always wanted to be a little heavier in sound and so did I . . . [Other members] wanted to be a lot more commercial. I was always an Iron Maiden and Judas Priest fan myself. So there was some infighting going on among Trauma as to what direction we needed to head . . .'

But whichever direction that was, it would be without their bass player. Following his meeting with Cliff Burton, and after seeing the musician onstage again with Trauma at the Troubadour, Lars Ulrich, that little engine that could, and did, marched up to Brian Slagel and delivered a direct injunction.

'That guy's gonna be in my band.'

✝

After Metallica's appearance at the Old Waldorf on November 29, the touring party and friends retired to a motel on Lombard Street to celebrate their first headline show in the city.

'It was then,' Lars Ulrich recalled, 'that we began to fuck girls who came to the concerts. I remember me and Dave Mustaine scored a few chicks together. It was the first time I was in a pile of bodies, there was someone on the bed, someone on the other bed, someone in the corner and someone in the closet. It was one of those times we would have only one motel room, then woke up the next morning with twenty people sleeping on the floor. But it was just like a dream . . . it was just so cool. It was everything we've ever dreamed of and more.'

Adrift in this drunken, ecstatic state, however, Ulrich failed to realise that he had shown his hand when it came to his plot to unseat Ron McGovney as his partner in Metallica's rhythm section.

'At the second Waldorf show Lars was already talking about replacing McGovney,' reveals Bill Hale, then a photographer for the *Metal Rendezvous* fanzine. 'I remember being back at the hotel with Cliff and a bunch of friends and Lars was drunk and saying, "When we get back to LA we're getting rid of Ron," . . . and Ron was right there in the room . . .'

'After I heard them talk about Cliff, I had some idea [I was going to be replaced],' admits McGovney. 'I remember after that show it was raining like a motherfucker and I saw Cliff, all in denim, just standing there in the rain. And I said to him, "Hey dude, do you want a ride home?" I kind of felt sorry for the guy. I kind of saw the writing on the wall . . . We played at the Mabuhay Gardens the next day, it was a little hole in the wall. That was the last gig I did with Metallica.

'On the way home we stopped at the liquor store, I was driving, and they got a whole gallon of whisky. James, Lars and Dave were completely smashed out of their minds. They would constantly bang on the window for me to pull over so they could take a piss, and all the sudden I look over and see Lars lying in the middle of Interstate 5 on the double yellow line. It was just unbelievable! And I just said, "Fuck this shit!" Then one of my friends told me that they witnessed Dave pour a beer right into the pickups of my Washburn bass as he said, "I fuckin' hate Ron." The next day my bass didn't work. My girlfriend at the time also told me that she overheard that they wanted to bring Cliff in the band.

'I never, ever heard them tell me, "You're out of the band." After Dave fucked my bass up, I confronted the band when they came over for practice and said, "Get the fuck out of my house!" I turned to James and said, "I'm sorry, James, but you have to go too." And they were gone within the next couple of days.'

'What bothered me the most was that James just kind of sat there and let it happen. He just kind of turned a blind eye to it.'

On December 10, 1982, Ron McGovney officially quit as Metallica's bass player. While Hetfield moved down to Huntington Beach to crash on Mustaine's couch, Ulrich redoubled his efforts to cajole Burton into joining his band. Shortly after his nineteenth birthday, he finally secured the present he had been coveting for the past two months, when Burton agreed to be in his band. His consent, however, came with one condition. If Metallica wanted Cliff Burton to be their bass player, the group would have to come to him.

3 – JUMP IN THE FIRE

As the winter of 1982 surrendered to the spring of 1983, a rash of
xeroxed yellow-and-black posters began appearing on the lamp
posts casting long shadows outside the strip clubs and shebeens
of San Francisco's Broadway district. The posters served notice of
a forthcoming show on March 5 at The Stone, a three-band line-
up unified under the billing 'The Night of the Banging Head'.
In truth, the promoters could have saved themselves the effort
of manufacturing hype. For the members of the Bay Area's metal
fraternity, this event had long since been pencilled into their
diaries as the occasion of Cliff Burton's keenly awaited debut
outing as a member of Metallica.

As arcs of bucking feedback brought Metallica's traditional
set-opener, 'Hit the Lights', to its conclusion on that warm spring
evening, James Hetfield peered through a fug of smoke and dry
ice into a club packed tight with familiar faces. Brian Lew and
Bill Hale stood stage front with their cameras, Ron Quintana
held court at the bar, while Rich Burch, Toby Rage and Exodus's
faithful 'Slay Team' prowled the periphery of the pit cracking
heads with impunity.

'How you doing?' enquired Hetfield with a smile. 'We're
ready to fucking kill!'

Indifferent to the ways of the music scene of Los Angeles,
onstage at an intimate club the logic behind Cliff Burton's
insistence on joining Metallica only if the group came to him
rather than vice versa was clear for all to see, and at the closest
quarters at that. Burton looked like a man not just born to appear
onstage, but born to appear onstage as a member of Metallica;

the bass player's charismatic authority, even regality, beggaring belief that this was the first time he had stepped onstage with his new band mates. This sight was met with equal emphasis by the few hundred people gathered to see the band perform. As with the animalistic roar that greets the end of 'Ace of Spades' on *No Sleep 'Til Hammersmith*, the sound from the people gathered in The Stone that March evening was informed not so much by adulation as by an energy that was reckless and emphatic. In 1982 Lars Ulrich would tell interviewers that, in Los Angeles, Metallica were 'the right band in the wrong city': now ensconced in the City by the Bay this, evidently, was no longer the case.

Writing in *Metal Mania*, issue ten, Lew was barely able to contain himself in his attempts to describe both the evening in question and, in a larger sense, the significance of the group whose name appeared as headliners on the ticket stub. 'Metallica, those Supreme Metal Gods, those Purveyors of Raging Sonic Decapitation, those Rabid Vodka-Powered Maniacs, blew our faces off as they stormed onstage,' came the writer's sentiment, delivered with a flurry of youthful energy not dissimilar to that summoned by the subject of his prose. 'As is their style,' he continued, 'the band went from power to power . . . leaving the headbanging horde thrashed and raging and it was only three songs into the set!' Before concluding this most effusive of notices, the author had volunteered the opinion that 'with the addition of Cliff Burton, Metallica now have the fastest and heaviest line-up ever assembled', and that 'their live show is now complete and is the most effective of any club band [the author had] seen!'

'The thing about Metallica is that they were *our* band,' says Doug Goodman, an original observer of the Bay Area metal scene. Goodman would in time come work as tour manager for such groups as Green Day and Smashing Pumpkins. His first job in this field was touring with Slayer, in front man Tom Araya's Camaro car. 'It didn't matter that they came over from Los

Angeles. As soon as they played here, even before they'd moved up to San Francisco, they were immediately *our* band. The people in the scene identified with them in the strongest way right from the start. Of course, in time they'd come to represent the whole area, but even before that it was obvious that there was a real connection between what they represented and what we wanted to hear.'

'There was this immediate intense connection,' agrees Doug Piercy, one-time guitarist in Anvil Chorus and Heathen. 'A lot of the bands in the Bay Area were more into the glammy, make-up, LA-influenced kind of thing, but there was a lot of fans that were interested in seeing some form of the British heavy metal scene without having to wait forever for Motörhead or Maiden or Saxon to come. There was a really diehard scene that was small, with kids who'd go to keg parties blasting New Wave of British Heavy Metal music on our ghetto blasters, but unfortunately there wasn't a band at all that the scene could support. So when Metallica came on the scene, it just clicked. Here was a real genuine American band that played all the shit that we understood: we'd all been tape-trading looking for the new noisy thing and suddenly here was a band of our own.'

Considering that Los Angeles and San Francisco are cities that reside in the same state – and are in a geographic sense relatively close neighbours – the differences between the two are marked. Despite its easy-going, languorous exterior, Los Angeles is a city of high achievement, a place that attracts people from all over the country hoping to 'make it'. As such, competition is fierce, while camaraderie is often merely a façade that goes no deeper than the sweat on each hustler's skin. Tales abound from the Hollywood metal and 'hair-metal' scene of the Eighties that would see band members roaming Sunset Boulevard and taping to lamp posts and walls flyers advertising their group's upcoming shows *over* those announcing appearances by competitors.

By comparison, for a band such as Metallica, San Francisco was day to Los Angeles' neon-polluted night. As Janis Joplin once observed, 'The first thing that defines the music scene in San Francisco is the freedom. For some reason people gravitate here and feel free to make any kind of music they feel like making.' Artists seeking a location that allows them to 'make any kind of music they feel like making' stands in marked contrast to people relocating to a city in order to play the kind of music they feel will enable them to *make it*. Metallica, though, made music that while feral was also finessed, and the band themselves were more than animals out on the loose and looking for trouble. In today's parlance people who claim to have 'a vision' are implying that they themselves are visionaries, but in the case of Lars Ulrich this could already be said to be true. Metallica may have worn their integrity like a patch on the sleeve of a denim jacket, but even in the group's earliest days Ulrich appeared not only to have had his eyes fixed on a larger prize but also to be possessed of the wit to appreciate the incremental steps required in order that he and his band mates might realise this achievement. Relocating to San Francisco may not have been the drummer's idea, but he was quick to realise the potential gain of such a move. The group's arrival on the streets of the Bay Area, though, was less a tale of two cities, and more the story of one implacable musician. That Cliff Burton was able to spirit virtual strangers away from the city in which they lived serves to signify the power of an enigmatic presence that seemed to be comprised of little more than human hair and flared denim.

As Dave Mustaine himself recalls: 'If there was any hand-wringing over this decision [to relocate to Northern California], I don't recall it. We all knew that Cliff was talented enough to present what would ordinarily be considered an outrageous bargaining chip: *Relocate the whole band? For a bass player!* He was that good. And we were that driven; we were willing to do anything to be successful. I think that we all recognised that by adding Cliff, we would become the greatest band in the world.'

Metallica's first rehearsal with Burton took place in the dead hours that separate Christmas Day from New Year's Eve. Although the move from Los Angeles to the Bay Area – the term 'San Francisco' is here misused, as the three émigrés actually lived outside the seven square miles that comprise that city's limits – took almost two months to complete, as soon as Hetfield, Ulrich and Mustaine arrived in their new zip code on February 12, 1983, the young men required a place to stay. In this pursuit, Hetfield and Ulrich were accommodated by Exodus manager Mark Whitaker, who allowed the teenagers house room at his two-bedroom home at 3132 Carlson Boulevard, in the small East Bay city of El Cerrito. Presumably drawing the shortest straw, or perhaps as evidence of a division in the camp, Mustaine found himself in the bizarre position of lodging with Whitaker's grandmother, an hour away from Ulrich and Hetfield.

It was in the living room of the house on Carlson Boulevard that Metallica first practised with Burton on December 28, 1982. Ulrich set up his drum kit in front of the couch while Hetfield's Marshall stack stood wedged by the kitchen door. Such was Ulrich's confidence in Burton's ability to fit seamlessly into the unit, that he invited Ron Quintana, Ian Kallen and Brian Lew and a handful of other 'Trues' along to document the day. Following the rehearsal, Lew conducted the new look quartet's first photo session. This was just one of many gatherings at 3132 Carlson Boulevard, an address that would quickly come to be known as the 'Metallica Mansion', a phrase used in jest given the dwelling's 'compact and bijou' one-storey appearance. At the time, Hetfield and Ulrich's new home on the working-class side of 'the Bay' – the East Bay, to be precise – was perceived as being in a less than desirable neighbourhood. This may have been the case, but today the home is a sedate-looking apple-green coloured bungalow positioned next to a petrol station on a thoroughfare that seems as unthreatening and unremarkable as any address in the Bay Area.

Unremarkable, that is, except for the young men who once lived there. Even allowing for the group's liking of their new environment, and that environment's love of the group, that Metallica would relocate themselves from Los Angeles to Northern California at the asking of a man with whom they had yet to play a single note of music displays either a level of faith that borders on the fervorous or else a sense of naivety that is not far shy of being reckless – and is possibly both. But as dysfunctional as the backgrounds of Hetfield and Mustaine may have been (and as short-lived as Ulrich's tenure in the City of Angels may itself have been), in this action the band's willingness to separate themselves from streets known to unknown, and to divorce themselves from family and friends, speaks of a single-mindedness that would serve them well. In plotting their course to Northern California, Metallica turned their cheek not only to a safety net of any kind but also to the notion that theirs was a union that merely 'played' at being a band. As immature and foolish as Hetfield, Ulrich and Mustaine were capable of being, in this regard at least their actions were those of men rather than boys.

'We knew that there was something about [Metallica] that was beyond all the rest [of the bands populating the Bay Area],' recalls Steve Souza. 'Exodus shows back in the day, even when I was not in the band, with [original vocalist] Paul [Baloff], were probably some of the most violent and brutal shows you've ever seen, way more violent than Metallica. But Metallica had the flair and the sound.'

'We started being more comfortable with ourselves, more confident,' is Ulrich's recollection. 'We started feeling that we were belonging to something that was happening, and that was bigger than ourselves, that we *belonged* instead of being on the outer fringes.'

That it was San Francisco and other cities in and around the Bay Area that provided the germ of an idea for thrash metal, as well as being the setting for its most fertile and violent breeding ground, at first appears to be an incongruous truth. Despite the vibrations caused by groups such as Exodus and Testament as well as a host of other frenetic and precise local metal acts, it was only Metallica whose appeal possessed sufficient force to break through thrash metal's ghetto walls and secure real estate in the mainstream. As such, the cultural movement that is still most closely associated with the area – then, as now – is that of the hippie and flower-power movement of the Sixties, where the sounds of bands such as the Grateful Dead and Jefferson Airplane could be heard along the drug-enriched thoroughfares surrounding the 'tune in, turn on, drop out' bohemian enclave of Haight Ashbury. Elsewhere, the 1967 song which took the city as its title found singer Scott McKenzie requesting, 'If you're going to San Francisco, be sure to wear some flowers in your hair.'

Audience members gathered to see Exodus at The Stone or at Ruthie's Inn in Berkeley – a club located next door to the Covenant Worship Center, a church on the steps of which, according to Ron Quintana, concert-goers would do 'many, many bad things' – wearing flowers in their hair could be certain of being the recipients of much unwelcome attention. The notion that the Bay Area, with San Francisco acting as shorthand for its varied and numerous streets and avenues, is a location that lacks teeth or knuckles is itself one that is short on attention to detail. Shipping, freight, railroad and canning industries provided work for thousands of employees on both sides of the bay, with working people represented by the International Longshoremen's and Warehousemen's Union, the International Brotherhood of

Teamsters and the Service Employees International Union, to name just three. Oakland was also the birthplace of the militant African-American Black Panther party, formed in the city in 1966 by Huey P. Newton and Bobby Seale. Less political but attracting scarcely less infamy were the Oakland Raiders American football team, and their legion of often unruly fans. Owned by Al Davis, a man capable of filing a lawsuit in an empty courtroom, and who often played to Oaklanders' sense of underdog grievance, the Raiders are the team beloved of James Hetfield, this despite the organisation moving from Oakland to Los Angeles just three months before Hetfield headed in the opposite direction (unlike Metallica, the franchise was to return from whence it came in 1994). But perhaps the most symbolic example of the Bay Area being a place other than a haven for the Free Love generation came on December 6, 1969, at the Rolling Stones' notorious free concert at Altamont Speedway in Alameda County. 'Just be cool down there, don't push around,' Mick Jagger implored of the crowd moments before eighteen-year-old Meredith Hunter was stabbed to death by Hell's Angels

Fourteen years later, the notion of not pushing people around at Bay Area thrash metal shows was as ridiculous as arriving wearing flowers in one's hair.

On the part of Metallica, or at least on the parts of James Hetfield and Dave Mustaine, such physical aggression was not confined to the dance floors of spit 'n' sawdust clubs filled with angry adolescents, but often spilled out on to the streets of the Bay Area itself.

'When Metallica first came to San Francisco I thought Lars's guitarists were either going to get him killed or else land him in jail,' is the recollection of Ron Quintana. 'Hetfield and Mustaine were just out of control. For a time it seemed like Dave would get in a fight every single night on Broadway. He wasn't always the instigator; he didn't always start the fights, but he usually finished them. He was a tough guy and was always drunk. I didn't expect him to last the Eighties. James was kind of quiet back then, and he'd only come out of his shell when drunk. But Dave was always out of his shell – and always out of his head!

'He was,' concludes Quintana, grasping for a suitable euphemism, 'a real character.'

As well as its obvious obnoxiousness, the picture painted by Quintana is not without its attendant humour. The image of the irrepressible and voluble Ulrich charging through the streets of San Francisco, in tow of two band mates, boiling with energy but of a kind different from Hetfield and Mustaine is, at the very least, striking. Lars, the born conciliator and natural diplomat, in company with a lead guitarist capable of starting a fight with a Salvation Army Santa Claus and a front man so shy that his hidden character only reveals itself under cover of darkness, and under influence of alcohol; and a drummer with an appetite for construction being undone by the opposing instincts of his band mates. Quintana is right when he says that Hetfield and Mustaine could well have succeeded in getting a drummer five inches shorter than themselves killed; what he also might have added is that it was surprising that none of the party ended up in rehab even sooner than they eventually did. This intemperance was not confined merely to nights out. On the rare occasions that the new kids on the block were not running wild through the streets of San Francisco, back in El Cerrito the 'Metallica Mansion' drew faces from the scene into which its tenants had recently parachuted, like filings to a magnet.

'We all hung out because they had their house,' recalls Steve Souza, '. . . and everybody would go there. I remember there was one night where we were drinking and we didn't have any chaser, so James pulls out fucking log-cabin syrup. We were drinking vodka and log-cabin syrup! But it was just like that, everyone was close knit and everyone went to each other's shows and hung out.

It was a great scene. It was strong. It wasn't anyone saying, "Oh, that band sucks!", not like in the glam scene in LA. We were together. We had the unity . . . But that house was a free-for-all. It was 24/7. Shit was going on constantly there, till three or four in the morning. It was infamous.'

†

Three thousand miles east of 3132 Carlson Boulevard, in New Jersey, Johnny Zazula (a man known to his friends as Johnny Z) and his wife Marsha were at work staffing Rock'n Roll Heaven, the rock record and tape stall the couple ran in a flea-market at the Route 18 International Indoor Market in East Brunswick, a small town in the centre of the Garden State. Despite its suburban location, the epicurean selection of rock and metal – particularly releases imported from Europe – available at the couple's stall qualified Rock'n Roll Heaven as a popular spot for informed metalheads from as far afield as the furthest boroughs of New York City, a two-hour commute. On a spring afternoon in 1983, a customer from San Francisco approached Johnny Z and handed him a cassette tape.

Ironically, given what was about to happen, Rock'n Roll Heaven had at the time a policy that it did not play demo tapes. The unnamed customer, however, was adamant that the stall's proprietor would love the music contained within. Zazula looked down at the object in his hand, and read the name on the inlay card – 'Metallica'. By deciding to lift the needle on the record that was playing on the stereo – an album by Angel Witch – and to begin playing a cassette tape by a band he had never before heard, Johnny Z made a decision that would change his life.

Occasionally music strikes with such a force that it seems as if a bolt of lightning has served to split the sky in two. When the Sex Pistols unveiled 'Anarchy in the UK' on an astonished United Kingdom in 1976, music writer Greil Marcus observed that Johnny Rotten's assertion that he was 'an antichrist' 'for a few minutes made it seem as if the rage issuing from his mouth could level London'. Fifteen years later, Nirvana's 'Smells Like Teen Spirit' took mainstream rock's play book and cast its pages to the hurricane they themselves had created. In terms of widespread amplification, in the first half of 1983 Metallica had nothing like this kind of impact. But as has been seen, many of those who heard the group on the tape-trading vines became not so much fans of the group as adherents to, even participants in, the cause. The trouble was, of this number few were in any position to do anything to further the group's cause other than nod, or bang, their head in appreciation.

That the proprietor of a stall in a flea-market in a small town in America's most widely derided state quickly became the most pivotal figure in their story so far shows the paucity of options open to Metallica as the days began to lengthen in 1983. Aside from running Rock'n Roll Heaven, Johnny and Marsha also operated the company Crazed Management, the live promotion arm of which saw UK proto-thrashers Venom and Canadian journeymen Anvil perform in the United States for the first time. But this operation was a labour of love rather than a business run for profit; its aim was to bring underground metal to an underground audience solely for its own sake. Such noble intentions go some way to explaining the course of action pursued by Zazula immediately after he first heard Metallica. Remarkably, the tape that so impressed the impresario was not *No Life 'Til Leather*, but rather its successor, the *Live Metal Up Your Ass* concert tape (a recording of the band's set at the Old Waldorf on November 29, 1982), a collection notable for its execrable sound quality. Asking his wife to mind the store, Zazula made his excuses and made his way to the nearest public pay phone. Inserting a fistful of metal into the coin slot, he placed a call to K. J. Doughton, the man who was soon to become administrator of Metallica's fan club, and whose number and address – actually, the number and address of his parents' home in the state of Oregon – featured as the contact detail on the demo's inlay card. The fact that Zazula recalled reading an article Doughton had written about Metallica fortified his decision to attempt to contact the band. It was to be the beginning of a fortuitous and fast-moving chain of events.

Zazula revealed to Doughton his desire to speak with a member of Metallica, and was told by the voice on the other end of the line that Lars Ulrich (inevitably) would be in touch. The following day, the proprietor received a phone call from a young man with a thick European accent. With this, first contact was made.

Zazula enthused to the drummer about his love for the music captured on a tape that was not even the best thing to which Metallica had put their name. In return, the drummer – ever the student of the underground metal scene – spoke of his familiarity with the activities of the husband and wife team on the East Coast. In a stroke resplendent in its chutzpah, Zazula then presented a proposition so startling that it might even have silenced Lars Ulrich. It was suggested to the Dane that his group transport themselves and their equipment across the United States from California to New Jersey. A practice facility in the New York borough of Queens was promised, as was accommodation at the Zazula family home in the Garden State, and a place on the bill for concerts headlined by Venom and The Rods

At this point in their career, Metallica can be thought of as being like a shark: if they ceased moving, they would die. While other bands existed only in the present, Ulrich for one had trained his eye to search for future possibilities, and no risk was deemed too large. The drummer relayed Zazula's suggestions to his band mates, all of whom agreed that it was a capital idea. There was, however, one significant obstacle to be overcome: Metallica lacked the means with which to embark on such an epic journey.

Ever resourceful, Johnny Z had a solution.

'We sent them fifteen hundred dollars to come across America,' he recalls. 'They got a one-way rental: a U-Haul van and a truck. Literally they had two drivers and they slept in the back with all their gear and they delivered themselves to my front door. It was basically, "Well we're here – what do we do next?"'

✝

The journey to New Jersey in the U-Haul trailer took place at the end of March 1983. Accompanied by Mark Whitaker, the party decided that rather than waste time and money sleeping in motels en route, they would instead sleep in shifts on mattresses placed in their ride, and for the driving to be undertaken in shifts. Aside from food and bathroom breaks, it would be a caravan of uninterrupted motion.

If the prospect of traversing a country the size of a continent had not previously struck Metallica as being a trepidatious, even ill-advised, endeavour, there can be little doubt that such thoughts did enter their minds once the journey was under way. To this day there is a culture in parts of the United States that finds it socially acceptable to drive while under the influence of alcohol; in the case of Dave Mustaine this tendency was indulged to a hazardous degree. Already a considerable drinker – in fact, the lead guitarist would subsequently claim that even at this point in his young life he was already an alcoholic – during the long journey from West Coast to East Mustaine failed to make the distinction between there being a time and place for getting drunk and its exact opposite. In the town of Laramie, in the border state of Wyoming, the group's caravan jack-knifed after their truck – or truck driver – mishandled in the snow, forcing the party off the highway. While the travelling party dusted themselves off on the side of the road, and as each man laughed with relief at their scrape with danger, the group were almost decapitated by a passing eighteen-wheel lorry passing close enough by that the human face felt the blast of cold air from its slipstream. In the wake of the truck came a Jeep Wrangler, only this time the ride was headed straight for the now bewildered and discombobulated evacuees. Each man dived for cover, with Mustaine pulling Mark Whitaker from the path of the oncoming vehicle at the last possible second.

'On the big continental trip from SF to NY it all kind of spilled over – there were a few things happening that became too much,' observed Ulrich. In the same interview Hetfield confirmed that Mustaine had been drinking while in charge of the group's vehicle, thereby risking the group's lives.

'If there had been a smash,' he noted, 'we could have all got killed.'

'Fortunately no one was hurt,' recalls Mustaine, while at the same time understanding that the near miss with him at the wheel quickly became a pivotal moment. 'But the mood had changed. There was less laughter, more hostility. It could have happened to any one of us. We were all stoned or drunk, and we all lacked the expertise to drive the truck through snow-covered mountain passes. Unfortunately, I was behind the wheel at the time, and so the weight of the incident – *the blame* – fell on my shoulders. For the rest of the journey I felt like an outcast.'

The reason for this is because what followed next has since become one of the most widely discussed and pivotal moments in the history of the group. According to Lars Ulrich, the decision to sack Dave Mustaine as lead guitarist was made during the journey to New Jersey.

'The guy [Mustaine] couldn't control himself under various situations,' the drummer said. 'On a long-term basis it would have become a problem. We decided [to find a replacement guitarist] somewhere between Iowa and Chicago.'

†

Metallica and Mark Whitaker arrived at Johnny and Marsha Zazula's home in Old Bridge, New Jersey, a week after departing the Bay Area. The group were unwashed, unkempt and uncouth. Offered something to drink, a number of the party simply helped themselves to whatever alcohol they could find in the house and drank straight from the bottles, carelessly discarding whatever scant concern they may have held regarding not having a second chance to make a good first impression. For their part, the Zazulas were wondering just what kind of venture they'd invested $1,500 of their own money into, not least because this sum accounted for virtually all of the couple's available funds. At the time of Metallica's arrival, Johnny Z was in the middle of serving a four-and-a-half-month sentence after being found guilty of conspiracy to commit wire tap fraud (to this day Zazula denies his culpability, and claims to have taken a 'pity plea' of guilty in order to avoid a costly trial that he could ill afford to defend). The result of this conviction saw the entrepreneur spending his week nights living at a local halfway house, a place he later described as being 'a prison without guards'. Meanwhile at his own home, his wife and young daughter, Rikki Lee, were left to cope with the arrival of a group of feral young men on whom they had never before laid eyes.

Today Johnny is the first to admit that the possibility that this was the start of a terrible mistake was a thought that had begun to journey across his mind. The first time Metallica were taken down to Rock'n Roll Heaven, Mustaine was so drunk that he spent much of the visit emptying the contents of his stomach on the floor of the International Indoor Market. Back at the couple's home, things were scarcely more agreeable. With the exception of Burton – who would help put Rikki Lee to bed in the evening, and would often read the child a bedtime story – Marsha found herself broke and sharing her home with people who, in the case of Hetfield and Mustaine, expended their energies bending the elbow, or else, with regard to Ulrich, were intent on consorting with every female in the tri-state area under thirty years of age. As if this weren't quite enough – and surely it was more than enough – in summoning these unruly charges from the other side of the United States, the Zazulas were without funds to pay either their mortgage or fuel bills. In a financial sense, the straits in which the couple found themselves were so dire as to require the delivery of food parcels from Marsha's father.

In a matter of weeks, Metallica's digs moved from suburban New Jersey to New York City itself, an arrangement certainly more agreeable to the Zazula family (the final straw having come after the visiting party drank an expensive bottle of champagne saved from the couple's wedding day). In order that his Californian guests have somewhere to practise for the shows Johnny intended for them to play in and around the five boroughs, the entrepreneur had secured for Metallica a practice facility in Queens. The Music Factory was a low-rent establishment in that borough's Jamaica region which offered individual rehearsal rooms for the kind of bands who were content, or at least willing, to pay their dues in the hardest of currencies. Approaching the establishment, visitors would be greeted by the sight of broken windows and piles of detritus, the aftermath of abandoned construction work; there was plaster board everywhere. In a city where the winter chill can be relied upon to exert its grip well into the early days of spring, the facility was both cold and foreboding. But with Metallica having long outstayed their welcome in Old Bridge, the Music Factory was for now their new home. Sleeping bags were laid out on the freezing practice room floor; jackets and T-shirts were employed as pillows. They were thousands of miles from home and in circumstances that at the time could only have seemed far less certain than history has proved them to be; Hetfield's assertion in 'Whiplash' that 'life out here is raw' could hardly have seemed more prophetic.

Help, though, was at hand. In 1983 Anthrax were a young New York power metal band managed by Johnny and Marsha Zazula. They were also ambassadors for both the fraternity of metal and the city in which they lived. Seeing their visitors newly arrived in a part of town in which they surely felt less than comfortable – in a way that Anthrax would have felt equally ill at ease had the East Coast band embarked upon a week-long journey westward, only to pitch up in the 'socially crunchy' location of Oakland's East 14th Street – the locals were quick to offer the hand of friendship to a band who were seeing a side of New York not often glimpsed by tourists. Recognising that Metallica were in need, Anthrax guitarist Scott Ian and bassist Danny Lilker arrived at the Music Factory armed with a toaster oven, ensuring that in a setting resembling a Siberian Gulag the Californians could at least prepare for themselves food of a temperature higher than the frigid floors on which they slept. On another occasion, Lilker bought a famished Mustaine two slices of New York pizza, an act of kindness of which the guitarist still spoke a generation later.

This generosity at the hands of virtual strangers was, though, the exception that proved the rule. Elsewhere, the problems witnessed by the members of Metallica in one of the saltiest neighbourhoods of New York's largest borough were in many ways symptomatic of the malaise in which 'Gotham City' found itself in 1983. Thirty years after the rubber-soled feet of Hetfield and Ulrich first trod the soil of America's largest city, NYC has become one of the safest urban conurbations in the United States. Under the mayoralty of Ed Koch, however, in the early part of the Eighties, the 'City That Never Sleeps' hardly dared do so for fear of violent attack. New York Law Enforcement Agency statistics for 1983 show that the murder rate in the five boroughs accounted for more than 5,000 deaths, more than twice the figure for 2011. In other reported crimes, more than 94,000 people were the victims of muggings, almost 60,000 were the subject of assault, while just shy of a quarter of a million homes were visited and plundered by unwelcome guests. Such activities were not confined to areas such as the Bronx or Alphabet City, two neighbourhoods that at the time had become shorthand for locations that required visitors to carry their own lives in their cupped and trembling hands. In fact, such was the extent of New York's social problems during this period that even iconic locations such as Times Square and Union Square had become, at least under cover of darkness, the kind of places that were not safe to visit. A year before Metallica's arrival in the city, the Los Angeles punk group Fear had arrived on the East Coast in order to appear as guests on the comedy programme *Saturday Night Live*, filmed at the NBC Studios in Rockefeller Center located between 5th and 6th Avenue in Midtown Manhattan. Upon returning home to California, the punk group penned a song telling of their experiences, titled 'New York's Alright If You Like Saxophones'. 'New York's alright if you want to be pushed in front of the subway,' sang front man Lee Ving, before adding that 'New York's alright if you want drugs in your doorway. New York's alright if you want to freeze to death. New York's alright if you want to get mugged or murdered . . .'

Of those who knew Metallica during their initial days and weeks in the city, few were privy to the rumours surrounding the imminent departure of Dave Mustaine. It is also telling that a group that for more than a year had featured among its number three young men whose energetic appetite for alcohol (among other things) mirrored the sense of wild abandon that could be heard in the music they made, should choose to eject a member for the behaviour he exhibited when under the influence of an intoxicant beloved of all. In making this decision, Hetfield and Ulrich at least (the level of influence Burton exerted in a change of personnel that took place just four months after he had joined the band remains unclear) showed that even though they spent much of their time pissed, they were nonetheless perceptive enough to regard Mustaine as one might an unpinned hand grenade. This represented a radical realignment of Metallica's internal balance of power. In the group's earliest days, it was Mustaine who was Metallica's principal guitarist, a role he eventually came to share with Hetfield. Similarly, while at first the singer's shyness found him reluctant to speak to audiences between songs, the lead guitarist fulfilled the role apparently without effort. But as time passed, so Hetfield's confidence grew. Not only this, but this confidence blossomed in tandem with a growing irritation and even embarrassment at Mustaine's sneering and carelessly provocative remarks made to members of the audience. Despite the fact that Mustaine once occupied a position of power within Metallica, in the crisp air of New York City the band's charismatic cornerstone was suddenly no longer as indispensable as he believed himself to be.

Although Mustaine had relocated himself and his life to Northern California, like his band mates, he did not live with Hetfield and Ulrich. En route to the East Coast, however, the two parties were thrown together without respite; upon their arrival, the members of Metallica continued to live cheek by jowl, first at the Zazulas' home in Old Bridge and then at the Music Factory in Queens. Problems that had merely simmered at a tolerable heat in California suddenly quickened to a rolling boil. Isolated as the source of this problem, Mustaine careered without care into Hetfield and Ulrich's cross-hairs.

'By now [life at the Music Factory had begun to take on] a pattern,' is his recollection. 'The more we drank, the more our personalities diverged . . . Lars and James would get weird, and by weird I mean silly – childish. The more they drank, the goofier they became. With me it was a different story. The more I drank, the more I sought an outlet for my rage and frustration. I wanted to get out and do some cruising and bruising.'

Dave Mustaine played two concerts in New York as a member of Metallica, the first on April 8 at the Paramount Theater in Staten Island, the second the following evening at the L'Amour club in Brooklyn; on both nights the band appeared first on a bill that also featured Vandenberg and The Rods. On the afternoon prior to the second date, the Californian group found themselves loitering on the venue's dance floor, waiting for their turn to sound check while onstage Vandenberg took an age to find their own sound levels. Despite the daylight hours, Mustaine was already drunk. As the musicians onstage continued to tinker with the music pulsing from the PA system, just fifteen feet in front of them stood Mustaine, impatient for his own group to take their place. But rather than tap his watch or offer an exaggerated shrug of impatience, Metallica's most volatile member chose instead to loudly insult Vandenberg's lead guitarist, Adrian Vandenberg. The musician onstage was told that he sucked, that no one gave a fuck about his band, and that he and his colleagues should remove themselves from the stage with immediate effect. Those watching this outburst were said to be amused and embarrassed in equal measure.

But as the seasons in New York City were soon to change, so too were Metallica. On the morning of April 11, Mustaine was roused from his sleep by Hetfield, Ulrich, Burton and Whitaker. The lead guitarist enquired as to the reason for his interrupted slumber and was told that he was no longer a member of Metallica.

'I said, "What, no warning, no second chance?"' Mustaine recalled. 'They just shrugged and said, "No."'

Shocked, yet unwilling to surrender whatever dignity he had to hand, the guitarist decided against appealing the decision with cowed and desperate pleas, and opted instead to enquire as to the time of his flight back to San Francisco. He was told that for him there was no plane. Instead, Mustaine learned that his transportation back to California would be provided by the

Greyhound Lines bus company and would take four days. As if this were not galling enough, the now former member of Metallica was scheduled to depart in just one hour's time from the Port Authority Bus Terminal on 8th Avenue in Manhattan. Hetfield drove the exiting musician to the bus station, and as the pair hugged goodbye the front man had tears in his eyes. He told his departing friend to take care of himself.

'Don't use any of my music . . .' spat Mustaine in return.

'It was a pretty sad time,' the guitarist later reflected. 'I remember James crying as he was driving me to the bus stop but Lars didn't care. I think that's when he started to blacken his heart and stopped being sensitive to people.'

'It wasn't really working,' says Ulrich. 'We weren't particularly emotional. We fired Dave at ten o'clock in the morning, by ten thirty we were halfway through our first bottle of vodka of the day. I liked Dave, I was the closest to him in the band emotionally, but he was too destructive. And he was going to take us down. At the time, relationships were second to the band, the communal good.'

As Mustaine prepared himself for a ninety-six-hour journey on public transport, he was struck by a thought that made his already awful day just that little bit worse: he had upon his person not a single dollar. As he began a 3,000-mile journey relying on the kindness of strangers for food and fluid, his replacement as lead guitarist in Metallica was heading in the opposite direction on a direct flight from San Francisco.

✝

Kirk Hammett as born on November 18, 1962, at St Luke's Hospital in San Francisco. His father, Dennis L. Hammett, was an Irish Merchant Marine while his mother, Chefea Olyao, was a government employee of Filipino descent. The Hammetts lived in the city's Mission district, on 20th Street and South Van Ness, a neighbourhood as ethnically diverse as the family themselves.

The address was also home to Richard Likong – a half-brother to Kirk on his mother's side, eleven years his elder – and sister Jennifer. By the time Hammett was seven years old, the family had swapped the vibrancy of melting-pot America for the homogeny of the suburbs, moving from San Francisco to El Sobrante in Costa Contra County. Hammett enrolled at Juan Crespi Junior High School and, later, De Anza High School. It was at the latter establishment that the youngster discovered an appetite not just for listening to music, but also for playing it.

In terms of rock alma maters, De Anza High School ranks as one of the most fertile breeding grounds for aspiring musicians in the United States, not least given that the population of El Sobrante at the time numbered fewer than 15,000 people. Despite this, the senior school has over the years seen its student year book feature the names and photographs of musicians such as Primus bassist Les Claypool, Possessed guitarist Larry LaLonde (who later found success as guitarist in Primus) and John Kiffmeyer, more popularly known as Al Sobrante, the original drummer with Green Day. In the clique- and status-obsessed world of the suburban American high school, the position occupied by Kirk Hammett on the totem pole was low, somewhere below the jocks and cheerleaders but above the members of the chess club. Bespectacled and dressed in a blue-down jacket, Hammett would each day ride to school listening to Jimi Hendrix on a portable tape recorder, stoned out of his mind. Other social groups at De Anza High School labelled him and his friends 'the acid rockers'.

Hammett obtained his first guitar as part of a trade, surrendering a copy of Kiss's *Dressed to Kill* album and a ten-dollar bill in exchange for a red Montgomery Ward owned by an acquaintance named Dan Watson. But Kirk's relationship with the instrument he would one day become famous for dominating was not quite love at first strum. Instead, his new guitar occupied its owner's attention for just a day before being discarded in his bedroom closet. One day, Richard Likong asked if his younger half-brother was persevering with the instrument; Hammett lied and said that he was. Pleased by this answer, the elder sibling suggested the two of them venture out to a local music shop in order to buy new strings, an idea the teenager felt unable to refuse. Given that these strings cost $5 – and took literally hours to affix to his guitar – Kirk Hammett reasoned that he may as well justify the expense by actually learning to play his as yet unloved possession. In pursuit of these aims, the young student spoke to one of his neighbours, a woman who played folk guitar, and from whom he learned his initial chords. The first song the aspiring musician managed to play was 'Calling Dr. Love' by Kiss.

Just weeks later Hammett began playing music with his 'acid rock' school friends, a union that featured Kerry Vanek on drums, Mark Lane on bass and vocals from Dan Vandenberg. The group would attempt such ambitious numbers as Jimi Hendrix's 'Purple Haze', their rendition not at all aided by the fact that their instruments were sourly out of tune.

By now Hammett's musical tastes had expanded to include such groups as Aerosmith, Rush, UFO and Van Halen. He would regularly board a Bay Area Rapid Transit (BART) train bound for Berkeley in order to visit specialist record shops such as Rather Ripped, Rasputin's and Leopold's. It was at such outlets that his ears and eyes would be opened to such releases as Motörhead's towering *Overkill* and Iron Maiden's pivotal self-titled debut album. As his musical tastes expanded – tastes that soon enough would include the kind of New Wave of British Heavy Metal acts that were whetting the appetites of Lars Ulrich and James Hetfield several hundred miles to the south – so too his musical capabilities grew. Such was his proficiency that Hammett was able to convince his mother to make a down payment on a blond 1978 Fender Stratocaster, by any measure a beautiful guitar. Ignorant of technical specifications, he decided to amplify his instrument through an amplifier designed for a bass guitar. Lacking the funds to buy a guitar case, he was forced to carry his precious new instrument in a black refuse sack.

But if an adolescence spent listening to hard rock bands and playing music with friends on a tasteful guitar the down payment on which was provided by a supportive mother suggests formative years that are enviable, even idyllic, it should also be noted that Kirk Hammett's young life came marred by activities which took place in the gloom of a darker shadow. For much of his childhood, Kirk's seafaring father would be absent from the family home for between six and eight months of each year; the fact that his mother worked meant that the couple's only son learned to fend for himself from a young age. Years before adolescence, Kirk would roam the streets of San Francisco, entirely comfortable with the energy and expanse of one of America's most significant metropolitan cities. With his father at sea and his mother at work, their son would rise in the morning, make himself breakfast and then walk his younger sister to school. A front-door key dangled from a chain around his neck. The family had a dog named Tippy, and one day Kirk witnessed his next-door neighbour having sex with the animal. Elsewhere on the streets of San Francisco, when Kirk was out walking with his sister, strangers would approach the pair and offer him money for the young girl. One woman insisted that she would be the pair's 'new mom' and once went so far as to physically grab Jennifer, before her brother wrestled her free.

Despite these travails, and despite relocating fewer than twenty miles from the City by the Bay, the Hammett's move to El Sobrante came as an unwelcome development in his life, with the young charge viewing his new home as being redolent of 'a small-town mentality [to which he] couldn't relate'. Denied the sense of escape offered by the city, the sedentary nature of suburbia forced Kirk to confront his often turbulent home life. When home from the high seas, the truth was that Dennis Hammett did not cut a reassuring or reliable father figure. 'My dad was somewhat of an alcoholic,' Kirk reveals, 'so when he was home you were always walking on egg shells because you didn't know what sort of mood he was in [given his] inebriated state. Sometimes he was happy; sometimes he was ragingly angry.'

An occasion when the man of the house was in the latter mood came on November 18, 1978. 'I'll never forget my sixteenth birthday because my parents got into a huge, huge fight,' recalls Kirk. 'I remember my dad being very, very abusive when he was drunk. He got very, very physical with me and my sister and my mother, and just about anyone else who was in his path. He was a full-blooded Irishman; he had that temper and when you added alcohol it was explosive. My dad beat the hell out of my mom.'

Elsewhere Hammett revealed, 'I was abused as a child. My dad drank a lot. He beat the shit out of me and my mom quite a bit. I got a hold of a guitar, and from the time I was fifteen I rarely left my room.'

As informed by cruelty and fear as this self-imposed isolationism may have been, Hammett's decision to retreat to a place of relative safety with an instrument through which he learned to express himself soon paid dividends. His first real group went by the name of Mesh, which in turn became Exodus. With an early line-up comprising Hammett and fellow guitarist Gary Holt – a man who would in time come to be viewed as being as skilled and ferocious a guitar player as any in modern American metal – drummer Tom Hunting, bassist Jeff Andrews and vocalist Keith Stewart, Exodus began playing cover versions of songs by Angel Witch, UFO and Judas Priest. The group truly began to mine its own seam, however, when in 1982 Stewart was replaced by firebrand vocalist Paul Baloff, a man whose charisma and strangled singing style lent the group a thuggish edge that spoke as much to hardcore punk as it did stylised and studied heavy metal. By now penning their own songs, Exodus recorded a demo tape and became not just regulars in the metal clubs of the Bay Area but also pace-setters for the emerging local thrash metal scene as a whole. To this day, those who bore witness to Exodus concerts at such clubs as the Keystone Berkeley, the Old Waldorf and Mabuhay Gardens speak in awestruck tones about the ferocious, often downright violent, nature of the audience the group attracted. But Metallica's second visit to the Bay Area made Hammett aware that his own band still had a lot of growing to do.

'I was at the Old Waldorf in San Francisco and they were opening up for Laaz Rockit,' he recalls of the evening of October 18, 1982. 'They came on and just blew the place apart. I was blown away by the aggressiveness, the velocity and the overall originality of their sound. By the time Laaz Rockit came to play, three-quarters of the crowd had left. After Metallica there was nothing else that could have been more interesting than that. Everyone who saw them that night was converted.'

'I thought to myself, "These guys are so goddamn original, but that guitar player isn't so hot, they should get me." I actually thought that within the first few minutes of seeing them.'

When Metallica returned to the Bay Area on November 29, they were billed to headline above Exodus at the Old Waldorf. The following evening, at a benefit gig held at the Mabuhay Gardens to raise money for *Metal Mania* fanzine, Hammett met the LA group for the first time. He spoke with both James and Lars and watched with silent unease as Ulrich changed clothes, undressing to the point of nudity in front of him. All the while, Hammett listened to the Danish immigrant as he was speaking, thinking of his accent, 'Wow, he sure has a weird way of speaking.'

As befits a tightly knit musical community concentrated in one area, the Bay Area underground metal scene in the early Eighties already had about it an incestuous nature, and one that would serve Hammett well. Baloff had introduced Mark Whitaker, manager of Exodus when they shared a bill with Metallica at the Old Waldorf, to Metallica. Whitaker was, of course, soon to be landlord to Hetfield and Ulrich at 3132 Carlson Boulevard and, following this, was the group's travelling companion in the week-long journey from the Bay Area to Old Bridge, New Jersey. As feelings during this trip hardened against Mustaine, Hammett's name began to hover into view. Prior to leaving for the East Coast, Hetfield and Ulrich had listened to Exodus's demo tape and heard for themselves the quality of Hammett's playing. As Ulrich himself says, 'James and I have always been the main thing in this band, and we always looked at Dave and Ron and thought, "This is fine for now, but . . ." We had a vision that these guys weren't going to last. We weren't going to kick them out, but if we found someone who could fit in, we'd get 'em in the band. We saw Cliff and went, "Woah! This guy should be in the band!" So we concentrated on him until we got him.' This done, in the months that followed Hetfield and Ulrich began to consider who might serve as a hypothetical replacement for Mustaine.

'[Hearing Exodus' demo tape] was the first time we'd thought about it,' says Ulrich. 'Then the next couple of weeks it was, like, "Kirk! Kirk! Kirk!" [But] it wasn't as if we were going to put him in the band and get rid of Dave . . . until we left for the East Coast later that month.'

Given that Metallica were only acquaintances of Kirk Hammett in the most casual sense of the term, the task of making first contact with the Exodus lead guitarist fell to Whitaker, who placed a call to Hammett's Bay Area home. Sitting on the toilet at the time, the guitarist picked up the receiver and listened to his friend's pitch. The voice on the phone told the listener that Metallica were having problems with Dave Mustaine. When Hammett enquired about the source of these problems, he was told, 'He fucking sucks, man. His tone sucks, his playing . . . he's a fucking drunk.' Whitaker then told Hammett that, if he so desired, the odds on him replacing Mustaine as Metallica's lead guitarist were so short that no bookmaker on earth would accept the bet. He was also told to expect a copy of *No Life 'Til Leather* to arrive at his home in short order, courtesy of Federal Express. As Hammett processed this information, a part of his mind was on guard to be told that everything he had just heard was nothing more than a joke, as the day of Whitaker's call was April 1.

At the end of this conversation, instead of placing the phone receiver back into its cradle, Hammett made another phone call, this time to secure for himself a copy of *No Life 'Til Leather* prior to the arrival of the tape being dispatched from New York City. By the time his clock struck midnight on April 1, the Exodus guitarist knew half of the songs contained within. In fact, from Kirk Hammett's perspective, the call from Whitaker could not have come at a better time. Despite having built up a strong and swivel-eyed following, Exodus had reached a point of stasis: not only had the group not played live for a time, but its members had even failed to convene in order to practise. Hammett was feeling frustrated and was thus not at all disagreeable to what might otherwise have seemed like an entirely crazy suggestion: that he embark on a five-hour flight to New York in order to audition for the role of lead guitarist in Metallica.

A little over a week after receiving Whitaker's phone call, Hammett found himself aboard a domestic flight bound for America's East Coast. In the aeroplane's hold sat his Marshall cabinet and amplifier head, packed in boxes that featured towels for padding and duct-tape for wrapping. As the plane began to make its final descent, the passenger, who had never left California before, looked out of the window and saw snow on the ground.

The guitarist was met at Newark International Airport in New Jersey by Whitaker and Burton. Arriving at the Music Factory, Hammett was greeted by a scene of human detritus devoid of human beings. He was told that Hetfield and Ulrich were asleep; looking at his watch, he saw that the time was seven o'clock in the evening. The guitarist took stock of his current circumstances and thought, 'Fuck, what the fuck did I get myself into?'

4 – SEEK & DESTROY

On the afternoon of April 23, 1983, James Hetfield and Lars Ulrich decided to call a brief time out on drilling their newly recruited lead guitarist in order to partake in a little unrest and recuperation. Their itinerary for the day was to be divided into three parts: the duo would first conduct an interview for Brian Lew's new fanzine *Whiplash* before heading out onto the streets of south Brooklyn to check out the latest import releases at Zig Zag Records. Their evening would end in the company of Toronto's Anvil at L'Amour, the self-proclaimed 'Rock Capital of Brooklyn' which had played host to Dave Mustaine's final Metallica show just two weeks previously.

On his right hand Hetfield was sporting six stitches on a freshly opened gash, the result of a drunken stumble while cradling a vodka bottle, after the new-look Metallica had opened for Venom at the Paramount. Onstage in New York's forgotten borough, the San Franciscans had found themselves performing to an audience that, while not as indifferent as those they faced in Los Angeles, were still some way south of being exuberant. Part of the reason for this was surely nothing more than the fact that New York, like London, is a city where people are spoiled rotten by the sheer quantity of live music on offer, a fact that renders its concert-goers a difficult body to excite. In addition, it is also fair to say that the tri-state area had never before seen a band of Metallica's kind. For while metal of a muscularity greater than that known to the mainstream did exist in New York in 1983, it did so with a sense of theatricality that bordered on the camp. Dressed in loin cloths and furry boots, Auburn act Manowar were scarcely less homoerotic than the Village People, while the heaviness of Staten Island's own Twisted Sister was somewhat undermined by the fact that its members chose to apply make-up to their faces, albeit in a slapdash manner that did nothing to obscure the fact that band looked more like dockers than rock stars. In fact, despite that group's thuggish, punk-tinged sound, Twisted Sister's music was far enough removed from that made by Hetfield's band that vocalist Dee Snyder found himself entirely bewildered after seeing the group perform at one of its New York concerts. Upon meeting the group Snyder opined that while they seemed like good people, he still reckoned their chances of 'making it' were nil. In the context of the time, it is not difficult to see why he arrived at this conclusion. In 1983 heavy metal was one of contemporary music's most flamboyant genres, yet here came Metallica dressed as if they lived in a squat.

But if New York was not yet entirely enamoured of the teenagers from California, the same could be said of the visitors' attitude to the Empire State. When *Whiplash* writer Trace Rayfield collected Hetfield and Ulrich in the parking lot of Rock'n Roll Heaven that spring afternoon, his first enquiries centred around the duo's impressions of the East Coast. 'The 'bangers out here aren't as fanatic [*sic*],' answers Ulrich, as his band mate can be heard belching in the background. Although the drummer does concede that the reception his group are afforded 'gets better with every gig', nonetheless the inevitable comparison comes not to Metallica's experiences in Los Angeles – 'LA was the fucking worst' being Hetfield's take on his home town, in some of the few words he manages to string together amid his drummer's dominance of the interview – but rather, San Francisco. 'They're not as crazy . . . out there in San Francisco the first ten rows are just hair and sweat and bobbing heads . . . almost like punk gigs. They're just all over each other and shit.'

One of the striking things about the interview is the certainty with which Ulrich speaks of the future plans set in place for his group. He confirms that, while Metallica are 'a San Francisco-based band', it would be unlikely that the quartet would perform in the Bay Area until the autumn (which they did, on September 1 at the Key Club in Palo Alto). He also states that his band are set to enter a recording studio on May 10 in order to record their debut album, the sessions for which would last two and a half weeks. So definitive and authoritative are the drummer's answers that the resemblance between the Lars Ulrich of 1983 and the drummer thirty years on is not so much striking as it is unsettling.

Ulrich also revealed that Metallica's choice of producer for their debut album – at the time, set to be titled 'Metal Up Your Ass' – was Chris Tsangarides, a man known at the time for his collaborations with Judas Priest and Thin Lizzy. For his services, though, Tsangarides reportedly requested a fee of $40,000, blue-chip currency indeed for a band who at the time dealt only in red cents. 'We just have to be patient with our first album and make the best of it,' confessed Ulrich in a tone of voice that suggested that even then compromise was to him fast becoming anathema. 'Every song we have we feel is good enough to put on [the] album – we don't have any filler songs,' he said, in a statement that at that time at least was true.

Despite the fact that one half of the band had been among its number for less than six months, as Metallica readied themselves to record their first vinyl LP they were by musical measure a professional group. The same, however, could hardly be said of the business operation established to support them. Johnny and Marsha Zazula worked hard, even selflessly, on behalf of their charges, but the cloth they were able to cut came woven from cheap materials. All expenses were spared, from the fact that the group recorded their first album not in New York City, or even in New Jersey, but at Music America Studios situated in Rochester, a minor American city some six hours' drive upstate from the five boroughs. Despite the fact that the studio costs reflected the location in which Music America found itself – that and the fact that the facility itself housed only the most basic of professional recording equipment – Johnny Z still lacked the funds to pay to record Metallica. Ever resourceful, instead he negotiated with Music America's owner and in-house producer Paul Curcio that the costs be spread over a period of time and paid in instalments.

From a professional point of view, the band that arrived at Music America in the second week of May 1983 were equipped with everything required to make a sound for sore ears. Recording music that will, for better or worse, last forever, is a job of work vastly different from the blink-of-an-eye business of playing live. While Metallica had mastered the latter task, when it came to making music in the studio the band were not up to scratch. The group showed up at the studio carting equipment that looked as if it had been in a mosh pit. Cliff Burton's Rickenbacker bass guitar was battered almost beyond repair, as was his amplifier; Lars Ulrich's drum skins were pock-marked and out of tune, with none of the band having the slightest clue as to how to go about *re*-tuning them. It was not an auspicious beginning.

'Metallica were obviously a very young band that didn't have a lot of money,' recalls Chris Bubacz, the man whose job it was to engineer the album the quartet had convened to record. 'They came into the studio with pretty poor equipment . . . Truthfully, I was quite concerned. I was concerned because they weren't real knowledgeable about the recording process and I wasn't really knowledgeable about what their real idea was, what it was they were trying to capture.'

At least in a creative sense, the union between Metallica on the one hand and Curcio and Bubacz on the other seemed like a match made in hell. The group's producer was not himself greatly enamoured by, or even particularly understanding of, the music the group were aspiring to record – with Bubacz recalling, 'Paul really didn't have any idea of what kind of sounds we should go for' – and it was left to the membership of Metallica to 'work together' in order to make decisions regarding the sounds they were recording. Bubacz was himself not a fan of heavy metal music, preferring artists such as Chick Corea and Blood, Sweat & Tears. But the engineer did at least attempt to locate common ground between what he as a technician hoped to record and what Metallica might desire to create. Upon learning that he was to be working with a metal group, Bubacz made it his business to research a number of albums current to that genre. That year's most successful hard rock album was *Pyromania*, the third LP from Sheffield's Def Leppard, a set recorded with a painstaking attention to detail by producer and notorious perfectionist Robert John 'Mutt' Lange. Both engineer and artists were in agreement that in a sonic sense this was the album to which their own recordings should aspire. Speaking almost thirty years after the fact, it is with a philosophical smile that Bubacz delivers his verdict that in pursuit of this aspiration both he and Metallica 'failed miserably'. This, though, is an unforgiving point of view, one delivered by someone equipped to hear things as they might have been rather than as they exist.

As unassuming as Bubacz's recollections of his part in the recording of Metallica's debut offering may be, his role was nonetheless pivotal. For when critics and audiences refer to a album's production, often they are confusing the term with the sound of its engineering. In studio terms, there are two kinds of producers: those who dirty their hands with the business of sound levels that have as much to do with mathematical theory as art, and those who assume the loftier position of plotting the musical course of a project as a whole. In many cases the person responsible for how a piece of music actually *sounds* is the engineer. In numerous instances, the term 'producer' is a misnomer – 'director' is a more fitting description. Having previously spent mere hours inside a recording studio, Metallica by definition required assistance in translating their music as it existed in the confines of a small club or rehearsal space onto the permanent grooves of a twelve-inch record. And in 1983 it seems as if Curcio was more jobbing hack than visionary director. At the same time as both producer and engineer were recording Metallica – sessions which took place from early evening until one o'clock in the morning – they were also, by day, producing a local group whose music would be best defined as 'easy listening'.

The project was beset by the kind of problems that nagged rather than overwhelmed. Early in the proceedings the producer halted a Hetfield guitar take to complain that the noise being committed to tape didn't sound normal. 'It's not *meant* to sound normal,' Hetfield muttered. The front man's relationship with Curcio did not recover from this miscommunication.

'Our so-called producer was sitting there checking songs off a notepad and saying, "Well, we can go to a club tonight when we're through recording. Is the coffee ready?"' Hetfield recalled. 'He had nothing to say about any of the songs. I don't think he'd dare say anyway, because we'd have said, "Fuck you, that's *our* song."'

To someone who earned a living from recording musicians, a glance at the stock provided by Johnny and Marsha Zazula could not have filled Curcio with confidence. Here was a group playing music of a kind the producer had probably never before heard, a sound both raucous and extreme. Such was the poverty of the group's circumstances that the relatively modest costs of recording at Music America could only be met by payment on the never-never. Metallica themselves had no real studio experience, and one of their number, Hammett, was of a tenure so short that he had not yet seen a single rainy day. Despite his undoubted technical proficiency, the parts the lead guitarist desired to contribute to his new group's first album were not yet up to the specifications set by his colleagues, to the point where Johnny Z ordered him to simply replicate Dave Mustaine's parts. When Hammett protested, his manager offered a compromise, whereby the guitarist would open every solo with Mustaine's phrasing and then take them somewhere new.

'As a twenty-year-old kid, put in a position like that, you don't want to rock the boat too much, especially being the new kid in town,' Hammett admitted. 'So I said, "Sure." I took the first four bars of most of the solos and changed them. When I changed them it was always for the better and everyone liked it.'

In an age before Pro-Tools, Hammett's guitar solos had to be compiled from numerous different takes and then dropped in atop the drums, bass and rhythm guitar from tape literally cut by hand and laid above the music at the allotted place in any given song. This was both a time-consuming and tiresome procedure. This process was not aided by the fact that the equipment Metallica had to hand, both instruments and amplification, to lay down this most precious of things, their debut album, was less than high end.

'It was really all done on a shoestring budget, to be honest with you,' says Bubacz. 'You could see that these guys were struggling to make something of themselves.' The engineer, of course, quickly came to understand that the music Metallica desired to record was both darker and wilder than was at the time the norm, but even allowing for this the engineer was still of the mind that 'proper recording techniques and playing techniques will help improve the sound. [Such techniques] certainly improved over the years and [today] you can record that type of music really well and still keep the same impact. But, yes, it was very raw and extremely distorted, and when you had a lot of the equipment not really working properly it lends itself to a pretty harsh sound, to say the least.' Despite this, Bubacz recalls the members of Metallica as being 'great', young men who were 'eager to be in the studio and do the recording'.

As was normal for the time, the mixing of Metallica's first professional recordings was overseen by Curcio and Bubacz. But when Johnny Zazula heard the initial mix of an album the costs of which had yet to be paid, he was displeased. To his ear, Metallica's sound as captured in Music America studios was unbalanced: the guitars were too low in the mix while the drums were too loud. Producer and engineer were instructed to return to the mixing desk and reset the sound in order that Hetfield's already forensic multi-layered guitars feature with greater prominence. 'So that's what we did,' recalls the engineer, adding that this direction 'wasn't positive [and] wasn't negative', rather it was merely a case of 'the guitars aren't loud enough'.

Thirty years after the fact, Bubacz says that the songs that comprise Metallica's debut album do not amount to 'one of his best recording efforts. In fact,' he says, 'I'm always a little bit disappointed when I hear it years later.' Despite this, the engineer surmises his experiences in the spring of 1983 as being 'a good experience', a thing that 'worked out fine'.

From the point of view of Metallica themselves, however, the recording of their debut album might have given the appearance of being a process where compromise came stacked on compromise. The group's members found themselves ignominiously excluded from the process of remixing their own songs, a state of affairs that must have been jarring for a union that even in 1983 was unyielding with regard its own creative defiance. Famously, the group had wanted their first album to be titled 'Metal Up Your Ass', a decision that was vetoed by US distributors who were fearful that record shops in many states of what was then, and in many cases still is, a conservative nation would refuse to stock such an item. Upon hearing this news, Cliff Burton damned the purveyors of this compromise with the words 'Fuck those fuckers' and surmised that the group, or at least someone, should just 'kill 'em all'. With these three words the bass player provided the band with an alternative title for their first record. This much is known by Metallica fans the world over. What is less often considered is the worth of the group's original idea. To accompany the album as it was originally to be titled, its creators envisioned a front cover featuring an image of a man sat on a toilet, with a metal spike emerging from the bowl and penetrating his anus. The group's creative vision may have been neutered by people interested in money rather than art, but this does not mean that in being censored in this way Metallica were not saved from the very people from whom in this instance they required protection: themselves.

†

Metallica were formally introduced to the world at large when *Kill 'Em All* was released on July 25, 1983, just shy of two months after the completion of its recording sessions. In place of the group's awful original idea for their cover artwork, instead record store browsers were met with a stark image of a lump-hammer strewn carelessly on a ceramic floor, a pool of blood gathering around this bluntest of instruments. While adhering to the metal clichés of cruelty and physical threat, the cover artwork that accompanies *Kill 'Em All* is effective in its starkness and simplicity, and stands in contrast to the more over-the-top covers favoured by metal bands of the day.

On the reverse side of the sleeve, the group photo finds the quartet of young musicians attempting to present themselves as street thugs. In this they fall some way short of their marker. For while it is possible to imagine a figure such as, say, Lemmy emerging from the womb dressed entirely in black, smoking a Marlboro red, his first actions on this earth being the act of slapping the doctor in the delivery room, as pictured on their first album Metallica resemble lion cubs more than kings of the jungle. Particularly unconvincing is Lars Ulrich's bum-fluff moustache and Hetfield's teenage acne. But despite the hesitant impression given by a group trying too hard to appear like the kind of men they desire, or imagine, themselves to be, in one sense the photograph of Metallica chosen to represent the group on *Kill 'Em All* is both resolute and striking. From the shining leather of Judas Priest to the spandex of Iron Maiden, at a time when even the most unreconstructed of heavy metal bands – the kind of groups who were not afforded the attentions of MTV and FM radio – tended to present themselves in a stylised and considered way, here Metallica stand in what appear not only to be the clothes they woke up in that morning, but also the same clothes they went to bed in the night before (if indeed they went to bed at all). In this sense, the group are portrayed in a manner as unvarnished as the music they made.

It is also to its authors' credit that Metallica's debut album has about it a rather counter-intuitive quality. With regard to the relationship that exists between songs as originally submitted in demo form and then as refashioned on a debut album, it is the norm that, come the second visitation, the tracks are given polish and shine, their rough edges sanded down with studio trickery and an abundance of professional sleights of hand. With *Kill 'Em All*, though, this process was placed on its head.

As with *No Life 'Til Leather*, *Kill 'Em All* begins with the track 'Hit the Lights', and immediately the difference between Metallica as heard on demo and the group as represented on vinyl becomes apparent. A telling quality with young groups is not so much how these acts handle their strengths, but rather how they deal with what they perceive to be their weaknesses. There is no doubt that the one aspect of the group's music about which Metallica (and Hetfield especially) was most sensitive and unsure were the vocals. Evidence of this can be heard with particular emphasis on 'Hit the Lights' as represented on *No Life 'Til Leather*, where Hetfield's voice comes shrouded to the point of obfuscation by reverb. On the same song on *Kill 'Em*

All, the voice that announces the questionable opening couplet, 'No life 'til leather, we are gonna kick some ass tonight', is not only prominent in the mix but is also unadorned by anything that resembles studio trickery. In later years Hetfield would dismiss his vocal contributions to Metallica's first four albums as amounting to nothing more than 'yelling in key', and while this may in essence be true his evaluation serves to undermine the effectiveness of such a strategy as it related to his band's music at this time. With regard to *Kill 'Em All* there is no doubt that, despite his own internal misgivings, the front man's voice resonates with both clarity and authority. Much of this authority is derived from the sincerity of many of the words that are being sung. On 'Whiplash', after describing a Metallica concert as being a site populated by people 'gathered here to maim and kill', the singer reveals to the listener that the reason for this is because 'this is what we choose.' Even as early as 1983, the notion that Hetfield viewed life as something to be lived either with liberty or not at all was already finding some form of expression.

Despite its descriptions of feral gatherings of young men who 'bang [their] heads against the stage like [they] never did before', by the standards of today *Kill 'Em All* is not a particularly heavy album. Part of the reason for this is that in setting the standard for what would soon enough come to be termed 'thrash metal', Metallica punched holes in walls through which other groups would follow with perhaps a more determined singularity of purpose (Slayer being the prime example). But while the band's debut album does not, as metal parlance would have it, shift much air, what it does do is announce its presence with a level of precision and clarity that is at times forensic. Metallica may have disdained Paul Curcio's role as producer, but to the outside ear at least the stridency and immediacy of Metallica's sound as represented on their first album serves the band well. For their own part, no small part of this credit should go to the musicians themselves. For while the production and engineering of the tracks might cause a lesser band to sound brittle and one-dimensional, Metallica's innate sense of musicality and melody means that their compositions actually benefit from the rather stark manner in which they are presented. Yet another by-product of the album's sound is that the production enhances rather than obscures the group's wild and compelling energy. Even in the short time that had elapsed since the ejection of Dave Mustaine, there were noticeable signs of progression. 'The Mechanix', with its double-entendre-laden lyric, was reworked as 'The Four Horsemen'. The new lyric – a fairly stock account of the coming of the four horsemen of the apocalypse that somehow manages to wrongly identify one of the riders ('Time' being nominated as one of the quartet, in place of 'War') – is not particularly impressive or even greatly superior to its predecessor; its subject matter is more fitting for a band whose energy at this time equated more to anger and intensity than it did to anything related to sex. Elsewhere the sheer chutzpah displayed by the decision to include on the album a bass solo in the form of Burton's much discussed 'Anesthesia (Pulling Teeth)' showed that when it came to displaying a taste for the unusual Metallica had chops to spare. However, the rarely spoken truth about this inclusion is that aside from what might rather harshly be described as the song's 'novelty value', an innovative bass solo is not as interesting as a good song. But when *Kill 'Em All* does take flight, it does so in soaring fashion. Even thirty years on, listening to the crisp-as-lightning pneumatic drill riff that precedes the opening lines of 'Whiplash' is exhilarating.

'From start to finish it's a complete package,' says Kirk Hammett. 'It's young, raw, obnoxious, loud, fast, energetic, and inspirational, and everything in between. When it came out, it was the achievement of our lives. We could hold it and show people and go, "Hey, look, we made an album! We're on vinyl." It was a great feeling.'

'I remember the first time I heard *Kill 'Em All*, I thought, "Blimey, this is a bit different",' recalls English rock journalist Malcolm Dome, who reviewed the collection for *Kerrang!* 'To me, it was Venom played by superior musicians. Musically, they were a better band than Venom. You could hear Motörhead in there as well. You could hear Diamond Head in there, and you could hear Iron Maiden and Judas Priest. You could hear all those traditional things in the make-up of the album. But clearly they were doing something a bit different. Now, you look back and listen to it and think, "Well, it's not really that fast at all." But at the time it seemed to have an incredibly fast pace. And also, the fact is, they had really good songs as well: they had a really good sense of structure, really good melodies, and although the production was comparatively non-existent, what that meant is that it allowed the band space in which to breathe. So to this day it sounds like a very sharp record.'

At the time the effect must have been piercing. While the once street-tough bands who populated the Los Angeles metal scene were preparing to tousle up their hair and water down their sound in preparation for an assault on the mainstream, here was an album released by a band whose hands were unlikely to ever uncap a can of hairspray (or deodorant, for that matter). For anyone paying attention, it would soon become clear that battles lines were being drawn between those who opted for a form of hard rock that often amounted to little more than pop music played loud, and a sterner form that required – in fact, insisted upon – greater commitment from the listener. In terms of musical circumstances not all of which were under their control, Metallica already represented a black flag raised high, around which adherents might gather to salute. Not only did they serve as standard-bearers for those whose musical tastes ran to groups with little mind for compromise, but they were also the first American heavy metal band to take the influence of

European groups and translate this into a new form.

But while it is certain that *Kill 'Em All* was a compelling calling card, what is equally sure is that in the summer of 1983 few rallied to their cause.

When Johnny Z had invited the group to New York just months earlier, his plans, such as they were, had been to secure for them a record deal. Quite what Zazula had in mind regarding this pursuit is unclear, but while his endeavours as a small-change (although in time undeniably important) tri-state metal hustler were admirable enough, it is unlikely that his work on the ground in the name of the musical underground went noticed by the men with expense accounts and corner offices of the major record labels of the United States. Johnny Z found that his enthusiasm for Metallica was not shared by the American music industry at large.

'I'd been all over to the record companies and they laughed in my face,' he recalled. 'They told me I was crazy, or said, "Please don't play this." Or just, "We don't want to see you."'

With a bill for recording costs from Music America Studios yet to be paid in full and no takers for *Kill 'Em All* from either major record labels or significantly sized independent imprints, the problems faced by Zazula were mounting like the clouds of a coming storm. The reality of his circumstances did not make for easy reading: he had a criminal record, a young child, and an unruly band for whom he was suddenly responsible.

What Johnny Z was to do next comprised an act of such audacity that his thinking appears to fall between the two stools of courage and lunacy. Unperturbed by the lack of interest in Metallica from the music industry at large – or perhaps realising that he had already reached the point of no return – Zazula refused to accept defeat and instead decided that he would forge his own path. Re-mortgaging his and Martha's home in Old Bridge, the impresario founded his own record label, Megaforce, on which he would release *Kill 'Em All*. The album would be distributed by the independent company Relativity.

'We just didn't pay our bills,' he shrugs. 'We'd come home from the studio and we'd be dealing with our electric or our mortgage would be sixty days behind. As far as finances go, it was crazy. Everything we had went into the band.'

✝

When *Kill 'Em All* was unveiled to the American public in the summer of 1983 there was nothing to suggest that the mainstream music industry had judged the state of the market incorrectly, or that Johnny Zazula would have the last laugh. Initial sales of the album were so pallid that the title did not graze even the lowest reaches of the US *Billboard* Top 200 album chart. This was a period when even acts that were viewed as being mainstream metal bands, as distinct from hard rock groups such as Van Halen or Quiet Riot, received little in the way of radio or video support in the US (in fact, a year later Iron Maiden's Bruce Dickinson would wonder aloud onstage at Los Angeles' Long Beach Arena why it was that his group was able to fill the 13,500-seat room for four nights without their music appearing on that nation's airwaves) and Metallica were no exception to this rule.

But while the reception afforded to *Kill 'Em All* did not warrant the attentions of the major record labels (at the time, such corporations usually came calling with contract and inducements to bands who had sold 100,000 albums on an independent label), by the standards of the style of music Metallica were making not to mention the fist-to-face nature of Johnny Zazula's business operations, the response to *Kill 'Em All* from the underground metal fraternity was encouraging. Despite an initial pressing of just 1,500 copies – a number surely necessitated by their manager's finances – *Kill 'Em All* took up where *No Life 'Til Leather* had left off and quickly found a small but dedicated audience within the musical underground. With nothing other than their own industry to propel them, as the choruses of 'Auld Lang Syne' resonated on the final evening of 1983 *Kill 'Em All* had been re-pressed four times and sold a not insignificant 17,000 copies in the United States.

More than any other musical form, the success of a metal band is determined by perspiration as much as it is inspiration. Groups such as Judas Priest and Iron Maiden had found success in the US by touring from coast to coast, and in doing so had shown a willingness to visit the kind of unheralded towns and cities that even in the early Eighties were beginning to decay. At the time, heavy metal was a form of music that attracted a solidly working-class audience; groups seeking success would find favour in blue-collar cities. Married to this was the fact that much of the mainstream media viewed metal bands and their audiences as being not so much off-limits as beneath contempt, forcing such groups either to accept defeat or else to plough on regardless. Given the adolescent sense of anger inherent in much metal music of the period, it is no surprise that many bands opted for the latter course of action.

Metallica's first proper tour of the United States saw them share a bill with the English group Raven. Formed in Newcastle in 1974 by brothers Mark and John Gallagher and Paul Bowden, the trio signed with the independent rock label Neat (also based in Newcastle) for their first two albums, *Rock 'Til You Drop* (1981) and *Wiped Out* (released the following year). The group's music might best be described as being prototypical, a mixture of high-energy rock, power-chord anthems as well as the occasional nod to more progressive elements. While both albums dented the lower reaches of the UK album chart, Raven gained most attention from their energetic live appearances. Concerts would see the band take to the stage wearing garments such as American football helmets and ice-hockey body armour, with the performers ringing every ounce of energy from their audience with shows they themselves described as being 'athletic'. Certainly, the group's commitment to giving their paying public value for money each and every night, regardless of the circumstances in which they found themselves, was to have a marked influence on the young group with whom they were about to head out on tour.

'We knew how to get a reaction, whatever it took,' says vocalist/bassist John Gallagher today.

As with Venom, Raven caught the ear of Johnny Z, who with his usual sense of derring-do invited the trio to the United States. The band made their American bow with Riot and Anvil at the Hallowe'en Headbanger's Ball at the St George Theater in Staten Island. Zazula released the trio's third album, *All for One*, on the new Megaforce label just a month after unveiling *Kill 'Em All*. Given this, the notion of placing the two bands together on one tour made perfect sense.

According to John Gallagher, Raven met their tour mates for the first time at the Zazulas' home just a day or two before the excursion began. The front man recalls Ulrich as having a 'stick of dynamite up his arse', as being 'the mover and shaker' who 'asked 20,000 questions'. The other members of the group he recalls as being 'very Californian . . . very laid back'. Yet to be unburdened of his offstage shyness, Hetfield is remembered for not speaking 'two words' all evening, while Kirk Hammett gave the impression of being a rookie draft-pick who was 'just pleased to be a part of the whole thing, this big adventure'. As ever, Cliff Burton's sense of serenity and magisterial remove registered as a quality belonging to someone who could lay claim to being 'the epitome of cool'.

Embarking on their first tour, Metallica found themselves in circumstances of such squalor as to make the Music Factory look like the Waldorf Astoria hotel. John Gallagher remembers the experience as being 'complete punk rock guerrilla warfare', the kind of operation that either makes bones or breaks spirits. All tours require their participants to surrender privacy and personal space for the communal confines of dressing rooms and tour buses. The more rustic the tour, the tighter its musicians are packed together. On the freeways of America, the members of Metallica and Raven lacked the space to even draw a picture of someone swinging a cat.

The Kill 'Em All for One excursion lasted for two months of the American summer and travelled from city to city in a Winnebago Johnny Zazula had procured for the occasion. As the tour was set to conclude with three concerts in the Bay Area, James Hetfield painted the words 'No Life 'Til Frisco' on one side of the vehicle. Inside the ride were packed seven musicians, five roadies – three for Raven, two for Metallica – as well as sound man Mark Whitaker; thirteen people crammed inside a vehicle designed for nothing like that number. For the first few dates of the tour the travelling party were not even afforded the necessity of hotel rooms in which to rest after each show. As the Winnebago drove through the treacle-thick air of an uncommonly intense summer, none of its occupants were able to sleep. Such were the levels of exhaustion that following the fourth date of the tour – an appearance at the Rat club in Boston – the groups demanded that the local promoter hand over the keys to her apartment in order that the visitors might recuperate. Gallagher recalls opening the front door and being met with a dwelling that appeared to be the habitat of 'a hoarder', a place with 'piles of crap everywhere' and 'a gigantic lump of human hair down the couch'. Taking stock of this sight – 'It was,' recalls the Englishman, 'just *filthy.*' – Raven decided that they would sooner take their chances back in the Winnebago. Coarsened by weeks sleeping at the Music Factory, Metallica, however, decided to stay.

Unsurprisingly for a tour of a vast country by bands whose profiles were in some cities microscopic, the Kill 'Em All for One tour was an excursion comprised not entirely of high points. Performing at the Cheers club in Long Island, just outside New York, Metallica found themselves seen by fewer than fifty people, none of whom, according to Gallagher, 'gave a shit'. At Harry's Bar in Roland, Oklahoma, Raven faced a scene 'totally out of the Blues Brothers', with the audience throwing anything they could lay their hands on in the Englishmen's direction. Used to performing before unruly punk crowds at home, though, the trio were equipped to deal with such situations and had by the end of their set transformed their fortunes to the point where the crowd were dancing on the tables. Witnessing this, Ulrich asked John Gallagher how on earth his group had managed to salvage the situation?

'I remember Lars afterwards going, "Hey, how did you do that?"' he says. 'I replied, "Well, we believe in what we do. Don't you believe in what you do? And [if you do] then why don't you go up there and show them?"'

Gallagher reflects that, as the more experienced touring group, 'it was cool [that Raven] were able to be mentors' to the young quartet. That said, the thirty-one-date tour was Metallica's first time at the rodeo, and it showed.

'A lot of time they were just borderline out of control,' he recalls. 'They'd have their act cleaned up for the gig, but once the gig was over all bets were off. They were a party band, that's for sure.'

To the outside eye the Kill 'Em All for One tour sounds like the kind of occasion where nightmares are lived and memories are made. Audience numbers in some cities may have been small, but the size of the impact made upon some in these audiences was significant. In Texas the package was seen by members of a then unheralded (and awful) glam rock band by the name of Pantera, who, witnessing the energy and ferocity emanating from the stage, took stock of their own music and decided to change direction. In time this group would become one of the most popular and uncompromising names in American metal. Elsewhere, on the fringes of the US Midwest, a young thrill-seeking photographer named Gene Ambo took possession of *Kill 'Em All* and discovered an album that for him smashed down a wall and presented metal with a tranche of new possibilities. 'The first time I heard [the record] I thought, "Woah, this is fucking heavy," ' he recalls. 'It was something totally different. It was like listening to your old Scorpions records on 45 [rpm], like Judas Priest but without all of the clichéd bits.' On the strength of his reaction to their first album, Ambo decided not to wait until the Kill 'Em All for One tour arrived in his home town for a date at the famous Metro venue – an appearance John Gallagher recalls being one of the highlights of the tour – but instead decided to equip himself with a six-pack of Old Style beer and a submarine sandwich and board a train for the long journey from Illinois to Maryland. There the photographer attended a performance at the Coast to Coast Club in Baltimore. After Metallica's set, Ambo headed backstage in order to introduce himself, and the two parties became fast friends. On subsequent visits to Chicago, the group would stay at the lensman's home in the central north of the city, and on one occasion Ambo went so far as to lend Kirk Hammett a set of clothes to wear onstage. The reason for this, according to the photographer, was that Hammett was dressed that day in tight leggings and slip-on black footwear of a kind worn when practising yoga. Ambo took one look at the lead guitarist's attire and said, simply, 'Dude if you go onstage dressed like that in Chicago, they'll kill you.'

But even as Metallica's reputation grew, the group's insecurities regarding their own abilities still nagged. Ambo recalls being asked by Hetfield whether he knew of any capable vocalists who might be willing to join the band, a question which caused its listener to respond with incredulity.

The photographer recalls that he 'looked back at [Hetfield] and said, "Dude no one wants to hear a singer. No one wants to hear melody. They just want you to yell at them!"'

Thirty years after this anti-musical advice was offered, it has become common for metal bands who display all the smooth edges of sandpaper not only to make a living from the music they make, but in some cases to make a killing. In 1983, though, Metallica were pioneering earth-shifters constructing a road that for all they knew may well have led to nowhere. At times on the Kill 'Em All for One tour their passage to the promised land must surely have borne a striking resemblance to a highway to hell.

As days turned into weeks, inside the Winnebago the touring party found itself in conditions more akin to the gruelling road trips undertaken by Sun Records artists such as Elvis Presley, Chuck Berry and Jerry Lee Lewis in the Fifties (where these now musical legends found themselves driving through the day and night in cars in order to show their faces in village halls in no-horse towns all over the United States), rather than the jet-propelled mile-high luxury of groups such as Led Zeppelin. In the middle of July, the party drove for thirty-six hours in temperatures of 110° Fahrenheit in order to reach the punchline-inviting town of Bald Knob in the central southern state of Arkansas. There the performers played their sets at the Bald Knob Amphitheater, a vast outdoor facility that on this occasion was populated by an audience that numbered in the low hundreds. Some thirty years later, the abiding memory of John Gallagher is of the bands sharing a stage with 'insects the size of helicopters' and of trucks selling fried catfish. It was, he reveals, 'a complete culture shock'.

Twenty-four hours later circumstances veered yet further towards the surreal, as the tour reached the Pine Bluff Convention Center in the town of Pine Bluff, Arkansas. Upon disembarking from their Winnebago, the touring musicians were met by a

local promoter who had recently dined on the misinformation
– perhaps supplied from a telephone caller in Old Bridge, New
Jersey – that earlier in the tour the bands had performed a show
at the 17,000 capacity Madison Square Garden in Midtown
Manhattan. In 2013 it is tempting to forgive the acceptance of
such a bald-faced lie by a gullible promoter with the defence that
in the days prior to the advent of the Internet greater latitude
was afforded to unscrupulous opportunists happy to discard any
facts that lay in the way of a good story. The reason for this is that
anyone raised in the age where all information is within the reach
of a fingertip tends to believe that prior to the computerised age
people were incapable of finding out anything for themselves.
The truth is, though, that the notion that Metallica and Raven
were in possession of profiles of sufficient size for them to perform
at 'the Garden' was a lie of such arena-sized proportions that it
could easily have been dispelled either with a phone call to the
venue itself, or even a glance at the *Billboard* album chart, on
which neither group could be found. Upon hearing the news of
the tour's popularity on the American East Coast, John Gallagher
thought to himself, 'Hmm, someone has been bullshitting.'

Owing to a claim even more odoriferous than that emanating
from the inside of their Winnebago, Metallica and Raven found
themselves booked in an arena built to accommodate 10,000
people. Come the evening of the concert, barely 300 people had
gathered for the performance, not all of whom were impressed
with the entertainment on offer. As it must, the show went on,
with both groups performing beneath two meagre lighting rigs
held aloft by trusses anchored by fork lift trucks. Whatever this
hot summer night resembled, it was not an evening at Madison
Square Garden.

The nearer the Kill 'Em All for One tour juddered towards
its denouement, the more the problems faced by its personnel
increased. Following an appearance at the Country Club in the

Los Angeles suburb of Reseda, a booking for which Lars Ulrich had been saving a consignment of brand-new cymbals (presumably believing LA to be the kind of 'special occasion' city for which his new equipment was suited) the travelling party headed north on Interstate 5 for the five-hour drive to San Francisco. There, the Kill 'Em All for One tour would draw to a climax with a triumvirate of performances at the Keystone Clubs in Palo Alto and Berkeley, and, finally, The Stone in San Francisco – three clubs that have since become notable simply for the fact that bands such as Metallica used to play there. En route to the Californian group's adopted home city, the wheels on their long-suffering and fully ill-equipped Winnebago completed their final revolution. The van's engine died not with a cough or a whimper, but instead exploded with a force sufficient to cause smoke to billow from the vehicle's every orifice. The sight of this was enough to propel Ulrich himself out of the ride and thirty yards up the freeway before anyone else had even exited the vehicle.

Temporarily stranded, the group convened in what John Gallagher recalls as being 'a weird little town straight out of the Twilight Zone' until alternative transport was sourced. Deciding to complete their journey not on Interstate 5 but rather on back roads leading south to north, at one point the party travelled along a road on which one side was abutted by a cliff edge and a sheer drop of several hundred feet. It was the kind of scene at which one which one might expect to see Wile E. Coyote in fruitless pursuit of the Road Runner. While some of the passengers reacted to this sight with gallows humour, others were less cocksure. From a seat in the rear, the voice of a young man with a Danish accent could be heard to say, 'Kirk, I'm really scared. Can I hold your hand?'

For musicians coarsened by the experience of a two-month tour that had seen them endure gruelling conditions, bear witness to backwater cities, and amass enough experience to gain a crash-course understanding that it was indeed a long way to the top for anyone desiring to rock 'n' roll, such a request did not fall on sympathetic ears. For the final hours of the journey to San Francisco, it was Ulrich who found himself in the barrel as everyone in the vehicle laughed themselves silly at the drummer's expense.

✝

Following an adventure that, if not quite a trial by fire was at least an ordeal in heat, the sight of the seven square miles that comprise the city of San Francisco came as a welcome relief to the members of Metallica. The three shows the band performed upon their arrival re-affirmed to the group that their five-month absence from Northern California had only served to make the hearts of the local underground metal community grow fonder. As with each of the quartet's previous Bay Area performances, the three appearances – on a bill strengthened yet further by the addition of Exodus as the opening group – were attended by audiences in possession of energy levels which surpassed anything seen in the preceding two months. For while the Kill 'Em All for One tour had been met with approval in cities such as New York, Chicago and Bridgeport in Connecticut, the sight of slam-dancers clambering on to the stage, only to immediately propel themselves on to the heads of those gathered in the front rows, proved that the Bay Area still contained the greatest number of hotheads of all the hotbeds that made up the emerging US thrash metal scene.

The travelling musicians marked the end of their great and surely never-to-be-forgotten adventure with a party at the Metallica Mansion on Carlson Boulevard. After a summer spent either asleep in a vehicle or else in motels of a kind where rooms were available for rent at hourly rates, this modest suburban bungalow may well have resembled the kind of luxury on offer at Claridge's. But if this was the case, the scene didn't bear this resemblance for very long. As drinks flowed fast, the party-goers listened to bands such as English punk thugs the Anti Nowhere League and responded to this music by slam-dancing through the living quarters and breaking just about everything in sight. At one point an unidentified guest decided it would be a good idea to start a fight with Raven drummer Rob Hunter, an undertaking the assailant was ill-equipped to finish. Instead the aggressor found himself knocked out cold by a punch of such force that it broke a number of bones in Hunter's hand.

With Metallica at last ensconced on home soil, the group turned their attentions to the business of composing new material. Even at this point in what could hardly yet be called their 'career', the group displayed character traits that could almost be described as being schizophrenic. This was a union that appeared not to be equipped with an 'off' button, but while Metallica's capacity for waking up in the morning having little recollection of what occurred at the end of the night before is without doubt, to portray the group as being one whose sole concern was the pursuit of a good time all of the time is a construct without foundation.

Indeed, before anyone had even heard his name, Lars Ulrich understood that in order to realise his dream – actually, his aim – of guiding Metallica to the position of being the biggest band in the world would require talent married to discipline and graft. In this he was aided by Cliff Burton, a man whose commitment to making music had been noted not just by his supportive parents but also by everyone he encountered. In Kirk Hammett Metallica had finally found a lead guitarist committed to mastering his instrument not as a means of securing fame but as an end in itself (and unlike his predecessor, these talents were not kept in time by the metronomic beat of a ticking time-bomb). Most impressive of all was the development of James Hetfield, who assumed the role of front man with an authority that belied his own uncertainties. With Dave Mustaine dismissed, Hetfield began to emerge from the monosyllabic shyness in which he had previously been cocooned. Coupled with this was his growing skill as a rhythm guitarist capable of composing first-class riffs with just a flick of the wrist. Together, the four musicians were starting to coalesce into a formidable unit.

As the nights began to draw in during September 1983, inside the cramped confines of their El Cerrito garage Metallica punched in shifts that would soon enough yield results that were both startling and surprisingly progressive. For once, the group could be said to have time on their side when it came to determining the direction their next musical steps would take. Although the quartet would once more play the Keystone Club in Palo Alto, this date was scheduled for Hallowe'en, some seven weeks after the completion of the Kill 'Em All for One tour. Following this, on the docket were a further four bookings at various Bay Area clubs, plus a return to the Country Club in Reseda, at which the group debuted the songs 'Fight Fire with Fire' and 'Creeping Death'. During the same set Metallica also performed a new composition, the final details of which they had yet to wrestle into position, a lengthy instrumental presented under the working title 'When Hell Freezes Over'. In time this track would metamorphose into the classic 'The Call of Ktulu'. Three days later at The Stone the band premièred another new composition, titled 'Ride the Lightning'. Unbeknownst to the people gathered to see the band play at either club, these audiences had between them heard what would become 50 per cent of the headliners' second studio album.

Armed with a cache of fresh material, as autumn hardened into winter, Metallica once again left San Francisco, this time for a short tour of the Midwest and eastern United States. After playing shows in Illinois, Wisconsin and Ohio, the group headed back to the Eastern Seaboard for dates in New Jersey and New York state. On January 14, 1984, the quartet were scheduled to perform their now expanded live set at the Channel Club in Boston. On the night prior to this appearance, Metallica's three-man road crew – a body of men that comprised the ubiquitous Mark Whitaker as well Dave Marrs and guitar tech John Marshall – drove a truck into which was loaded the group's backline of amplifiers, drum kit and guitars four hours north from New York City to Massachusetts. Arriving in a city gripped by frigid weather and what Marshall recalls as being 'four feet of snow', the crew parked the truck outside the hotel in which they were booked to sleep. Given the frigid temperature of the outside air, rather than leaving Metallica's guitars to potentially warp in the cruel night air, instead the party carried the instruments up to their rooms for safe-keeping. With New Jersey as their starting point, Metallica themselves were scheduled to travel up to Boston the following day.

On the morning of the performance, however, Kirk Hammett was awoken by the sound of a trilling telephone. Picking up the receiver, he was confronted by a confusion of voices, one of which was saying 'Oh no, oh no, I can't. No, I can't. No, no, I can't . . . I can't do it.' Despite being just seconds into his waking day, Hammett inferred that this panicked voice was not the bringer of good news. 'No, I can't tell 'em, I can't tell 'em,' the speaker continued. 'Tell us what?' wondered Hammett? Eventually the speaker was replaced by someone capable of placing sentences together in something approaching a cogent order. Hammett listened as the voice at the other end of the line delivered a message the gravitas of which brought Hammett's day into the sharpest of focus.

'Guys,' he was told, '[all of your] equipment has been stolen.'

In the exchange that followed Hammett learned that at some point during the night thieves had broken into the band's equipment truck and not only relieved the ride of its entire cargo, but also nicked the truck itself. This raid, under cover of darkness, saw Ulrich dispossessed of his drum kit, Hammett relieved of his Marshall head cabinet, and Hetfield bereft of his much-loved modified Marshall head cabinet and speaker. Also stolen was a suitcase containing books dedicated to music theory, as well as technical matters relating to the production of live music. Suffice to say, Metallica's appearance at Boston's Channel Club was promptly cancelled.

Receiving this news from a prone position in New Jersey, Hammett took possession of the facts and replied with a single word.

'Fuck.'

5 – FIGHT FIRE WITH FIRE

With snow on the ground, and a truck filled with drums and amplifiers God knows where, for Metallica the new year blues of 1984 bit hard. Following their cancelled appearance in Boston, they were scheduled to fly to Europe for their first tour of the continent. But as a consequence of the actions of light-fingered New Englanders, these plans were placed on ice.

'We were very depressed,' admitted James Hetfield. 'We were stuck in New Jersey, bumming.'

So dispiriting were their circumstances that Hetfield was inspired to write a lyric which eclipsed anything he had penned before. 'Fade to Black' tells the story of a life so hopeless that suicide is presented as a valid means of escape. The perspective from which this tale unfolds takes the form of a first-person narrative. 'I have lost the will to live, simply nothing more to give,' wrote Hetfield. As the lyric expands into metaphor, it showcases an early example of the author's underrated poetic ear, with the assertion that 'growing darkness [is] taking dawn' and that 'I was me, but now he's gone'.

For Hetfield a lyric that came from a sense of self-imposed powerlessness broke new ground. Other words written for Metallica's as yet untitled and unrecorded second album also shifted position from the tough-guy bravura that splattered the lyric sheet of *Kill 'Em All* to scenarios where the narrator finds himself trapped in circumstances beyond his control. The recently premièred 'Ride the Lightning' takes as its subject matter a condemned individual whose last moments on earth see him constrained beneath the leather straps of an electric chair. Terrified that the state is acting to switch off his lights in this manner, he asks, '[Can] someone help me? Oh, please God, help me, they are trying to take it all away.' As when Johnny Rotten asked of the citizens on the east side of the Berlin wall to 'please' not to be waiting for him (in the Sex Pistols' 1977 song 'Holidays in the Sun'), the appearance of the word 'please' gives 'Ride the Lightning' a quality different not only from the material its author had written before, but also from the music with which Metallica's own stood comparison. Notions of vulnerability and helplessness were, and are, prospects about which Hetfield held genuine fears. Even when couched in the metal-friendly narrative confines of state execution (and in another instance, of being trapped under ice), songs sung from this point of view lent the material a level of authenticity that had been absent from the group's earliest work.

But with 'Fade to Black' Hetfield had taken an extra step towards revealing feelings of failure and futility. Here was a narrator left powerless not by outside forces, but rather by the ghosts that haunted the corridors of his own mind. One should not confuse the circumstances faced by the narrator of 'Fade to Black' with those of Hetfield himself – 'I'm sure I wasn't really thinking of killing myself,' the front man conceded – but what can be said is that in translating and transposing personal misfortune into a convincing scenario of a much darker hue, the lyricist did successfully complete the alchemical process of turning real life into art.

'It was my favourite Marshall amp, man!' he said, by way of explaining the giant leap that saw a stolen speaker and amplifier-head provide the catalyst for a song about suicide.

Armed with an album's worth of new material in various stages of development – from songs that had been rehearsed at length and committed to demo tape, to others still under construction – Metallica set about the business of finding both a studio and a producer who might translate their music to a twelve-inch oil-based canvas with greater care and skill than that shown by Paul Curcio on *Kill 'Em All*. In this pursuit, the band – or, in all likelihood, the band's drummer – had aced their homework.

In the winter of 1984 Copenhagen-born Flemming Rasmussen was co-owner and in-house producer of Sweet Silence Studios, a recording facility then located on the outskirts of the centre of his home town, the Danish capital. Born on New Year's Day, 1958, Rasmussen joined the staff at Sweet Silence and was only eighteen when in 1976 the facility was bought by fellow Dane Freddie Hansson. Just four years later he was invited by Hansson to buy into the business, and in 1980 the engineer became joint owner of the premises. Despite having attracted the business of artists such as Ringo Starr, Van Morrison and Cat Stevens, not to mention being established as a favourite location of Danish jazz ensembles, it was Ritchie Blackmore's decision to record his band Rainbow's fifth studio album *Difficult to Cure*, at Sweet Silence in 1981 that brought the establishment to the attention of Lars Ulrich. Featuring a hit single in the form of the Russ Ballard-penned 'I Surrender', the nine-song set was produced by Rainbow bassist Roger Glover, but inspection of the album's small print reveals that the credit for recording *Difficult to Cure* belonged to one Flemming Rasmussen, a fact that did not go unnoticed by a group in San Francisco who were quickly learning not to miss a trick.

'In those days there was no email or anything, so a call came into the studio, which was taken by [Freddie Hansson],' recalls Rasmussen. 'I was told that there was this band coming over called "Metallisomething", and I went, "Yeah, yeah, I'll do it."'

Not for the first time in their short life, Metallica found the stars aligning in their favour. Despite its underwhelming if not entirely disastrous commercial performance in the United States, *Kill 'Em All* had found a receptive audience in Europe, and in the United Kingdom in particular. The album had been released in Britain on the fledgling independent rock and metal label Music

For Nations, which licensed the record without signing the band directly to the label. When it came to the matter of a second album, however, Music For Nations were sufficiently impressed by *Kill 'Em All*'s commercial performance to place its creators under contract. With these rights came responsibilities. When Johnny Zazula inevitably ran out of money needed to pay for the studio costs incurred in recording *Ride the Lightning*, it would fall to his band's new record label to settle the account.

Music For Nations was launched in 1983 by music industry insider Martin Hooker. Hooker had earned his wings in the trade at the blue-chip corporation EMI, where he worked with such artists as Paul McCartney, Elton John and Kate Bush. To his delight, in 1976 the label – at the time, the very embodiment of the British establishment – signed the Sex Pistols, only to hurriedly discard them following the storm of notoriety surrounding the song 'God Save the Queen'. Hooker realised that as long as he was in EMI's employ he would have little control over the artists with whom it was decided he would work, and so determined to take action. While still working at the company's offices in South Kensington, he secretly established his own independent imprint, fittingly titled Secret. Within six months, he had sufficient confidence in his new venture that he decided to devote himself to it in full, and handed in his notice at EMI.

The roster amassed by Secret could hardly have been more different from that of Hooker's last place of work. While his previous employers had hurriedly hit the eject button on the Sex Pistols, Secret signed the Exploited, a Glasgow-based punk quartet so unreconstructed as to make the Pistols look like the Charlie Daniels Band. Despite not being in possession of a single artistic bone in their bodies, in 1981 the Exploited scored a Top 40 hit with the song 'Dead Cities', an occasion marked with a startling appearance on the BBC's flagship early evening music programme *Top of the Pops* (a booking which suggested that, in an age where the musical mainstream was becoming increasingly timid, 'Auntie Beeb' was still capable of stirring shards of glass into a bowl of vanilla cream).

'I just loved [that period],' recalls Hooker today. With not a little sarcasm, he adds that 'just for a change' the financial straits through which Britain was sailing were 'crap', a state of affairs that meant that the music offered by his label spoke more to the kids on the dole rather than to a nation hypnotised by the sinister fairy tale of the 1981 wedding of Charles Windsor and Diana Spencer.

'Bands like the Exploited, who were our big act at the time, were having hits with the likes of "Dead Cities",' remembers Hooker. 'And when you went on tour to places like Sheffield and Liverpool, you really did see horrific poverty. Everywhere places were closed down, there were kids sitting in gutters sniffing glue. It was quite the eye-opener. So [the kind of music made by the Exploited and others like them] had a valid place at the time. We put out nine albums and all of them went Top 40.'

At the same time as the Exploited were thrilling football hooligans and those for whom Johnny Rotten's proclamation that there was 'no future' had become a deadening reality, listeners who preferred to grow their hair long rather than spike it to the rafters with sugar and water were rallying to the sound made by groups lumped together under the awkward acronym that was NWOBHM (New Wave of British Heavy Metal). But while Hooker admits that the sound made by Iron Maiden was that of a 'great band', for the most part the collective whole as represented by the New Wave of British Heavy Metal left him cold. That this was so might have made Hooker's decision to take *Kill 'Em All* under licence on his new label, Music For Nations, an odd choice, what with so many of that album's component parts bearing such close resemblance to the sounds that had emerged from the United Kingdom just a year or two earlier. But while Hooker recognises this irony, he is also quick, and correct, to point out that Metallica brought to their sound 'an excitement and energy' that gave their music a sense of uncharted vitality, if not quite originality. For while even the most frenetic of New Wave of British Heavy Metal turns did carry with them a whiff of something hoary, Metallica roared from the speakers with the pure amphetamined energy of the kind of punk that had never been near an art school.

So smitten was Hooker with Metallica that in his pursuit of the group the label owner broke a number of his own rules. 'Unusually I went against my own instincts,' he admits. 'Usually I'd have long talks with the band and go and see them play live, but time-wise I wasn't in a position to do that. I just wanted to get them signed up before anybody else was interested. So, yeah, I went about it a bit arse-about-face, and it was a bit of a gamble. But obviously it was one that paid off for me.'

But as with his decision to leave EMI in order to build Secret, and then Music For Nations, Hooker understood that in order to accumulate first he must speculate, and that Metallica were a prospect upon which it was worth placing a bet. The Englishman liked the fact that the group themselves were not English, observing that US bands were so much more to his personal taste.

'American musicians were so much easier to work with than English guys,' he maintains. 'They were so much more hard-working, Lars Ulrich being a perfect case in point – you just wound him up and let him go. Whereas a lot of English bands that I worked with would be, like, "Right, I've signed a record deal, now make me a star." They would just sit back and let it all happen around them. But the American bands were more inclined to put in a twelve-hour day to make things happen.'

†

Metallica's decision to record their second album not in America but at Sweet Silence was aided by the fact that February 1984 saw the band perform their first live shows in Europe. Ticket holders who attended the Volkshaus club in Zurich, Switzerland, on February 3, 1984, can lay claim to being members of the first audience to see the quartet perform outside the United States. The group had travelled to the mainland as special guests on Venom's Seven Dates of Hell tour, a tour which confusingly comprised of just six dates. As well as visiting Zurich, the caravan also made noise in the cities of Milan, Nuremberg, Paris, Zwolle and Poperinge.

The quartet were guided through this short European trek by tour manager Gem Howard. A friend of Martin Hooker's and a colleague since the days of the Secret label, in 1984 Howard held the position of general manager of Music For Nations. The aspect of the job that Howard most enjoyed, however, was being out in the field, travelling with and taking care of bands touring Britain and mainland Europe. This he had been doing since 1976, when as an employee at Secret he would shepherd around the continent the kind of groups parents dread their daughters might one day bring home. Eight years on, Howard was still traversing the motorways and autobahns of his home continent in the service of Music For Nations' growing roster of bands, many of whom were not just young and American but also in Europe for the first time.

It was a life free of any particular luxury. But as the man in charge of a tour – a role he describes as being 'part parent, part babysitter, part boss and part organiser, all rolled into one' – Howard was afforded his own room in the low-rent guest houses in which his charges were invariably booked. The reason for this was that as tour manager it was his responsibility to guard the money from light-fingered groupies and other flotsam and jetsam attracted to the dim lights of rock bands.

In this regard at least, though, Metallica differed from the norm. Howard remembers the group as being one rather more interested in 'the process of playing gigs' than 'the groupie side of things', noting that he had 'met so many bands who just want to get on the road and get laid as much as possible, and who have no real interest in anything other than that. But [Metallica] were always interested in other aspects regarding the craft of what they were doing. They still got trashed on the road and all of that, but they were always primarily interested in the musical side of things. Everything else was just kind of a bolt-on.'

Metallica's expectations came without frills. In 1984 the group desired only a venue in which to play, enough money to buy food and (understandable given the events in Boston just a month earlier) musical equipment. These criteria were met. Perhaps realising he was in the company of a man who even in the mid-Eighties was beginning to bear the hallmarks of a grizzled veteran, Lars Ulrich even managed to keep a lid on his oft-repeated assertion that Metallica were destined to become the biggest band in the world. But while Gem Howard has no recollection of such brazen talk from the smaller man, twenty-nine years after the fact other seemingly insignificant details have been filed to memory.

'There's one thing that always stands out,' he says, 'and this can be related to really any young band. It actually comes down to what they listen to. I've been out [on tour] with lots and lots of bands. I've sat in tour buses with them, minibuses and all the rest of it. And the ones that tend to come through are the ones who are listening to stuff that isn't necessarily what you'd expect them to listen to. If you go out with a very average British thrash metal band, all they tend to listen to is thrash metal; so all of their influences come from the same kind of music that they're making. There's nothing new in there. But with Metallica, at one minute they'd be singing along to the Misfits, while the next minute they'd almost be crying their eyes out listening to "Homeward Bound" by Simon & Garfunkel. And they'd be listening to Ennio

Morricone, which, of course, they used as their intro tape before they came onstage [in the form of "The Ecstasy of Gold"], and in time they'd develop acoustic intros to their songs that were influenced by Ennio Morricone. They really were picking up stuff from all over the place, which is how they developed. They were listening to all this different stuff that they then figured out a way to incorporate into their music. And that made them stand out above the others.'

The difference between a band that John Gallagher viewed as being 'borderline out of control' and the at least semi-professional young men encountered by Gem Howard just six months later is striking. There is a notion that if people are treated like animals then they will act accordingly, a self-fulfilling prophecy that was afforded full expression on the Kill 'Em All for One tour. But in Europe at least, three-quarters of the group were suddenly strangers in a strange land, and there are few types of people more easily discombobulated than young American musicians who find themselves in a foreign-speaking country for the first time. They were under the wing of a tour manager equipped with a sense of calm and authority. They were riding around, not in a Winnebago propelled by the wind and reliant on WD40 but rather in a minibus that, while sparse, was amenable. At the end of their working day, the bed linen underneath which their bodies rested may have crackled with static electricity, but it was at least clean.

Metallica were also a different band in a musical sense. During that autumn of 1983 in San Francisco, the group had done more than drink beer and vodka while imagining themselves to be an all-conquering force. Instead, they had worked to amass material that stood years rather than months ahead of the compositions heard on Kill 'Em All.

'The Hetfield/ Ulrich/ Mustaine/ McGovney Metallica was a pretty one-dimensional musical unit,' says Ulrich. 'When Burton and Hammett joined in the space of three months, they added a lot to our sound. Cliff joined in February '83 and right away we started working on songs that expanded our horizons. Cliff was studying music at college and he talked about Beethoven or Bach as much as he talked about ZZ Top or the Misfits. And Kirk also added a lot of elements. And we realised that we could be "heavier" by actually slowing down.'

Metallica arrived to begin work on the album that would become *Ride the Lightning* in a freezing Copenhagen on February 20, 1984. As with its predecessor, time was not the band's friend. Not only were the sessions constrained on one side by the kind of limited budgets familiar to any young group recording on the dimes afforded by an independent record label, but allied to this Metallica's window of opportunity was also hemmed in by a series of European live dates scheduled to begin just twenty-nine days after the band had convened at Sweet Silence. Clearly, then, time and money were both in short supply.

'I'm pretty sure that what Metallica paid to record in [the studio] would have been more than it would have cost to get into the studio today,' says Flemming Rasmussen. 'Prices for studios then were a lot more than they are now, actually. We're roughly talking Eighties prices right now, so this is not a lucrative business. Everybody and their uncles thinks they can do it on their computer, but then they can't understand why what they've recorded doesn't sound like Metallica.'

The producer then leans forward and with the air of one who knows, and the timing of a natural comedian, says, 'Well, then let me tell you why . . . '

On a bright and warm early September morning, Flemming Rasmussen met this book's authors on the arrivals floor of Copenhagen's International Airport. Of slim build and medium height, with his fine sandy hair and discreet eyewear the fifty-four-year-old producer has about him the cultured air of a university lecturer rather than someone who has spent his adult life attempting to set and record a perfect guitar tone. As is the case with almost all Scandinavians, Rasmussen's spoken English is fluent and crisp, with verbal intonations that remind the listener of a slightly older Lars Ulrich (whom the producer reveals he is to visit in San Francisco in just a few days' time). Unlike Ulrich, however, Rasmussen has no qualms about depositing sentences in an order that causes the sentiment held within to come crashing down with immediate force. Of his first impressions of the group that gathered to record *Ride the Lightning* he recalls 'I thought they were pretty childish. I thought they were kids.' Pausing to consider this memory, the producer allows himself a small smile and says, 'I liked them.'

Today what was Sweet Silence Studios is an unremarkable-looking apartment block situated beside a main road that leads to the centre of Copenhagen. Parking his car, Rasmussen walks to the walls of number 85 Strandlodsbej and paints an image with words and pointed fingers. 'You see that room over there?' he asks. 'Well that's where Lars recorded his drums. The guy living in that apartment is living in the exact spot where Lars used to play.'

By agreeing to produce Metallica, Rasmussen reached a point at which all working people arrive: that is, for the first time in his professional life he was older than the people with whom he was collaborating. At the time of the recording of *Ride the Lightning*, Rasmussen was still a relatively green-horned twenty-six years of age. His charges, though, were younger still, with Cliff Burton being the oldest member of the group at twenty-two, and with both Lars Ulrich and James Hetfield having yet to celebrate their twenty-first birthdays.

The first task Rasmussen faced was to ensure that Metallica were not choked by the mouthful of ambition on which they were attempting to chew. The producer quickly and rather astutely recognised that the band had in their minds a clear and resonant idea of exactly how their second album should sound. What he also realised was that the quartet lacked the fundamental skills required to realise what could justifiably be described as their 'vision'.

'My job was just to get them to perform as well as possible,' remembers Rasmussen. 'The reason for this was because at the time Metallica's ambitions were higher than their technical abilities.'

One of the first challenges came in the diminutive form of the person who might well have understood most clearly what it was the group were striving to achieve. In the years that have elapsed since the release of *Ride the Lightning*, Ulrich's technical abilities as a drummer have been both greatly discussed and largely derided – mostly by people who have never themselves held a pair of drumsticks. There is something rather gratuitous about the blood-lust that surrounds what has now long been the self-fulfilling prophecy that not only is Ulrich Metallica's musical weak link, but that the Dane lacks the proficiency of even the most inadequate of drummers. There is to this scenario a subtext of the 'tall poppy syndrome', that to counteract Ulrich's indefatigable energies and his unquestionable success as 'the little engine that could' a weakness must be found. Given that his own capabilities as a drummer are one of the few subjects about which the musician has not publicly voiced an opinion, it is into this vacuum of silence that a derogatory consensus has swept.

That said, the case for Ulrich's defence is not entirely aided by Hetfield's observation that his band mate and occasional friend 'will admit' to not being a particularly accomplished player. (Hetfield is also of the belief that he himself 'is not a very good singer' – itself a statement that isn't quite just – but that when he and Ulrich combine forces 'there's something that [just] happens . . .') What can be said with some certainty is that in learning to play his instrument, Ulrich took care to master certain elements of the craft while paying no heed whatsoever to other, more fundamental aspects: minor things, like the ability to keep time.

'Lars's drumming wasn't quite up to the standards needed for the recording studio,' is Rasmussen's recollection, a state of affairs the producer reckoned to be 'really really strange'.

'I think the first recording we did was [a rough take of] "Creeping Death", and after they'd done it I got the band into the control room so they could check the sound,' remembers the producer. 'They were delighted with it. So then we took Lars into the back room – a big ten foot by ten foot room where the drums were set up with mics all around the kit – and the first thing I asked Lars was, "Why are you starting on an upbeat all the time?" And he looked at me and said, "What the fuck is an upbeat?" . . . [But] I quickly realised that Lars – and this pretty much defines his attitude to drumming – what Lars lives for in his playing is doing all the fills. All of the stuff in between, he never gave a thought to. But all of his fills were fabulous; they sounded really good and they were in time. But every time he had to do something simple, that's when we'd have problems. Lars is a good drummer, but he's not a good timekeeper.'

In the years that have elapsed since the recording of *Ride the Lightning*, it has become almost a hanging offence to utter a single negative word regarding the musicianship of Cliff Burton. For his part Rasmussen describes Burton as being 'the best bass player I ever worked with', while at the same time acknowledging that he too 'had some issues when it came to keeping time'.

As drummer and bassist hacked their way towards some kind of rhythm (with Ulrich receiving guidance from Flemming Larsen, then the drummer in Danish thrashers Artillery, who later became his drum tech) in Sweet Silence's other studio, Freddie Hansson, Rasmussen's business partner and studio co-owner, would be recording Danish jazz musicians. These players would hear the music being played in the other room and react with vociferous disdain. 'These musicians would hear Metallica and

go, "God it's so fast, it's so loud and it's so untight",' remembers
Rasmussen. 'And I'd be going, "But it's fucking brilliant!" Me, I
didn't just like it, I loved it. And the jazz musicians were saying,
"Yeah, but they can't play!"'

Rasmussen begged to differ. Not only that, but he recognised
qualities in Metallica's music that went unnoticed by the more
formal ears of the jazz musicians, qualities such as 'energy and
attitude'. The producer took particular pleasure in finding himself
in the orbit of Hetfield, whose talents the producer believes stand
equal to the title of 'the greatest rhythm guitar player in the world'.
For his part, Hetfield was sufficiently impressed with Rasmussen's
work on *Ride the Lightning* that to this day it remains the front
man's favourite album of the three on which the Dane was the
producer. Following Paul Curcio's inattentive supervision of *Kill
'Em All*, the rhythm guitarist was encouraged by Rasmussen's
attention to detail. One of the first tasks asked of him was that he
help Hetfield replicate the tone of his guitar as it sounded when
played through the amplifier-head stolen in Boston. To do this,
the producer assembled in a room 'nine or ten' Marshall stacks
and cabinets – the result of him 'calling pretty much everyone I
knew in Copenhagen' – and spent 'two or three days' in concert
with Hetfield attempting to navigate their way towards the
perfect tone. Once found, the guitarist then not only recorded
his rhythm parts with forensic precision, but also overlaid them
with two or three further takes played live rather than replicated
by overdub, as is usually the case. For a man who just three years
earlier had no desire to play guitar for Metallica, this was talent
showcased to a precocious and even unique degree.

From component parts that might be described as being
'uneven', in Sweet Silence Studios both producer and artists quickly
located each other's wave lengths and worked with tenacity, speed
and purpose. Sessions took place under cover of darkness, with
work beginning at seven in the evening and finishing some ten

hours later. Band and producer would then unwind over bottles of beer and hands of poker, before retiring (Rasmussen to his home in Copenhagen, Metallica to Ken Anthony's apartment in Brondby) to sleep the day away. This routine was adhered to on a daily basis for four weeks and a day.

'The whole recording of the album was quite a smooth process, I think,' is the producer's recollection. 'I mean, it was hard, but the energy and power they had meant that they were just going for it all the time.'

Rasmussen was not only capable enough as a producer to guide Metallica's ideas into a permanent form, but also young and enthusiastic enough to connect with the immediacy and energy of the group's genetic code. With freezing temperatures outside the studio walls and little else to do other than work, minds were focused on a job of work both parties inherently understood to be one worthy of seriousness.

'I could tell from early on that the album was going to be very good,' says Rasmussen. 'I could tell we were on to something.'

Soon enough, this would be an opinion shared by many of the people who heard *Ride the Lightning*. In the thick of a Danish winter, however, the group had only their own and their producer's instincts to guide them. But while the music was coalescing with certainty and fortitude, outside the studio walls Metallica's business operation continued to judder in an alarming manner. As ever, the question was one of money, or, rather, the lack of it. According to Johnny Z, the budget for recording his charges' second album had risen from $20,000 to $30,000, an escalation that caused the manager's spirits to plunge. Phone calls to a lackadaisical Lars Ulrich did little to calm Zazula's fears, with the drummer blithely asserting, '"Who can say how much a record costs? When it's done, it's done."' For his part, Johnny Z admits to being 'pretty broke at the time', the result, he says, of being 'ripped off by our distributor in a major, major way'.

'It was only later that we realised exactly how much we were ripped off for,' he says. 'But at the time all we knew was that Metallica were doing really well and yet we weren't seeing the kind of money we should have been seeing.'

In a state of increasing desperation, Zazula decided to fly to Copenhagen in an attempt to make first-hand sense of the situation.

'It was my first time abroad and I was just eaten up,' he recalled. 'I was a Bambi in a forest full of hunters – all these English businessmen with their pots and pots of money, and me running up debts I didn't even know I could pay. Not only had the album cost more than it was supposed to, but the band had blown all of their European money on the Venom tour. So I was going, "Woah, this is getting out of hand."'

On Metallica's behalf Zazula discussed the possibility of a record deal for the United States with the Bronze label, an imprint which could lay claim to being the home of the Damned, Hawkwind and Ulrich's heroes Motörhead (this despite the fact that the company was held in low esteem by the music industry at large). So confident were Bronze that they had secured Metallica's services that the label decorated a bus with a banner announcing their new signings and parked the vehicle in full display of the ticket holders and music industry insiders gathered to see the Aardschock Festival in Zwolle, Holland, on February 11, 1984.

In point of fact, representatives of Bronze were the first people outside Metallica's camp to be afforded a listen to *Ride the Lightning* at Sweet Silence, an occasion which saw the label founder Gerry Bron and his son Richard deliver a crash course in how to make a calamitous first impression. In the presence of the album's producer the pair asserted that *Ride the Lightning*'s sound was 'crap'. Winning no prizes for diplomacy, the Englishmen declared that the work might be best salvaged by sacking Rasmussen, scrapping the entire session and drafting in Eddie Kramer, a producer and engineer famed for his work with Led Zeppelin and Kiss, to oversee a new mix. Hearing this, Rasmussen looked over to Ulrich and said of his guests, 'they're idiots'.

Twenty-nine years after the fact, the producer is philosophical enough to realise that had Metallica ceded to Bronze's wishes it would have been 'just business'. Nothing personal. That said, Rasmussen was also of the opinion that the songs on which he and Metallica had collaborated featured 'the fattest drum sound ever recorded', and that the work 'sounded killer'. Having punched in night shifts on behalf of Metallica and been close enough to the group to have ordered Kirk Hammett to take a shower because the guitarist had been wearing the same clothes 'for a week', he admits that had the group accepted Bronze's thirteen pieces of silver he would have been 'offended'.

'Let's put it this way,' he says. 'They were certainly not people I would trust.'

In the end Ulrich decided that the Brons were not the kind of partners he wanted to climb into bed with either, and the label's entreaties were politely rebuffed.

'We decided,' said the drummer, 'that maybe we would be better off in the long run if we waited to see what else would happen.'

The group's decision to hold their nerve in the face of Bronze's advances was a wise one: just two years after failing to secure the signatures of Burton, Hammett, Hetfield and Ulrich, the label went bust. At the time, however, Metallica's hope that they would be 'better off in the long run' must have looked like a gamble even to their ever optimistic drummer. Following the completion of *Ride the Lightning*, the band headed to the United Kingdom for a proposed tour with The Rods and Canadian proto-thrashers Exciter, with the San Franciscans set to occupy the evening's middle slot. Appearing under the banner of the Hell on Earth tour, the three-band package will be remembered, if it is remembered at all, as being one of the most grievous miscalculations in rock music history. Scheduled to run from March 21 to April 3, and booked into venues built to accommodate in excess of 3,000 people – rooms such as the Apollo Theatre in Manchester and the iconic Hammersmith Odeon in west London – the eleven-date tour made advance ticket sales that were so anaemic that audiences could have been transported to the concerts in a single minibus, and in some cases a taxi. A proposed appearance at the Newcastle Mayfair club on March 30 captured the imagination of just fourteen people, a figure rendered all the more remarkable for this being one of the tour's more successful dates in terms of advance ticket sales. The number of people who paid money at the box office of the Hammersmith Odeon in anticipation of a concert booked for March 22 was just fifteen, this in a room that at the time held space for 3,300 people. To no one's surprise, the Hell on Earth tour was cancelled.

This left Metallica with time on their hands. The band were scheduled to make what would now be their debut appearance in the United Kingdom with a date at London's Marquee club on March 27, with a second engagement at the same venue booked for April 8. In light of time being called on the proposed tour with The Rods and Exciter, rather than incur the expense and inconvenience of placing the four musicians on a return flight to San Francisco, the decision was made to keep the quartet stationed in London. It was left to Music For Nations to find accommodation for the visitors, which they did with a short-term let on a flat in Earl's Court/Olympia. Safely ensconced in this picturesque quarter of the city, Metallica swiftly set about ensuring that their record company lost the deposit paid to secure the property.

'I remember visiting them at the flat itself and, to be honest with you, I've seen better squats,' remembers Gem Howard. 'And this was quite a nice flat as well. They made a real mess of it. No washing up had been done whatsoever. All the plates were piled up on the coffee table in the front room. In the kitchen, someone had obviously buttered some toast and the pack of butter had fallen on to the floor, and whoever was responsible had just walked away from it and left it there. It was just disgusting.'

For young bands visiting London for the first time in the early to mid-Eighties – particularly groups raised in locations such as Los Angeles and San Francisco – London resembled a city where only the language spoken by its citizens reminded them of home. The United Kingdom in 1984 was a place of turbid skies, boiled vegetables and pubs that not only stopped serving their customers at 11 p.m. sharp but which also closed in the afternoons. Were Metallica to have turned on a television set they would have had the choice of programmes from just four channels, while a stroll down the King's Road on a Saturday afternoon might have attracted the unwanted attentions of Chelsea Football Club's then significant hooligan element. America may have been the land of the gun and of violent crime delivered with terminal force, but when it came to bare-knuckle nastiness England in the Eighties was a hard act to follow. A pawn in the ideological battle between Margaret Thatcher's Conservative government and the Left-leaning Greater London Council controlled by 'Red' Ken Livingstone, the nation's capital was a city in stasis, populated in part, as Paul Weller observed in The Jam's 'Down in the Tube Station at Midnight', by people a number of whom 'smelled of pubs, and Wormwood Scrubs, and too many Right-wing meetings.'

But if London, compared with California, was a culture shock that assaulted all of the senses, another distinction between the New World and the Old Country did serve Metallica well. Unlike in the United States, the music industry in Britain enjoyed the benefits of a powerful music press. Magazines such as *New Musical Express*, *Melody Maker* and *Sounds* sold hundreds of thousands of copies each week and featured voices of such editorial independence and strength that they could either propel a group towards domestic stardom or else grind their faces into the dirt. The latter action was a pastime which the music press often particularly relished, rightly gaining for itself an international reputation for callousness and even brutality.

But while in the spring of 1984 the likes of the *NME* and *Melody Maker* would not dream of dirtying their hands or the minds of their readers with the likes of Metallica – not yet, that is – there was a corner of the UK music press occupied by two fledgling titles that did view the group as being subjects worthy of mention. One of these was the small independent title *Metal Forces*, a publication dedicated specifically to heavy metal and hardcore punk's fervent and burgeoning underground. Beloved of tape traders and other inhabitants of these genres' lunatic fringe, the monthly publication was sold at the underground (in both the literal and figurative sense) Soho record shop Shades and via mail order. But while the circulation of *Metal Forces* may have been small to the point of insignificance, its influence in its field of expertise was nonetheless substantial. Usually excitable and often not fully literate, under the editorship of founder and editor Bernard Doe the title catered to its obsessive readership with opinions that were not so much forceful as tyrannical. In his review of *Kill 'Em All*, Doe himself wrote that the album was 'one of the most awesome, fastest and heaviest pieces of vinyl' he'd ever heard.

'I'd urge every heavy metal fan to grab a copy of this album, and if when you've heard it you dislike *Kill 'Em All* then you can no longer call yourself a heavy metal fan,' he declared. 'You just don't understand what heavy metal is about.'

More significant in introducing metal's feral new order to the genre's rather stolid and conservative-minded mainstream was the contribution made by *Kerrang!*, which emerged every fortnight from an office on the South Bank of the Thames that was part music magazine HQ and part insane asylum. *Kerrang!* featured a cast of characters, many of whom would rather drink vodka than breathe and one who would be derelict in his professional duties to the extent of tossing a coin in order to determine whether or not to afford an album a glowing or scathing review. Nevertheless, the magazine put in much good, if sometimes untidy, work in heralding rather than merely defending the kind of groups derided by the more respectable members of the fourth estate. Many of the groups eulogised in *Kerrang!*'s garish pages were not up to much in either style or substance, but while the publication could not always be said to possess discriminating taste, it did resonate with a defiant conviction that harmonised with the appetites and temperament of its readership. It was in the magazine's pages that Metallica found their spiritual home. From the point of view of *Kerrang!*'s staff the advent of the San Franciscan outfit and others following in their slipstream heralded the emergence of a slew of acts younger than the magazine itself which the title could claim as their own.

'Personally, I've always preferred the American metal scene to the British metal scene,' says Geoff Barton, the New Wave of British Heavy Metal champion who became *Kerrang!*'s first editor. 'You had the Seventies monsters – Aerosmith, Kiss, Ted Nugent, Van Halen – but they couldn't really be accessed then. But when the whole Bay Area thrash movement came about these bands were much more accessible. After a while, once you learned more about it, it was plain they had a lot more affiliation with the groundswell of what was going on at that time than perhaps their peers from the 1970s had.'

In 1984 *Kerrang!*'s stock as measured by the London-based music industry was not high. Access to major label groups was offered first to the editors of the *NME* and *Melody Maker*, even if the music made by these groups was a bespoke fit for *Kerrang!*'s readership. With Metallica, though, this changed, with Music For Nations recognising that their energetic young charges were ideal material for the energetic young magazine. With this union, *Kerrang!* secured the jump on music publications that just a few years earlier had both the ear and the wherewithal to both announce and articulate the emergence of punk.

While stationed in London, the members of Metallica kept company with journalists and employees of *Kerrang!,* but not always harmoniously. On one visit to the magazine's offices James Hetfield became embroiled in a fist-fight with Steve 'Krusher' Joule, then the magazine's abrasive designer. Barton recalls being confronted with the two men entangled on the floor, a startling sight even by the wayward standards of the magazine he then edited. During the same period, *Kerrang!* journalist Malcolm Dome invited Lars Ulrich for an evening's libation at the St Moritz club in Soho, a location so befitting the phrase 'dive bar' that the words could have been paired together specifically to describe it. On this particular evening the pair were joined by Lemmy, then as now a man with a constitution as unbreakable as a diamond. Self-possessed to the point of insanity, Ulrich announced to his companions that when it came to the night's drinking he would match the Motörhead front man 'shot for shot'. Predictably, this did not end well for the younger man.

'He didn't quite make it,' remembers Dome. 'At the end of the night I had to pour him into a cab. At the time the band were staying in west London and I remember him getting into the cab and the driver asking him, "Where to, mate?" He didn't reply at first, so I asked him, "Lars, where are you going?", to which he announced, "Denmark! Take me to Denmark!" So there's me asking, "Lars, seriously, where are you going?", and him answering "Denmark!" And, of course, there's Lemmy, completely sober, totally fine.'

On another occasion Cliff Burton decided to occupy a free day with a shopping trip to Oxford Street. He was joined by Anthrax guitarist Scott Ian, who was in London to discuss plans for his band's second album with Music For Nations. Ian accompanied Burton into the centre of town in order that the bass player could purchase a new Walkman. Waiting for an underground train at Tottenham Court Road station, the pair were approached by two policeman, one of whom asked, 'If we were to search you right now, would we find any drugs?'

The pair's answer, 'No', was not taken at face value by the two representatives of the thin blue line. Instead Burton and Ian were arrested on suspected possession of a controlled substance and were taken to the nearby Albany Street police station for questioning. Locked inside a windowless cell for hours on end, Burton found himself growing increasingly frustrated that the one free day afforded by Metallica's schedule found him imprisoned in a Metropolitan Police nick. When the door to the cell finally did open, it was only to permit the entrance of two policeman, who instructed the suspects to strip to their underwear in preparation for a thorough body search. This search revealed a number of pills, belonging to Burton, which the officers suspected to be drugs of an illegal kind. Despite the bass player's protestations that these tablets were nothing other than medicine for the treatment of allergies and a cold, he was told that neither he or his friend would be re-acquainted with their liberty before the items had been subject to testing in a police laboratory. While this took place, Burton was driven in a police van back to the flat he and his band mates were sharing in order that police could search the property for more 'contraband'. Answering the door, Kirk Hammett was startled to see his band mate accompanied by six uniformed officers, and even more surprised when (without a warrant) the officers began to search the flat. When this exercise unearthed nothing, and the forensic lab report duly identified Burton's seized property as being a phlegm expectorant, both young Americans were told they were free to go, sent on their way with a back-handed apology from the station's commanding officer. Saying that he was sorry for their inconvenience, the policeman added that had this event occurred in the United States the suspects perhaps could have expected worse treatment. Not one to suffer such foolishness, Burton retorted that that in United States most officers had the wherewithal to differentiate between cold medicine and Quaaludes and would instead quickly have shifted their attentions to the business of catching real criminals.

If Cliff Burton could hardly have been said to be viewing the sights of London (at least not while locked inside a police cell), the same held true for James Hetfield and Lars Ulrich. With the band's first date at the Marquee fast approaching, on March 23 the pair travelled to the not at all picturesque neighbourhood of Walthamstow, a north-eastern suburb of the city known locally for its art deco dog-racing stadium and very little else, in order to drum up interest in their debut UK performance set to take place four nights later. To do this, the pair handed out flyers to fans gathered at the Royal Standard pub where that night Exciter were playing a headline show.

'Lars and James were just giving out flyers inside of the venue,' says Malcolm Dome, who was with the pair that evening. 'They were just walking around asking people if they'd come down to the Marquee to watch them play. I don't think it was a case that they necessarily thought that no one would come, but more a case of the fact that they just didn't know what was going to happen. No one knew what was going to happen. There *was* a bit of a buzz about Metallica but this had taken a knock from the fact that the tour with The Rods had been cancelled. Suddenly from [a proposed date at] the Hammersmith Odeon, Exciter are playing the Royal Standard, which is a tiny place. And while Exciter got a good crowd that night, it wasn't a huge one. So you can see why no one quite knew what to expect.'

Hetfield and Ulrich's willingness to hustle on behalf of their own band in this way – an enterprise one imagines came more naturally to the drummer than it did the front man – lends credence to Martin Hooker's observation that American bands were willing to work harder than their British counterparts in an effort to engineer some kind of forward momentum.

The significance of Metallica's appearances at the Marquee would also have been something that was not missed by the band. Originally opened in 1958 on London's Oxford Street, since moving the short distance to Soho's Wardour Street in 1964 the 400-capacity room had established itself as the most iconic live music club in the world, eclipsing the profiles of even New York's CBGB and the Fillmore in San Francisco. By 1984 the Marquee's small stage had supported the weight of such acts as The Who, Led Zeppelin, Jimi Hendrix, Pink Floyd, The Police, The Jam and Iron Maiden, to name but a few. For any group equipped with any degree of knowledge of musical history, an appearance at the Marquee was an occasion that amounted to more than just another date on a tour schedule. As if this weren't enough, the headline act on March 27, 1984, might also have been feeling an added degree of pressure. For Metallica to have failed to honour their undercard appearance at the Hammersmith Odeon with The Rods was one thing; to then have managed only a timid splash over two nights at the Marquee would be quite another. A failure of this kind would have done nothing to encourage the charge of electricity that was beginning to crackle around their name.

They needn't have worried. As tour manager Gem Howard remembers, 'pretty much everyone from *Kerrang!*' attended the first of the two performances, 'everyone from the receptionist to the editor'. The band had also managed to attract paying customers in numbers sufficient to fill the room in which they were playing, a feat they would also accomplish less than a fortnight later. As the English winter ceded territory to a more agreeable spring, Metallica placed their first marker in the heart of one of the world's greatest and most musically significant cities.

'It was quite a typical mayhemic Marquee experience with sweat pouring down the walls,' remembers Geoff Barton. 'But I don't know if I necessarily saw the potential of Metallica at that point, because to me it was just a barrage of noise. It would be great for me to say, "Yes, I could see they were megastars in an instant," but I don't think that was really the case.'

'They blew the place apart,' is the rather more effusive recollection of Malcolm Dome, who bore witness to both of the group's performances on Wardour Street. 'The thing I remember most about them was just how commanding a presence James Hetfield was onstage. His personality was still developing at that point, but even then he had a great deal of stage presence. Live, he drove that band. And I remember Cliff looking odd and not seeming to fit in with the group that he was playing with, but in a good way. He just seemed to be a bit different, like a Southern rocker in a thrash band. But you just looked at what was happening on that stage and got the sense that you were watching something monumental.'

'At that time there were a number of American bands who were coming over to England and playing club shows,' he continues. 'Y&T had been over, as had The Rods and Twisted Sister. All of those bands had been really very impressive. But this was something different. The music Metallica were playing seemed to offer a whole new direction. And onstage, they sounded even heavier than they did on record.'

✝

But if Metallica's visceral live performances were of a power capable of thrilling audiences from San Francisco to London, when it came to the recording studio the group were ready to unveil a more nuanced and textured interpretation of their sound. *Ride the Lightning* met its waiting public on July 27, 1984, a mere one year and two days after the release of *Kill 'Em All*. The eight-song set was more than the sound of a band growing into their own skin; it was also the work of a group whose musical inquisitiveness had taken them far from the point at which they stood just twelve months previously. Odd, then, that one of its creators spoke of the band's effort with some hesitation. Informed by an ear trained on what he believed the album lacked rather than what it was outside parties would hear – itself always the sign of a restless creative force – when asked his opinion on *Ride the Lightning* Lars Ulrich explained with a perspective that suggested he viewed the bottle of vodka as being half-empty rather than two-quarters full.

'We're as happy [with the album] as we [can] be,' he said, adding that 'a few of the songs were only written just before we had to do the album, so I think we might have arranged them a little differently if we had had the opportunity to put them down on tape first, and then gone away and listened to them before doing the album.'

The very fact that Ulrich is making reference to musical arrangements offers a clue as to the distance traversed by the group over the course of the previous months. While the musicianship on *Kill 'Em All* is often accomplished in an individual sense, in 1983 Metallica's technique for summoning volume and force was to emphasise their power by layering instruments atop each other in a manner that produced heat rather than light. As Ulrich himself rather astutely observed, in effect the band's debut album was like 'one complete track', whereas its successor proved that 'You don't have to depend on speed to be powerful and heavy.'

With *Ride the Lightning* Metallica showed that they could transcend the boundaries of *Kill 'Em All* with some ease, a point that is made before the album's opening track, 'Fight Fire with Fire', has even really begun. While the main body of this song sees Metallica rallying to a riff that is both precise and relentless, the tracks opens not with power chords or a bass drum beat but rather with the swell of beautifully textured acoustic guitars. The contrast between what is heard in the first seconds and what soon follows is not only deliberately startling, but also serves to set the parameters within which the album itself operates. In 1984 the acoustic-then-electric technique displayed on 'Fight Fire with Fire' was sufficiently revolutionary and effective as to be quickly seized upon by thrash metal's chasing pack and copied to such an extent that within two years it would be rendered a cliché.

Not that Metallica themselves were above resorting to cliché. Despite displaying a level of musical progression that is rarely less than striking, *Ride the Lightning* is not an album free from the banalities particular to heavy metal at the time. Twenty-nine years after the fact, 'Creeping Death' remains a classic of the genre, and it is a testament to the song's remarkable musical power that it manages to obscure a lyric – the Biblical tale of the curse of the death of the first-born from the book of Exodus – that while poetically competent is in essence not a good deal smarter than a rock. The same might be said of 'For Whom the Bell Tolls', a tale of medieval men fighting to the death over a patch of land, a sentiment accompanied by music of such quality that to this day it remains a particular favourite of Metallica's audience and a staple of the group's live set. It is, though, somehow more than magisterial music that rescues a lyric that might have been both brittle and daft; here, the notion that James Hetfield has established an emotional connection between himself and the characters in the song is a difficult one to shake.

Throughout *Ride the Lightning* the presence of Cliff Burton permeates, his authoritative but never insistent technique adding texture and depth to songs such as the instrumental composition 'The Call of Ktulu', a piece that owes as much to nineteenth-century European classical music as it does 1980s European heavy metal. A glance at the songwriting credits reveals that along with Hetfield and Ulrich (credited as co-authors of all eight tracks) the bassist co-wrote three-quarters of *Ride the Lightning* – Kirk Hammett is also listed as co-author of four songs – suggesting that Burton's contribution to Metallica's ever-developing sound was more fundamental than merely stepping on a Crybaby wah-wah pedal and making a noise that sounded like a lead guitar.

In fact the two songs on which Cliff Burton's name does not warrant a writing credit are the album's weakest selections. As a power-metal anthem that declines to engage thrash metal's top gear, 'Trapped under Ice' – a track that had its roots in the riff Kirk Hammett wrote for the early Exodus number 'Impaler' – is a song that manages to be effective without ever quite becoming *affecting*. That said, compared to 'Escape', 'Trapped under Ice' suddenly assumes a mantle of unparalleled artistic genius. With its ponderous tempo, uncharacteristically timid chorus and insipid lyric – where the narrator aspires to 'break away from . . . common fashion' desiring instead to be 'out on [his] own, out to be free' 'Escape' holds the ignominious honour of being Metallica's first artistically dishonest song.

'In terms of progression [the band] were speeding along,' remembers Flemming Rasmussen. 'Their songwriting was just getting better and better. And they did the "Escape" song, which was supposed to be their single. Big mistake. [It was them saying] "This is how much we're willing to suck up to get a hit." That was them saying, "This is how much we want to progress in the music world." But it was their own stuff that did that for them, not a song like "Escape", which is good . . . I think they recorded the song to try and get some kind of commercial break. They didn't realise that that was a total waste of time.'

The folly of 'Escape' is not that it attempts to locate musical ground which its authors may explore, but rather that it does so with a degree of calculation and compromise ill-suited to

Metallica's instincts. In a just and fair world, if one song from *Ride the Lightning* were to have been regarded with suspicion and even opprobrium by the band's growing constituency, this would have been it. Clearly this was an opinion shared by Metallica themselves, who declined to play the song in concert for twenty-eight years. In 1984, though, 'Escape' was shielded from injurious brickbats by 'Fade to Black', a song greeted by many Metallica fans with all the enthusiasm one might associate with being run over by a car.

Whether consciously or otherwise, 'Fade To Black' takes Lynyrd Skynyrd's 'Freebird' as its structural template. In no hurry to make its point, the song weaves its way through a current of subdued guitars and graceful melodies, before the band eventually flood the dam with layer upon layer of rhythm and lead guitars. Despite it being possessed of both grace and fluency, many of *Ride the Lightning*'s initial recipients viewed the song not as a natural progression but as an outright surrender, a sop to those whose tastes did not run to metal finished to the point of razor sharpness. This would be the first occasion when the intensity felt by some sections of Metallica's audience would – in principle at least – prove to be a blessing that carried with it a hint of a curse. Those who disliked 'Fade to Black' did not react to the song with a sense of disappointment, they did so with thoughts of betrayal.

'When they played "Fade . . ." for the first time in [San Francisco] on the Ride . . . tour, some of us waved Kleenex at the band,' remembers Brian Lew. 'Cliff was pissed [off]. They lost some of the original fans over it.'

But if Metallica's artistic determination was shaking loose some members of their fan base, with *Ride the Lightning* the group also managed to attract the attentions of a new and wider audience. On Friday August 3, 1984, Metallica joined headliners Raven and opening act Anthrax at the 3,500-capacity Roseland Ballroom in Midtown Manhattan for A Midsummer Night's Scream, the concert promoted by Johnny Zazula. Located on

West 52nd Street and Broadway, just ten blocks north of Times
Square, Metallica's first appearance on the island of Manhattan
was an occasion to remember in more ways than one. Performing
a ten-song set in front of a sold-out crowd, each member of whom
appeared eager to eat raw meat from the palm of James Hetfield's
hand, Metallica were once again met with tangible evidence that
their efforts were beginning to pay dividends. And with regard to
one member of the audience in particular, the San Franciscans'
appearance at the Roseland Ballroom became the location of a
landmark occasion.

In the summer of 1984 Michael Alago was an ambitious
twenty-two year-old A&R man employed by Elektra Records.
Alago decided that he would pursue a career in the music industry
after passing the doors of the Ritz club on East 12th Street in
Manhattan in the spring of 1980. At the time a college student
working part-time in a nearby pharmacy, the teenager did not
let the fact that the venue was closed for renovations deter him
from what was by any standards an audacious hustle. Entering
the Ritz, Alago announced that despite the fact that he possessed
no previous experience and no CV, he desired to pursue a career
in the music business. Impressed by the young man's chutzpah,
the club's owner handed him a first job in rock 'n' roll. Not so
much living the dream as learning his trade, at first Michael Alago
spent his working day making coffee and fetching sandwiches
for colleagues higher up the food chain. Soon enough, though,
he was dealing with the acts booked to play the 3,000-capacity
venue. He spoke with the artists and liaised with promoters and
agents. When the time came for a move from concert hall to
record label, Alago could now claim to be in possession of both
a CV and feet-on-the-ground experience. It was enough to land
him a job in the A&R department of Elektra Records.

It was here that Michael Alago first met Johnny Zazula, who
presented him with copies of Raven's *All for One* and Metallica's

Kill 'Em All. While believing the former LP to be 'very good', Alago felt it was the American band's debut album that made the deepest impression. Such was the strength of the band's impact that in late 1983 Alago flew to San Francisco to see the quartet play at The Stone, an experience he remembers as being 'so exciting and so confrontational [but] in a positive way' that 'I lost my mind'. At the culmination of the group's set, he made his way backstage and introduced himself to Lars Ulrich, with whom he had spoken on the phone just a few days previously. The drummer took possession of the A&R man's telephone number and learned that the visitor from New York had his ear on the band.

'Being a young A&R person I didn't know what to do at first,' admits Alago of his first meeting with the drummer. 'So we shook hands and I said, "You know, man, I love the record, this is incredible, just please keep in touch with me." '

Possessed of an instinctive eye for opportunities, Ulrich did keep in touch with Alago, albeit on an intermittent basis. But with Metallica set to play Manhattan in 1984, the drummer was sufficiently thoughtful and politic to remember to invite the A&R man. For his part, Alago had not forgotten the impression Metallica had made on him at The Stone. But if the sight of the group in a cramped club in their adopted home town had provided the young industry insider with a frisson of excitement, not to mention a hint of commercial opportunity, the sight of thousands of New Yorkers queuing along West 52nd Street in the crushing heat of a New York summer must have brought to mind the image of an untapped oil well.

The occasion of A Midsummer's Night Scream was nothing less than a coming-of-age party for what a number of people were beginning to describe as the New Wave of American Heavy Metal, a moniker that would be quickly eclipsed by a term already making an appearance in the pages of *Kerrang!* and *Metal Forces*: thrash metal. And while the bill at the Roseland had as its headliners an English band – for it was Raven that closed the show – the noise that greeted the arrival of local representatives Anthrax and later Metallica showed that in the city that never sleeps a new audience was waking up to the sound of domestic, cutting-edge metal.

Despite his tender years, perhaps, even, *because* of them Alago's instincts were given full licence by his superiors at Elektra Records. Following the band's set, the executive headed to the band's dressing room to discover that he was the only A&R man within hustling distance. Despite Metallica holding to their hearts a healthy and innate distrust of outsiders in general and of much of the music industry in particular, the fact that the A&R man was the same age as the band he was by now attempting to woo (not to mention the fact that the previous year he had flown five hours coast to coast on his own dime in order to watch them play) meant that Alago was afforded a warm reception. In response, Metallica were met with an invitation to a meeting at Elektra's New York offices the following afternoon.

'Literally that night, I told them how over the moon I was about them,' he recalls. 'And [then] the next day I got beer and Chinese food and the band arrived in the early afternoon. At first we sat in the conference room, which was bigger than my office . . . and we sat there for a long time and talked about the music. The guys loved that there was a history to Elektra . . . So I think that excitement, my knowledge of their music, the fact that we were the same age, and that Elektra had a reputation kinda cemented the deal then and there. I don't remember there being any complications at all in signing them.'

In a move that speaks of a bygone age for a music industry that today finds itself in rapid decline, Metallica committed themselves to Elektra (and vice versa) in a contract that spanned eight albums. Another remarkable aspect of this union is that the courtship began without any kind of guidance from the band's management. In fact, Johnny Zazula learned that contact had been made between band and label *after* the fact, news he greeted with an uneven temper.

'John was *furious* with me,' recalls Alago today. 'Because you know what, I had to fucking tell him, "John, I've been talking to Lars." And [the manager] went off at the deep end. It was almost like I was stealing his first born. He wanted to sue Time Warner [Elektra's parent company]. He was going to get me fired. He was going to talk to [my superiors] – you know, how dare I, and all that kind of stuff. And of course what happened in the end was that our business affairs people talked to their lawyers, we agreed that the Megaforce logo would be on the next record, and they got a nice percentage . . .'

Alago goes on to say that he 'adores' the Zazulas, observing that Johnny and Marsha 'were such incredible people' who 'love music the way we all love music. So once we got past that little hiccup, the band was signed to the label.'

For Zazula, though, this was not so much a 'little hiccup' but rather the beginning of the end. The manager's anger at Michael Alago was misdirected; and the man who supposedly was in charge of Metallica's business operation could hardly have failed to appreciate that the group on whom he had staked the home in which he and his family lived had in effect taken the biggest decision of their short career without seeking his counsel. Wearily he agreed to pass over the rights to *Ride the Lightning* once sales of the Megaforce release exceeded 75,000 units.

As if this weren't enough, over the horizon troops were beginning to marshal themselves in opposition to Johnny Z's exhausted forces, as Metallica caught the eye of a man who was quickly emerging as one of the largest and most formidable beasts in the music industry's feral jungle.

Then, as now, along with his business partner Cliff Burnstein, Peter Mensch was the co-owner of the management company Q

Prime. The pair met in Chicago in the Seventies, when Burnstein launched the Blank label, an imprint of Mercury Records (for whom he had worked for a number of years, signing both Rush and the Scorpions to the company) and invited Mensch to run the label on a day to day basis. The two made for an effective if unlikely couple, with Burnstein possessing the aura of a Buddhist monk adhering to a vow of semi-silence while his partner handed out first impressions of an urban hustler who did not so much suffer fools gladly as leave them filleted and twitching on the floor. When invited by Aerosmith manager David Krebs to take up the position of that band's tour accountant, Mensch sought his friend's advice, and was told by Burnstein to 'take the fuckin' job, have fun and learn a lot'. Working his way up from this starting point in the company, soon enough Mensch was handling operations for bands such as the Scorpions, Def Leppard and Michael Schenker. Asked in 1979 to take charge of an emerging Australian band called AC/DC, Mensch extricated the quintet from their long-standing deal with producers Harry Vanda and George Young and instead paired them with Robert John 'Mutt' Lange, who had recently recorded the UK no. 1 single 'I Don't Like Mondays' with Dublin punks the Boomtown Rats. *Highway to Hell*, the first fruit of their union, duly became AC/DC's first million-selling album in the United States. After moving to London in order to be nearer Krebs's European-based roster, in 1980 Mensch invited Burnstein to leave Mercury Records and move to New York in order that the pair might handle his charges' business operations in tandem and on two continents.

Both being capable and ambitious men, it followed that the two friends would soon enough fly their employer's coop in order to master their own destinies. This they did in 1982 with the formation of their company, Q Prime. But while it is customary music business practice that parties striking out on their own be accompanied by a number of bands with whom they already work, in the case of Burnstein and Mensch only Def Leppard shared the courage of their managers' conviction. This was small fry indeed. In 1982 the Sheffield quintet had to their name two uneven, commercially underwhelming albums and little about them to suggest that a brighter future lay ahead. Since the managers received only a percentage of the money earned by those they represented, the first twelve months of Q Prime's existence offered slim pickings indeed. Reflecting on this period, Cliff Burnstein recalled that their budget at the time would afforded only a diet of 'peanut butter and jelly sandwiches for a while'.

The pair's fortunes, however, were soon to change, and peanut butter and jelly would quickly be replaced by caviar and truffles. In 1983 Def Leppard released their third album, *Pyromania*, a set that would sell more than seven million copies in the United States alone and make the name of both its creators and the men who managed them. Produced by Mutt Lange and propelled skyward by the video clip for the song 'Photograph' being placed on heavy rotation by MTV, the quintet from the Socialist Republic of South Yorkshire found themselves with both a smash hit album and, in Burnstein and Mensch, representatives who understood the crucial distinction between a successful record and a successful career. For their part, the men who had founded Q Prime also understood that their own fortunes depended on the longevity not only of Def Leppard, but also of other bands whose legs were built for marathons rather than sprints.

Although Q Prime harboured a suspicion of music journalists that has at times been known to cross the border into outright contempt, their initial advances to Metallica were facilitated by a bridge built by *Kerrang!*'s Xavier Russell. Having spotted a brace of youths in Shades record shop sporting Metallica T-shirts during a summer scouting mission in London, Burnstein sought out *Ride the Lightning* and heard in its eight tracks a unit with the potential to sell records to both underground and mainstream metal audiences. In the autumn of 1984 a call was placed from New York City to Russell's flat in London: the man on the American end of the line was Mensch, who told the Englishman that he was thinking about making an approach in Metallica's direction. Russell's response was both adamant and incredulous.

'I said, "Thinking? Thinking! You should go for it, they're going to be absolutely massive,"' he recalls. Mensch told the journalist that the reason for the delay in connecting with his quarry was that he lacked a contact number via which they might be reached. This was the reason for his call – could Russell act as conduit? 'I said, "I haven't got Lars's number, but I've got Kirk Hammett's mum's number, so I can phone her up and see if she can get them to phone you or phone me,"' he remembers.

'So then I got through to Kirk's mum and said, "Are any of the band about?" She said, "No, but I can get a message to them." So I said, "Can you get Lars or Kirk to phone me urgently, because it's to do with management." Following this, I then get a phone call at about three in the morning. It was the operator saying, "Will you accept a reverse-charge call from a phone box in California?" I asked, "Who is it?" and I was told, "It's some guy called Metallica." So I said, "Yeah, okay," and then, of course, I heard, "Hey, hey, this is Lars – have you got some news?" So I told him about my conversation with Peter Mensch, and he said, "Can you get him to phone us? I'll hang on here."'

Xavier Russell took the number of the phone box in which Ulrich was standing, said his goodbyes and placed a call to Peter Mensch. The next day the drummer phoned the Englishman once more, and told him that 'I think we're going to sign [with Q Prime].'

At the time Metallica were still based on the East Coast. Mensch suggested to Ulrich that the two parties meet at the home of Cliff Burnstein in Hoboken, New Jersey. Picturing in their minds the kind of luxury befitting a man now in full possession of music industry muscle, instead the group were surprised to discover that their prospective co-manager resided in a neighbourhood which by the standards of California was 'pretty urban'. Along with this revelation, Metallica also found out that despite having owned the property for a year, Burnstein had yet to fill its space with much furniture. Instead of finding themselves held in the comfort of leather chairs in a space designed to executive specifications, instead the house guests were invited to perch themselves on wooden packing crates. While this setting may not have instantly suggested that Q Prime would offer a fast track to the high life, Metallica nevertheless decided to stay.

'I instantly felt that [this set up] was right for [us],' remembers Ulrich. 'I was very surprised how down to earth it was. That was a very big word back then, "down to earth". And Cliff [Burnstein] was really down to earth – we hadn't met Peter yet – but it just seemed so right for Metallica.'

Burnstein was struck by the impression made by a band who 'while only being twenty-one or twenty-two years old' were in possession 'of a pretty goddamned good idea of what they wanted'; not only that but had learned from experience 'how some things can go bad because [a manager] doesn't have enough money . . .'

And so it was that in the shortest space of time opportunity had come calling for Metallica. In order that this might happen, however, a door was closed in the face of Johnny Zazula. Despite having offered the group their first real breaks, and having striven on their behalf almost to the point of bankruptcy, Johnny Z's role in the story of Metallica was placed into the past tense with immediate effect. It would not be the last time that the band would make difficult but wise choices with both a direct stare and an air of unflinching ruthlessness.

With a new infrastructure now supporting them, Metallica's bandwagon began to roll with increased speed and purpose.

Speaking to Bernard Doe of *Metal Forces* as 1984 drew to a close, Lars Ulrich was bullish as to the road ahead.

'Cliff Burnstein who signed us to our new management deal in the States has this big belief that what we are doing will be the next big thing in heavy metal – especially in the States which is something like 80 per cent of the market – and this whole Ratt, Mötley Crüe, Quiet Riot, Black 'N Blue thing will get kinda old and die out, and that Metallica will lead the way in a sort of new "true metal" trend,' he gushed. 'One step further out than say Iron Maiden, who are at the moment the most extreme metal band with major success.

'I honestly believe that the kids who are into the Priest, Maiden, Kiss, [Twisted] Sister will take on to what we're doing. I'm not saying it's something that's going to happen overnight, but it could start developing and Metallica could be the front runners of a new branch of heavy metal.'

6 – CREEPING DEATH

Each member of any given band carries with them on tour items that help ease the burden of weeks and months away from home. Some have video cameras with which they document the activities of their colleagues and friends. Some have phone numbers of people in each city from whom they may secure drugs, or of women with whom they may keep intimate company before departing for their next port of call.

Cliff Burton, though, was, in this regard as in so many others, different. Whenever on tour, the bass player kept among his possessions a hammer. On one of Metallica's early European excursions, as band and crew were negotiating customs at Calais en route to the United Kingdom, a French customs officer plucked the item from Burton's luggage and regarded first it, and then the young American in front of him, with a quizzical look. Burton nonchalantly met the official's gaze.

'Hey, you never know when you might need it,' he drawled.

Le douanier gave the most Gallic of shrugs and carefully set the hammer back in Burton's bag, before methodically denuding each band member of their stash of freshly acquired European pornography.

When the quartet returned to France for the opening date of the Ride the Lightning European tour in November 1984, custody of Burton's favourite hardware item was entrusted to James Hetfield's guitar tech Andy Battye, one of a clutch of road-hardened young Englishmen newly appointed to Metallica's crew by Q Prime's Mensch and Burnstein. Sound engineer 'Big' Mick Hughes, a garrulous and likeable built-like-a-bomb-shelter

Brummie who had learned how to translate mush into live music by manning the sound desk for the English punk band GBH was another new addition to the team, while Sheffield-born Robert Allen, Def Leppard drummer Rick Allen's witheringly sarcastic older brother, came in to take over the duties of tour manager.

Four weeks into the tour, on December 14, the party arrived in Lieto, a Finnish city with a population numbering fewer than 17,000 people. The group were booked to play at the Ijoharo club, a venue which by day served as a school gymnasium. To no little consternation, the American visitors saw that they had been booked to play the room as the live act in what appeared to be an end-of-term school disco. At one end of the hall stood a DJ of a kind heard and seen at the budget end of the wedding reception market. The disc jockey would play records at a distorted volume, while speaking excitedly into his microphone in an accent of soft consonants and vowels that stretched like melted cheese. Ticket holders were left with spots in front of their eyes from the glare of disco lights blinking to the beat of the music. At the opposite end of the room was the stage on which Metallica would later perform, a space sufficient to accommodate the group and their equipment, but not necessarily at the same time.

Outside the venue sat the visitors' tour bus, one berth of which belonged to lighting director Tony Zed. Zed was not only older than the other members of the travelling party but also louder; influenced by a scene from Mel Brooks' comedy classic *Blazing Saddles* – a film watched repeatedly by band and crew as they were ferried from city to city – the roadie had adopted the practice of announcing his entrance to a room by whooping at the summit of his lungs. This he did in Lieto as he opened the door to Metallica's tour bus, only to discover that his actions had caused consternation with a Finnish schoolgirl seated in the vehicle's front lounge. If the presence of a female yet to reach the age of majority aboard a bus chartered by a band not known for its decorum was a sight to raise eyebrows, this was quickly eclipsed when the girl stood up and punched Zed hard in the face. In what can either be seen as a blow for sexual equality or else the actions of someone old enough to know better, Zed reacted by striking the schoolgirl – also in the face – causing the young student to exit the bus in tears.

Outside the doors of the tour bus, the girl wasted little time in telling her classmates that she had narrowly escaped the attentions of men who desired to cause her harm. By the time Metallica took to the stage, displeasure with the visiting party had escalated to such an extent that midway through their set the room exploded into a mass brawl, while at the side of the stage a bass speaker was set on fire.

'The whole fucking place was just this big scrap going on,' recalls Mick Hughes, 'and everybody was in the audience, all the band and crew. It was madness.'

Looking out upon this scene, Cliff Burton decided that he had had enough. Attracting the attention of Andy Battye, he said, simply, 'Andy, fetch the hammer!' The guitar technician ran to the tour bus, found the blunt instrument, and returned to place it in the bass player's hands. This done, Burton then strode through the mêlée of bodies, whirling his hammer in arcs of 360 degrees and telling those in his path that they had better back off. The sight was sufficiently startling to put an immediate end to the wall-to-wall donnybrook, as those who only seconds before had been throwing punches instead made way for Burton as if they were waves at the feet of Moses. Mick Hughes recalls the sight of the hammer-wielding bassist wading into the stramash as being 'fucking legendary'.

But while a winter's night in Finland was the site of a nadir equal to anything experienced on the Kill 'Em All for One tour, elsewhere Metallica's march into the sightlines of a wider public was beginning to take form. In the United States the initial Megaforce pressing of *Ride the Lightning* had made it presence known on the lower reaches of the *Billboard* album chart, selling in excess of 30,000 copies, no mean feat for a record released on a fledgling independent label. On the continent to the right, by the autumn of 1984 the album had been bought by more than 85,000 listeners, with a significant proportion of this constituency residing in the United Kingdom. Such was the impact of this impression that in December *Kerrang!* decided to honour the group with its first cover story. In doing this, the magazine not only gambled on the fact that sufficient numbers of its readers would accept an emerging group as being worthy of the title's front page, but also chose to mark this occasion not with a photograph of the entire band but rather a solo picture of Lars Ulrich spray-painted silver and holding in his hands a cake adorned with metal nuts and bolts.

This shot, along with the images which partnered the story, was taken by Ross Halfin, then, as now, one of the rock world's best known and most prolific photographers. A complicated man possessed of a temper that made Dave Mustaine look like Archbishop Desmond Tutu, Halfin had come of age in the pages of the rock fortnightly, most notably for his work with Iron Maiden. Despite the entreaties of Peter Mensch, however, as the days began to shorten in 1984 the photographer had yet to focus his camera in Metallica's direction. Increasingly exasperated with this state of affairs, Mensch finally demanded of Halfin that he 'stop being an asshole' and come shoot his new band.

'My original idea for the photo shoot was to reference the Rolling Stones' *Beggars Banquet* cover, as frankly I couldn't think of anything else to do with them,' remembers Halfin. 'Sadly, there was no stuffed venison or wild boar in sunny Oakland, so I had to make do with a Chinese takeaway. Actually, we had to order two as the first lot that arrived, the band ate . . . Then I looked at Lars and thought, "I know, let's spray him silver with a metal cake" . . . I still have no idea where the cake came from or the nuts and bolts we put in it. To this day, I think it's possibly one of the worst photos I have ever taken; but, look, it seemed like a really good idea in 1984. I cringe now thinking about it.'

Kerrang!'s decision to place Ulrich on its front cover was a bold plunge into the unknown. Although the magazine's sales figures averaged 40,000 copies per issue, this figure was a tally aggregated from sales of thirteen issues combined. Even now it is unknown whether the only issue of *Kerrang!* ever to feature a drummer alone on its front page sold well or otherwise. Despite this, Metallica would appear on the front page of the publication a further fifty-three times. For his part Geoff Barton recalls that Ulrich 'was instrumental in getting a lot of the journalists on board, with his sheer enthusiasm, persistence and his general nuisance-ness, shall we say. At that point he was the most recognisable member of the band; he was the face of Metallica. It was Lars who was really banging on about them all the time, and promoting their cause. It was his single-handed persistence that got them on the cover.'

At the same time as his face could be seen grinning in newsagents from Edinburgh to Exeter, in December 1984 Lars Ulrich and Metallica landed once more at Heathrow Airport for the occasion of their third London concert. The group's final live performance of 1984 took place at the Lyceum, at the time a Mecca-owned ballroom situated on Wellington Street in the heart of London's theatre district. A Grade II listed building built in 1834 to the specifications of architect Samuel Beazley, despite laying a justifiable claim to being one of Westminster's loveliest structures the Lyceum had in recent years staged concerts by bands as unruly as the Clash and Killing Joke. For Metallica to be appearing in a venue more than five times the capacity of the Marquee – this despite their music being played only on Radio 1's late-night *Friday Rock Show* – provided hard evidence that their bandwagon was beginning to take on the form of a steamroller.

Fittingly for a band who are often defined by their flaws, Metallica responded to this upturn in fortunes by delivering a set that remains one of their worst performances on British soil. Writing in *Kerrang!,* reviewer Howard Johnson confessed that 'a poor sound didn't help me make much punch-drunk sense of [the band's] assault', adding, 'There are those in the know that profess that this wasn't anywhere near Metallica at their hip-swingin' best.'

One of those not only 'in the know' but also in attendance at the Lyceum was Malcolm Dome, a man fast becoming the Forrest Gump on hand to witness the significant moments of Metallica's early years. Dome concurs that while the group's appearance in Theatreland did not amount to the 'best performance the band has ever played . . . in fact, it was far from it', nonetheless he is of the opinion that the concert was 'a seminal gig because it came at the time when everything was clicking into a higher gear. The music they played, the size of the audience, the business side of the band, it was all going up a notch.'

So much was this the case that an underwhelming performance on a Thursday night in central London offered no impediment to the band's first flush of success. As Big Ben chimed a dozen times and ushered in the winter solstice, at the Lyceum the members of Metallica were each presented with a silver disc of *Ride the Lightning* commemorating sales in excess of 60,000 in Europe. This they had achieved with no promotional video, no seven-inch single and without a single note of their music being played anywhere on any radio station during daylight hours.

†

In 1985 Metallica turned their attentions from the shores of Europe to the vast expanse of the United States. In the previous twelve months, the group had performed live on home soil on just three occasions, causing Ulrich to admit that 'we have rather overlooked America recently,' adding that 'our timing has been rather bad because heavy metal is taking off there in a big way.' With his usual attention to detail, the drummer also confessed that it was possible that Metallica 'may have lost a little ground to other bands'.

It is difficult to identify the 'other bands' to whom Ulrich is referring. At the start of 1985 Metallica's forward momentum had propelled them beyond the horizon of thrash metal's chasing pack. That this was so is no surprise, with the genre as a whole being not only nascent but also somewhat neutered. Slayer gnashed away merrily enough on *Show No Mercy*, the group's debut album released in 1984, but did so with milk teeth. Meanwhile, Anthrax had to their credit the debut album *Fistful of Metal*, a set comprised of a skipful of clichés and not a single song worthy of the name. Elsewhere Exodus had yet to disentangle themselves from a legal quagmire that would delay the release of the band's debut album, *Bonded by Blood*, by almost a year, while Dave Mustaine's Megadeth were at the time seconded at Indigo Ranch Studios in Malibu recording their first LP, *Killing Is My Business . . . And Business Is Good!*

In spite of their prolonged absence from North America, Metallica's status on domestic soil was beginning to elevate. Re-released on Elektra Records on November 19, 1984, *Ride the Lightning* (despite an almost total media blackout), loitered for weeks at the lower end of the *Billboard* Top 200 album chart, much to the delight of both band and producer. As the LP sat atop the turntables of an ever increasing audience, in Oregon K. J. Doughton was taking receipt of up to 300 letters addressed to the authors' fan club each week . A number of these correspondents were female fans who wrote that their attachment to Metallica sprang from a love of the song 'Fade to Black'. Other communiqués, however, said quite the reverse, and chastised the group for having 'sold out', at the time the gravest assertion in the musical underground's uncodified constitution. Other contributors, however, were rather more unhinged in the lengths to which they would go in order to display their commitment to Metallica's cause. One such individual was a Texan gentleman rejoicing in the sobriquet 'the Green Slime', who wrote requesting that he be employed as the band's official photographer. Enclosed with the letter were examples of his work, in the form of pictures of mutilated animals. Among these was a Polaroid of a rat that only seconds before had been the Green Slime's pet, until it was decapitated. The photograph showed it lying next to an axe and the image was accompanied by the words 'Goodbye Scooter'.

Metallica began their second tour of North America at the Concert Hall in Toronto on January 19, 1985. The excursion would occupy the band's time for the next two and a half months and would see their tour bus park at the stage door of no fewer than forty-five venues, ranging in size from the spacious Aragon Ballroom in Chicago – known locally as 'the Aragon Brawlroom', due to the often unruly nature of its patrons – to the rather more intimate Headliners pub in Madison, Wisconsin. Alongside Metallica, ticket holders were promised an evening's entertainment from Armored Saint, a Los Angeles quintet with a growing reputation as an impactful power-metal outfit who would open the gig, and the headliners were W.A.S.P. ('We are Sexual Perverts'), from the same city, a theatrical schlock rock turn with an act that comprised stage blood, fireworks, female nudity and songs so knowingly stupid as to have surely been written with a glint in the eye ('Fuck Like a Beast' being just one example). Led by bandleader Blackie Lawless – cruelly dubbed 'Bluey Clueless' by the wags at *Kerrang!* – W.A.S.P. were equipped with a muscular sound and a good ear for a chorus; for their part, Armored Saint were a group whose music was of a quality that spoke of both a commitment to musicianship and a love of the genre in which they operated. Despite this, and unbeknownst to either party at the time, Metallica were beginning to drag metal into heavier waters in which both bands would eventually drown.

Recalling the tour, Lawless remembers looking out into the audience on any given night and seeing division.

'[It was] like an invisible line [had been] drawn down the middle of the room,' he noted, 'and half was theirs and half was ours. It didn't matter what we were doing onstage. It looked like two opposing armies. Sometimes we just stopped what we were doing and watched.'

'It was', he remembers, 'a war.'

This image is striking, and is perhaps the first manifestation – and a physical one, at that – of Metallica as a polarising force operating within the parameters of a genre that in itself polarised opinions.

Compared to the travelling horror show that was their first North American tour, the caravan with W.A.S.P. and Armored Saint offered proof that the San Franciscan group's station had risen. The venues in which they appeared were larger than before, the crowds more vociferous; transport came in the form of a chromium steel tour bus rather than a pock-marked Winnebago; hangovers from the night before began under cover of hotel linen. Things were looking up.

As was the case with Raven, Metallica got on well with the other bands on their 1985 tour of the United States and Canada, especially with Armored Saint, who apparently did not hold a grudge about the fact that their new friends had once attempted to steal their singer.

'Right away we felt like [both groups] had a lot in common with each other,' remembers Joey Vera, Armored Saint's bass player, 'and that's probably what sparked the friendship to begin with. We had way more in common with them than, say, the guys in Ratt, for instance. We became quite close, especially on that tour. We would ride on each other's buses and have nights drinking and hanging out.'

Life on the road can equate to a prolonged, sometimes perpetual, adolescence, and in the case of Metallica this proved to be true. The band's tour bus was christened 'The Edna Express', 'Edna' being the name given to the kind of young woman willing to spend the night with drunken, long-haired strangers.

'Girls would come on the bus and just blow the whole bus,' Lars Ulrich recalls ungraciously. 'Like, "OK, here's two girls, everybody get in line." People would say, "Eww, she just blew that other guy . . ." "So? You don't have to put your tongue down her throat."'

'They enjoyed what they did,' says James Hetfield. 'And, heh-heh, they were good at it. Back then, we all shared stuff. "I did her. Dude, here! Have my chick." Lars would charm them, talk his way into their pants. Kirk had a baby face that was appealing to the girls. And Cliff – he had a big dick. Word got around about that, I guess.'

'We all had pretty good pulling power, but some of us got a little more desperate than others,' laughs Ulrich. 'There were certainly times where it was about quantity rather than quality.'

With their night's work done, the group would behave in a manner befitting their new nickname of 'Alcoholica'. Lars Ulrich would claim that he knew that Metallica were being viewed with a measure of success by the fact that promoters would comply with their booking's request for vodka by supplying bottles of premium Absolut rather than common-or-garden Smirnoff. With the band lit like fuses, the settings in which they found themselves were often ripe for misadventure.

Following a performance at the Rainbow Club in Denver on March 5, Hetfield found himself bending the elbow in the company of Joey Vera in the Armored Saint bassist's hotel room. Hung over the back of one of the room's chairs was Vera's leather jacket, which the visitor regarded with an appreciative eye. Asking if he might try on the garment, Hetfield was told by Vera to be his guest. Placing his arms inside the sleeves, the guitarist walked over to the window of the room as if to inspect himself in the reflection afforded by a dark sky. Vera nodded in agreement when told that his possession was a fine piece of apparel. His head ceased this motion, however, when he learned that his guest intended to throw the jacket out of this window, in order to see if it were capable of flight.

Vera's leather jacket caught the cold night wind and glided towards earth like a raven. Its owner watched in bewilderment; in a manner good-natured rather than confrontational he chided Hetfield for being 'an asshole'. The bassist did, however, insist that his friend accompany him down to the hotel's swimming pool, beside which this most beloved and essential component of the metal fan's wardrobe now lay. This done, the pair rode back to Vera's room, eight floors removed from the terra firma of the Mile High City. As the carriage ascended, Hetfield thought it a capital idea to hit the red emergency button and stall the lift on its pulleys, a course of action that heralded the loud attentions of a ringing alarm. Their minds focused by the insistence of this cacophony, the occupants stared at one another and wondered, 'Holy shit, what is going on?' Within minutes, they could hear the voices of hotel security workers shouting on the other side of the lift's closed entrance. The employees then proceeded to bang on the elevator's steel doors in an attempt to prise open a space through which the trapped guests might escape. To the sound of screeching steel, Hetfield and Vera were met by the sight of black shoes at eye level and realised they were trapped between floors. A member of the staff crouched down, looked the men in the face and asked, 'What the fuck are you guys doing?'

'So we're looking up at this guy from the hotel and thinking and saying, "Oh shit, man, sorry,"' remembers Joey Vera. The bassist was told to wait where he was, and that the workmen were going to descend to the floor below in order to better secure his release. Rather than viewing this news as being just one example of the kindness of strangers, instead the two men saw their chance to escape. As the employees made their way to the hotel's concrete stairwell, Hetfield and Vera eased themselves out of the bottom of the lift, dropped on to the carpet of the lower floor and ran in the opposite direction from the men headed down to set them free. While a more sensible man might have viewed this incident as amounting to enough foolishness for one night, Hetfield decided that his work in Denver was not yet done. Pulling a fire extinguisher from the one of the walls in the hallway, the guitarist began spraying water all over Vera, chasing him through the hotel's corridors and 'squirting this shit everywhere'. As he did this, some of the liquid found its way into the sensors of the building's sprinkler system, immediately activating not only the sprinklers but also the piercing sound of a fire alarm. Suddenly, the wacky high jinks at the hands of a travelling rock musician had become a matter of emergency protocol, not to mention a security risk. The author of songs about fighting to death and refusing to live by the rules laid down by mainstream society, Hetfield responded to this escalation of events by scurrying to his room in order to hide. Meanwhile Vera entered his own room, switched off the lights and lay, fully clothed, beneath the covers of his bed, feigning sleep.

'I'm just laid there pretending I'm oblivious to all this commotion going on,' remembers the bassist. 'In the meantime the fire department shows up and evacuates the entire hotel. So there are, like, 250 or 300 people in their pyjamas and underwear sprawled out in the parking lot and I'm still in my room looking out of my eighth-floor window going, "Holy shit! What the fuck just happened?" We got into a lot of trouble for that; I remember we had to pay some fines and James and I got a good talking to. I would say that Denver was the most memorably stupid night of the entire tour.'

Five days later, with W.A.S.P. having left the caravan in order to support Iron Maiden on the English band's World Slavery tour, the two bands arrived in Los Angeles for a sold-out performance at the 4,000-capacity Hollywood Palladium. Situated at the east end of the much eulogised Sunset Boulevard, the Palladium is a rather drab-looking, sun-bleached art deco structure that from the street at least gives the appearance of being more a forgotten picture house than a venue with a storied and glittering past. Inside, however, the room resonates with the memory of feet gliding atop a vast circular dance floor and of cocktails sipped by patrons seated at tables positioned on either of the venue's twin balconies. Opened in 1940 (and re-opened following an extensive renovation in 2008), the Hollywood Palladium has hosted events ranging from concerts by the Grateful Dead and hometown punks Bad Religion, to performances by Richard Pryor, to political events featuring John F. Kennedy and Doctor Martin Luther King Junior (the appearance of whom in 1965 led to the LAPD discovering 1,400 lb of explosives in a nearby apartment).

Alongside occasions such as these, the arrival of Metallica in their 'Edna Express' may have been viewed as amounting to very small beer indeed. But the performance that evening qualified as a triumph not only in the sense of being the best and most successful appearance in the city in which the group formed – admittedly, not a high bar to clear – but also in its significance with regard to the battle lines that were being drawn in the world of music played with distorted guitars by young men in need of a haircut. On the same street as the Palladium, two miles west the musical mindset of bands hustling on the Sunset Strip saw them smearing yet more gloss both over the music they were writing and on to the lips through which they mimed these songs on music television. As successful as this strategy may have been – at least in the shorter term – authentic it was not. After years of rejection by many of Hollywood's musical taste-makers, down at the Palladium Metallica were finally finding an audience in the market for music powerful enough to slap the bitter taste of hairspray from the back of their throats. A jubilant James Hetfield duly celebrated the occasion by back-flipping into a sea of outstretched hands at the climax of set closer 'Motorbreath'.

✝

As gratifying as all this must have been for Metallica, without question, their two most significant live appearances of the year took place in the warmer months of 1985. The first of these saw the band fly once more to England in order to honour a booking on the bill at the Monsters of Rock festival held at Donington Park, a motor racing circuit just outside Nottingham in the East Midlands. The brainchild of promoters Paul Loasby and Maurice Jones, the then annual, then day-long, event had been born in 1980 as an outdoor concert, the line-up for which had been designed to appeal solely to fans of hard rock and heavy metal. The first Monsters of Rock bill was headlined by Rainbow, atop a docket that also featured Scorpions and Saxon. Other groups that appeared at the muddiest festival site of the English summer in the early to mid-Eighties included AC/DC, Ozzy Osbourne, Van Halen, Mötley Crüe, Whitesnake and Twisted Sister.

With a line-up of headliners ZZ Top, English progressive rock quintet Marillion, Ratt, Bon Jovi, Metallica, and Brummie pub rock footnotes Magnum as the day's opening act, the roster for the 1985 Monsters of Rock festival remains the most muddled bill of the festival's first decade of existence. Despite the world-class quality of the headline act – a group which featured the talents of one Billy F. Gibbons, a player once described by no less an authority than Jimi Hendrix as being the finest guitarist of his generation – too often the 55,000 people gathered on the uneven ground within the inside corners of a concrete racetrack on Saturday August 17, 1985, were subjected to music that tended

Portraits of the artists as young men (*clockwise, from top left*): James Hetfield, Lars Ulrich, Cliff Burton, Kirk Hammett.

Early LA gig fliers: note the mention of the non-existent 'Metallica EP', the recordings for which surfaced on the *No Life 'Til Leather* cassette. *Below left*: Metal Blade CEO Brian Slagel's copy of the *No Life 'Til Leather* demo, with handwritten track titles and notes by Lars Ulrich. *Below right*: The back cover of the *Metal Massacre* album, Metallica's first vinyl outing. Spot the unfortunate spelling errors . . .

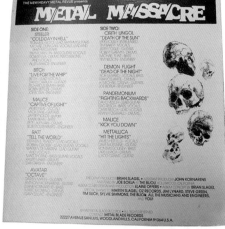

Above left: Dave Mustaine backstage at The Stone, San Francisco, March 5, 1983, the night of Cliff Burton's first gig with Metallica. *Above right*: James Hetfield photographed at 13004 Curtis and King Road, the home he shared with Ron McGovney in Norwalk, California. *Below*: The Young Metal Attack: Metallica backstage at The Stone, March 19, 1983.

Cliff Burton onstage at the Marquee club, London, March 27, 1984.

Alcoholica: Drunk and disorderly in Paris, August 29, 1984. *Below*: Award winners: receiving silver discs marking 60,000 sales of *Ride the Lightning*, backstage at the Lyceum, London, December 20, 1984.

Cliff Burton, sound checking in Stockholm, December 12, 1984. *Below*: The Little Prince: Lars Ulrich meets his public after an Iron Maiden show at the San Jose Civic, California, July 3, 1985.

An early photo shoot with new bassist Jason Newsted in 1986. *Below*: James Hetfield, onstage during the Master of Puppets tour, 1986.

Lars and Torben Ulrich in Copenhagen, Denmark, *c.*1991. *Below*: Ready for lift off: an early 'Black Album' photo session, 1991.

towards the ponderous and mediocre, lightweight in its tonality and occasionally plain inane. Among this number, Metallica stood out like a severed thumb. The group may have had just nine songs and less than an hour to make their point, but in front of the largest crowd they had yet faced the San Franciscans proved they were fast becoming masters of a first impression of a form both defiant and unyielding.

'If you came here to see spandex, eye make-up, and the words "Oh baby" in every fucking song, this ain't the fucking band,' announced Hetfield to those in attendance. 'Forget that Spandex shit, we came here to bang some heads for fifty-five minutes.' The front man then added that if the audience planned 'to throw shit up here, just make sure that you don't hit our beer – that's our fuel!'

More than a generation removed from the Monster of Rock festivals of the Eighties, it is difficult to re-create in words the kind of sight that met the eye at Donington Park. Suffice to say, it was no place for the faint of heart. Before the racetrack's gates had even opened to the public, the roads leading to the site would be strewn with the bodies of young men already drunk to the point of unconsciousness. Whereas festivals in the twenty-first century see literally hundreds of bands spread over several stages for three or more days, in 1985 rock fans gathered at Donington were provided with just one stage and a handful of acts; anyone not partial to the group occupying the stage at any given time had no choice but to listen to the music being played until something better came along. Ticket holders did not always accept this state of affairs gladly, and would bombard the stage with whatever objects happened to be at hand. During Metallica's first visit to the site, the component parts of an entire pig were hurled onstage; other objects that met the faces and fingers of more luckless groups included plastic bottles filled with warm urine in numbers sufficient to warrant the drawing of a black mesh curtain across the stage after each set in order that the stage could be swept clear of detritus. Needless to say, Metallica loved the place. But by the time Hetfield bid the English crowd farewell on the penultimate Saturday of August 1985, the group had found their spiritual home.

'I'm still trying to work out why I love this band so much,' wrote Xavier Russell in his *Kerrang!* review of the group's Donington set, before adding in his distinctive and uniquely irritating style, 'I have to put it down to one word: ENERGY. Even though [next act on the bill] Bon Jovi were surprisingly half-way decent, there was no way they could follow Metallica. [The San Franciscans possess] a natural ability to drain an audience, their music is so intense that one kan't [*sic*] help but be moved, shocked and stunned by the noise they churn out.'

Two weeks on from an appearance beneath the grey skies of an English motor racing track, Metallica would mark their second outdoor performance of the summer on the bill of the first night of the prestigious Day on the Green festival. Spanning two nights and headlined by the Scorpions, George Michael and Andrew Ridgeley's English pop duo Wham!, Day on the Green was the signature event of the German-born music promoter Bill Graham, the man responsible for staging that summer's United States Live Aid concert at RFK Stadium in Philadelphia. Resident of the Bay Area since the early Sixties, Graham staged his first Day on the Green in 1973, after which the event took place each August for the next nineteen years and attracted performances from such names as the Grateful Dead, the Rolling Stones, Fleetwood Mac and the Eagles, to name but four of many.

The site for the late summer festival was the Oakland–Alameda County Coliseum, a now ageing but not entirely charmless concrete bowl of a stadium that has as its principal tenants the Oakland Athletics baseball team and the Oakland Raiders American football franchise (in 1985, the Athletics were the facility's sole sporting tenants). On the final day of August, however, an audience in excess of 50,000 people gathered not to witness home runs but to see an event that would immediately be recognised as the Californian coming-of-age party for a group that were locked in on the title 'hometown heroes'.

Alongside headliners Scorpions, the bill for the first night of 1985's Day on the Green comprised Ratt, Oakland's own Y&T, Rising Force – a group led by the Swedish guitar virtuoso Yngwie J. Malmsteen – and German metal group, Victory; Metallica's slot was just two positions beneath that of the headliners.

Regarding the bill for that first night today, one is struck by the fact that, of all the bands who played, Metallica were the only group whose circumstances continued to improve from this point on. Theirs is also the only name that might cause a ripple of excitement among rock fans younger than twenty-five (or even thirty-five) years of age. The rest of the day was committed to groups who would soon come to be seen as yesterday's men. While Scorpions would continue to perform in arenas in the United States, it is fair to note that by 1985 the group had ceased to attract to their cause the allegiance of new and younger fans. Instead, this constituency surged towards Metallica. Despite the fact that *Ride the Lightning* was yet to secure a position in the US Top 100, its authors were nonetheless already casting covetous glances at Scorpions and Ratt's ivory towers.

More than a headline slot at the Hollywood Palladium, more than a place on the bill at Donington Park, even, Metallica's appearance on the stage of the Oakland–Alameda County Coliseum confirmed to scores of thousands of people gathered in one stadium that the ground on which they stood was shifting.

From the front row to the back of the stadium's third tier, Metallica's set was met with emphatic acclaim. The level of volume summoned by the crowd – a gathering that included Mike Dirnt, future bassist with Green Day, and Robb Flynn, who would go on to form Machine Head – exceeded that reserved for the bands that followed. As if to emphasise their allegiance, by the time Ratt began their set the Los Angeles quintet faced volleys of clumps of grass and mud torn by hand from the baseball field and hurled by the audience in their direction.

'I remember watching the band's set that day and being made really aware of just how popular this band might eventually become,' recalls Malcolm Dome, who was once again in the correct place at the appointed hour, in order to review the festival for *Kerrang!* 'The response they got from the crowd was phenomenal. It would have been phenomenal if they'd had an album that was in the Top 20, or if they'd had a single on the chart, or a video being played on MTV – but they had none of these things. All they had was a growing word of mouth, which meant that people in the stadium who hadn't seen them play before had a real sense of anticipation about what might be in store. It was obvious that this wasn't just "A. N. Other band".'

Backstage, following their nine-song set, Metallica basked in the glory of being afforded a reception befitting rock stars by acting like rock stars, or at least by acting in a manner they believed befitted a rock star. On a trestle table in the band's dressing room sat a platter of cold cuts as well as a tray of chilled fruits. Seizing this produce in his hands, James Hetfield attempted to force the food through the air vent in one of the walls of the dressing room. Realising that the laws of physics were not on his side and that this quantity of food could not pass through such a restricted space, Hetfield instead decided passage would be best secured by smashing a larger hole into the wall. His decision attracted the attentions of Bill Graham himself – not a man with whom any sensible person would choose to tangle – who took the singer aside for a frank de-briefing. 'The attitude you have – I've had the same conversation with Keith Moon and Sid Vicious,' said Graham. If Hetfield's first response was to offer up his patented goofy grin at being associated with such VIP-room rock-star company, his elation soon subsided upon recognising that the 'attitude' of which Graham spoke had led directly to each man ending up dead.

Elsewhere on site Cliff Burton was allowing Lars Ulrich to feel the sharp side of his tongue. Dome remembers hearing the Dane wondering aloud why he was the only member of his group not to have a girlfriend, and Burton replying, 'Lars, there might be a reason for that. Go and take a look in the mirror.' That same day, the English journalist recalls the bassist telling the drummer that if he heard 'one more word from you then I'm gonna fucking punch you'.

'Lars was a spoiled brat,' says Dome, with a shrug. 'In fact, he still is.'

This he may have been, but as the Scorpions climbed into limousines for the twenty-yard journey from their dressing room to the stage, Ulrich was, as ever, plotting the moves that would take his group from third on the bill to the position currently occupied by the German group.

✝

The day after the group's appearance at the Oakland–Alameda County Coliseum, the members of Metallica flew from San Francisco International Airport to Copenhagen. Or rather three of them did; Cliff Burton, for reasons known only to himself and never fully outlined to his colleagues, failed to report at check-in and missed his flight. Two days later, when the bassist finally appeared at Sweet Silence, the group began work on the album that would eventually succeed *Ride the Lightning*. Following the culmination of the tour with Armored Saint, the quartet had spent months at work inside the musty confines of the garage in the grounds of 3132 Carlson Boulevard exploring musical avenues, leaving no riff unpicked. As if completing a complex jigsaw puzzle, the group pieced together ideas, guitar parts, verses and choruses until material of a quality and duration sufficient for a studio album had been sewn in place.

'I would like to say that there was something magical in the air in the summer we wrote *Master of Puppets*, something that hasn't been there before and has never existed since,' recalls Ulrich. 'But that would be a lie. I guess we just had the right attitude and the right openness to ideas. The whole band was getting more confident.

'Most of the record was written in May and June of 1985, from the best ideas that were kicking around on our riff tapes from the previous year,' he continues. 'It really wasn't any different this time than before – it'd basically be me and James sitting down with a bunch of tapes and sorting through the details of his ideas and Kirk's ideas. But Cliff had [also] been in the band for a few years and he brought in a lot of harmonies and melodies. It took a little while for James and I to open up to some of Cliff's ideas about harmony and melody because we'd never played stuff like that before. But after a while we got it and that's when we started experimenting more.'

For his part Kirk Hammett recalls the songs on which Metallica were working coalescing into form in Metallica's practice garage and recalls, 'When [the group] started getting the songs together and rehearsing them, I can remember getting a huge lump in my throat, just from the emotion from playing these great tunes.'

Metallica then committed these songs to demo tape, a copy of which was sent from Oakland to Copenhagen to be heard by Flemming Rasmussen.

'Lars phoned me up and told me that they'd written the [next] album,' the producer recalls. 'Then when they sent me the demos it was pretty obvious that they wanted me to produce it.'

There was, however, one caveat. After spending four weeks in the frigid embrace of a Danish winter making *Ride the*

Lightning, for their next album Metallica desired a warmer location in which to record their next collection of songs. Los Angeles was nominated as the city of choice, a place far enough away from home that the group would not be distracted from their work but close enough to the Bay Area that the four men might fly home on any weekend they desired. To their laconic and unflappable producer, this sounded like an idea he could not only accommodate but also to which he could be sympathetic. Recalling the recording of the band's second album, Rasmussen is of the opinion that 'It must have been really boring for Kirk, who didn't play anything on the album apart from his lead guitar parts', adding that the idea of returning to Sweet Silence Studios for an even longer period was a prospect to which the guitarist would respond with the words 'I really don't want to go to Denmark again!'

In preparation for the making of the album that the world would soon enough know as *Master of Puppets*, Rasmussen flew to Los Angeles so that he and Lars Ulrich might spend a week scouting studios potentially suitable for the task. In this pursuit the pair had little luck. As with every single aspect of Metallica's operation, the group's drummer held in his mind an exact image of what it was he was looking for, in this case a sound room similar to that of Sweet Silence in which he could replicate the drum sound heard on *Ride the Lightning*. But beating a path from Redondo Beach to the San Fernando Valley, the two men could find no facility that matched these specifications. By default Sweet Silence Studios – quite apart from the declining temperatures of Copenhagen as the city headed towards winter – began to shift into focus as the place at which Metallica would convene.

'I think it's a pretty safe bet that Lars was instrumental in persuading the rest of the band that they had to record the new album in Sweet Silence,' says Rasmussen, not without humour.

This being so, at least Metallica could take solace in the fact that in the autumn of 1985 the group's improved commercial standing equated to a higher class of creature comforts. Rather than laying their bodies inside sleeping bags in someone else's apartment, instead the visitors were ensconced in the relative luxury of the Scandinavia Hotel in Copenhagen's lovely city centre. Here the band split into two camps, with Ulrich sharing a junior suite with Hetfield, while Hammett roomed with Burton. As with *Ride the Lightning*, recording sessions stretched through the night, beginning at seven in the evening and lasting until first light of the following morning. Before each shift would begin, though, Metallica would first eat dinner at the home Rasmussen shared with his wife, Pernille, who cooked for the musicians throughout the making of the album.

'They were really quiet and really nice,' remembers the producer, an impression that suggests this was a band quite adept at modulating its behaviour to accord to the circumstances in which it found itself. 'At the time I lived with my sister, so we had my sister there as well, and at times there'd be quite a crowd there for the evening meal. But [Metallica] all had really long hair, and I remember the first time Cliff came over, when we put the plate down in front of him he'd just put his head down to eat and his hair would just fall all around the plate. You couldn't see the food or his face; he just stuck his fork in and started eating.'

Rather than dine for months on end with such an image in her line of sight, instead Pernille decided to invest in scrunchies in order that her guests could tie back their hair while eating at the dinner table. This, though, was not quite sufficient to fully domesticate the dining habits of a group who in 1985 could still lay justifiable claim to the title of America's most feral metal band. As is traditional in Scandinavian countries, the meals fed to Metallica each evening comprised more than one dish; and as is traditional in the United States, the guests would then pile the different items on to one plate before not so much eating the food as inhaling it. Ironically, however, the worst offender for this happened to be Danish, not American. So egregious were Ulrich's eating habits that on one occasion his evening meal was served to him in a blender.

At Sweet Silence Studios, the sessions for *Master of Puppets* began with the recording of covers of Diamond Head's 'The Prince' and 'Green Hell' by the Misfits (with these versions of both tracks remaining unreleased to this day). The decision to run through songs authored by other groups was taken in order that Metallica might re-acclimatise themselves to the rigours of studio recording without this relearning curve coming at the expense of their own material. The process also served to identify any teething problems with regard to equipment and quality of sound. One such issue concerned Lars Ulrich's snare drum, which, according to the producer, 'sounded like shit'. Rasmussen suggested to his countryman that they see if a better sound could be found among the drums belonging to the studio, or else that the pair could head out to look for a replacement in the music shops of Copenhagen. Ulrich, though, had a better idea. He placed a call to Q Prime and requested a loan of Def Leppard drummer Rick Allen's Tama 'Black Beauty' snare, widely regarded as the finest (and rarest) model of its kind on the market. At the time Allen was recovering from a car crash so serious that it had severed his left arm at the shoulder. According to Rasmussen, Ulrich reasoned that the English band's drummer was 'in the hospital so he's not going to need it!'

Metallica's managers duly shipped the snare drum from America to Sweet Silence Studios (it can be heard on each of the eight tracks on *Master of Puppets*). They need not have bothered, though, as Ulrich managed to locate not only the same model in a Copenhagen music shop, but also one which had attached to it a price tag which had not been altered since 1979. 'That was just typical of the kind of luck Lars has,' believes Rasmussen.

Of course, there is a school of thought that believes you make your own luck. As this relates to the business of making of music, no location offers fewer places to hide than a recording studio, where art is nothing without effort. Many are the musicians who dread the process of making albums, as distinct from the spontaneous joy of playing live before an audience. For their part, even from their earliest days, Metallica appeared to understand by instinct that not only were the two disciplines polar opposites, but that it was their recorded work that would go furthest towards securing their legacy, and which they had to work hard at.

'They had made such massive strides,' remembers Rasmussen. 'Technically, as musicians it was very obvious that they'd spent most of the time since we'd recorded *Ride the Lightning* on tour. It was very obvious that their technical abilities had really improved, especially Lars who was just miles better than he was before.'

Albums are not so much made as constructed, with effects and touches often almost imperceptible to the outside ear being recorded and layered subtly beneath louder instruments as a means of adding depth to the textural whole. On *Master of Puppets*, band and producer experimented with volume-control and echo. As well as this, sounds were recorded on to tape that was then played backwards, the results of which can be heard in the shimmering and ominous swell that forms the beginning of 'Damage, Inc.'. Elsewhere, the natural talents of Hetfield as a rhythm guitarist helped propel the band's third album into focus, albeit at a pace that often seemed incremental. None of the eight original compositions the band recorded at Sweet Silence in the darkening months of 1985 featured fewer than six rhythm guitar parts; and as with *Ride the Lightning* Hetfield played each track live rather than adhering to the more conventional practice of merely overdubbing one take atop itself as many times as was required to attain the desired tonal depth. Hetfield's approach amounted to a technique that Rasmussen remembers 'took forever', even if the talents of the man being recorded were justified in being described as 'phenomenal and unbelievable'. Interviewed twenty-seven years and three days after the recording of *Master of Puppets* began, today it seems as if its producer's abiding memory of the entire process is that of watching James Hetfield track one devilishly precise rhythm guitar part on top of another.

'I've never seen anything like that since,' he says. 'And neither do I expect to.'

'I'm always saying, "It's not tight enough,"' Hetfield laughs. 'People think I'm nuts. It's something that absolutely haunts me. After we recorded "Hit the Lights", which appeared on the *Metal Massacre* compilation [in 1982] . . . this guy heard the song and told me, "Oh, the rhythms aren't very tight, are they?" Man. That was it! That started my lifelong quest. That was the Holy Grail for me – being tight.'

Slowly Metallica's new work began to take form. Inside the studio walls the alpha male personalities of James Hetfield and Lars Ulrich battled for territory, their sometimes discordant creative visions coalescing to the point where no aspect of the music being made was left unexamined or unsubjected to alternative methods of interpretation. The pair were learning that in order that an instrument in a song be emphasised, by definition another instrument must be *de*-emphasised, thus beginning a battle between guitarist and drummer, the energy from which would fuel the group for years to come.

Realising that Metallica's engine was quite combustible enough, Cliff Burton and Kirk Hammett took up positions as first mates. As keen as their colleagues in the desire that their union's third album be completed to the highest possible specifications, the pair nonetheless accepted that almost all groups are hierarchical in nature and often for good reason. Not just room-mates at the Scandinavia Hotel, while Hetfield and Ulrich combined to lock horns Burton and Hammett also united to bend the elbow. After many a recording session, having been awake for up to twenty-four hours the pair would then play poker for another eight hours, or would head out in search of a seafood restaurant at which they would eat raw oysters, drink cold beer and shout heated words at bewildered Scandinavians. These times, recalls Hammett, 'are some of my best memories of [Burton]'.

This fun, though, would not last. Short of funds, low on humour and without an appetite for the plummeting temperatures of the changing seasons, Burton stayed in Copenhagen only long enough to record his own contribution to Metallica's emerging album, before absenting himself with leave and boarding a plane home to the Bay Area. Lars Ulrich recalls that the band's bass player 'was the biggest home boy of the four of us' and that 'after he did his bass parts he was, like, "Fuck this, I'm off home."'

For his part Burton was of the opinion that the recording of *Master of Puppets* 'took too long', observing that while 'the songs were real good' the band 'could have managed [its] time a lot better'.

In the years that have elapsed since the recording and release of *Master of Puppets*, a proportion of Metallica's audience have ascribed to the bassist not just the mantle of being the group's artistic conscience but also that of being its silent and authoritative leader. This assertion is one that has been made without recourse to anything that might qualify as even the most circumstantial of evidence. Burton's decision to down tools early might well have resulted from the belief that his continued presence in Copenhagen would have made little material difference to the shape and sound of *Master of Puppets* (as opposed to the musician placing a premium on his own material comforts and thus caring not a jot either way) and thus realising that his work at Sweet Silence was done. As understandable – as justifiable, even – as this position is, it is certainly not one that would be taken by someone who believed themselves, or was seen by others as being, a leader. Given the group dynamic of the time, it is inconceivable that either Hetfield or Ulrich would have abandoned their post in this fashion.

As events would have it, it was Ulrich himself who was the last member of Metallica left standing in the sound room of Sweet Silence Studios, but only by a matter of days. On December 23, 1985, Hetfield and Hammett flew home to San Francisco, while their drummer spent the holiday with family in Denmark. Following Christmas Day, however, the Dane was back in the studio, working with Rasmussen to position the final overdubs that would complete the recording process of *Master of Puppets*. On December 27, one week shy of three months after entering the facility, the hardcore pornography Metallica had sellotaped to the walls of Sweet Silence Studios was removed and the levels of the sound desk were reset to their original starting points ready for the next set of musicians to enter its doors.

For the group, the final days of 1985 saw them shift focus from the recording studio to the demands of a paying audience. With just three days to prepare themselves, Metallica were to headline a New Year's Eve bill that also included Exodus, Seattle power-metal quintet Metal Church and an opening slot for Megadeth (an invitation that can be viewed as being informed by kindness but which might have been seen by Dave Mustaine as a reminder of an enforced inferiority). It was to be the most prestigious headline booking of the group's career to date.

If Metallica sought a portent that 1986 might be their year, the sight of both the exterior and interior of the San Francisco Civic Auditorium would surely have sufficed. Built in 1915 and with a capacity of 7,000, 'the Civic' –a building that in 1992 was renamed the 'Bill Graham Civic Auditorium' following the promoter's death in a helicopter crash – stands proud as one of the Bay Area's loveliest structures. Constructed from snow-white stone and standing in sight of the equally magnificent City Hall, the venue features wide carpeted staircases and a balcony lined with crushed velvet. With a sense of architectural majesty akin to London's Alexandra Palace, the San Francisco Civic Auditorium is many miles removed from venues such as The Stone or Ruthie's Inn in every sense, save for the geographical.

As with the Day on the Green festival just four months previously, Metallica's appearance at the Civic quickly became the kind of event about which fans would ask one another, 'were you there?' Despite the band being under-rehearsed, the success of both the headline act and of the evening as a whole provided yet further evidence that a musical movement born in the Bay Area had transcended its roots.

Backstage the musicians celebrated their fortunes in their usual way, by getting drunk. As ever, this tactic worked better for some than it did for others. Steve 'Zetro' Souza, a man who within two years would become the singer in Exodus, remembers Dave Mustaine being 'very mean', so much so that the tour manager for his future band mates 'turned round and just slapped him in the face and made him cry'. Onstage his old band tore through 'The Four Horsemen', while offstage the song's co-author continued to display the kind of behaviour that had forced his ejection from the group in the first place. But while Mustaine found himself wrestling with a cause for regret that would occupy him for years to come, onstage his former band mates rewarded the 7,000 people who had gathered in their name with the first public airing of the song 'Master of Puppets'. For both band and audience, the song promised a glorious future.

7 – DAMAGE, INC.

James Hetfield and Lars Ulrich had not been planning a big night out. The pair were in Los Angeles during the first month of 1986 in order that they might argue over the smallest details regarding the sound levels of *Master of Puppets* with Michael Wagener, the German-born studio technician charged with mixing their band's third album. Their work at Amigo Studios on Compton Avenue in North Hollywood had been temporarily stalled, however, by an intervention by the US Customs Office, who had impounded the master tapes of the track 'Battery', the next song on which the trio were set to begin work, en route to California from Copenhagen. Unexpectedly, the two musicians found themselves on shore leave.

With Hollywood as their playground, Hetfield and Ulrich were spoiled for choice as to locations at which they might share a drink. But with *Master of Puppets* still a work in progress, the pair eschewed the temptations offered by iconic rock 'n' roll drinking sheds such as the Rainbow Bar & Grill and the Roxy, opting instead to place their orders at the Cat & Fiddle, a British-style pub favoured by expat Englishmen, located on a section of Sunset Boulevard on which the magic dust of 'the Strip' did not sparkle. By Metallica's standards at least, such a setting would provide the perfect backdrop for a quiet night out.

Or so it seemed. Unbeknownst to Hetfield and Ulrich, also gathered around one of the many wooden tables inside the Cat & Fiddle that evening were Black Sabbath bassist Geezer Butler, Judas Priest guitarists K. K. Downing and Glen Tipton and Rod Smallwood, the likeable yet blunt West Yorkshire-born manager of Iron Maiden. This quartet did not merely represent the high table of the British heavy metal industry, but also the English working class and its desire to get pissed. This the party duly did, with Hetfield and Ulrich playing the roles of kids in a liquor store.

The momentum of the evening was such that when the bar staff at the Cat & Fiddle called time on their customers at 2 a.m., the party decamped to Rod Smallwood's home just above the Rainbow. Had the hour not been so late, and had he been less drunk, Lars Ulrich might have been rather more reticent regarding his decision to place into the tape deck of Smallwood's stereo a cassette featuring rough mixes of a selection of the songs that would in just a few a weeks' time be unveiled to the public under the banner *Master of Puppets*. Ulrich, however, was very drunk indeed, and caution had been damned.

For a man with a home in the Hollywood Hills, Smallwood could hardly have appeared less typical of a Tinseltown music industry insider. With a Huddersfield accent as hard as granite and directness of manner typical of one from the north of England, had Smallwood disliked the music he was hearing for the first time, he would have had no qualms about saying so. Having thrown discretion to the wind by commandeering Smallwood's stereo in the first instance, Lars Ulrich decided that if he were going to be hung it may as well be for stealing a sheep as a lamb: he turned the stereo's volume fully to the right. As Iron Maiden's manager took in the sounds being played for him, Metallica's front man and drummer found themselves exchanging smiles as both noticed their host nodding his head in appreciation for the music.

'We could be kind of obnoxious, but in a silly, drunken, cynical kind of a way,' remembers Ulrich. 'We never thought we were particularly hot shit. But this was the first time that I felt this album might connect on a different level than before. When "Welcome Home (Sanitarium)" came on, Rod was, like, "Can you play that again? That's a really good song." And I started thinking, 'Hmm, maybe there's hope for us here . . .'

As a form of music, metal often takes as its subject matter notions of dominance and supremacy, of overpowering an enemy, or else of rebelliousness in the face of an oppressive force, whether this be 'The Man' – to whom Dee Snyder of Twisted Sister announced, 'We're not gonna take it' – or, as is the case with 'Welcome Home (Sanitarium)', the allegorical setting of an insane asylum. For their part, Iron Maiden had made their name with songs such as 'Run to the Hills', a romp through the Wild West of nineteenth-century United States cavalry and Cree Indians that offers numerous lyrical perspectives of the story being told and is thus more complex and nuanced than it is usually given credit for being. That said, throughout the familiar themes of heavy metal remain strong, with the frontiersmen arriving on the shores of an indigenous population and 'selling them whisky and taking their gold, enslaving the young and destroying the old'. In 1986 Maiden's most recent studio album was titled *Powerslave*, released two years previously; the eleven-month tour that supported the release was dubbed the 'World Slavery tour'. In Darwinian terms beloved of so many metal groups of the time, by inviting Hetfield and Ulrich and their cassette tape of their soon-to-be-finished new album, Smallwood had taken the enemy from the gates and invited it in for a cold beer. In the middle of the Eighties Iron Maiden were at their commercial zenith in the United States, a point to which they would not return until well into the following century. This decline might have found itself under way even without the attentions of a younger, emerging audience being held in sway by the arrival of a younger, more thuggish-looking, sharper-edged and musically more ambitious group, not least because in the late Eighties and Nineties Iron Maiden released a succession of albums that lacked the quality and energy of their earlier work. But with their third album Metallica would light a fuse that would burn a slow but determined path towards a charge of such force that it would change the sound and nature of metal's mainstream forever.

Master of Puppets was released in the United States through Elektra on February 26, 1986, and on Music For Nations in the United Kingdom on March 7. The eight-track album was preceded by no seven- or twelve-inch single and no video clip was filmed for use on MTV or the music programmes of terrestrial television. In Britain the fifty-four-minute forty-six-second album entered the Gallup album chart at no. 41. At the time heavy metal albums followed a strict sales trajectory: the first week of release saw the largest number of copies sold, followed by a decrease in subsequent weeks that was often precipitous. It seems odd to reflect that an LP that has come to be viewed as one of the greatest – occasionally as *the* greatest – of the genre actually failed to secure a position in the Top 40 albums not only on its first week of release but at any point over the next twenty-seven years.

But while the response to *Master of Puppets* was hardly remarkable in terms of its width, in depth the reaction to the album was noteworthy. Writing in *Sounds* magazine, journalist Neil Perry was of the opinion that the LP constituted nothing less than 'a landmark in the history of recorded music', a statement that seems startling even by comparison with the kind of hyperbole that was fast becoming associated with the Metallica name. Among the group's older constituents, opinions were not quite so effusive. Despite having beaten a drum for the group for more than three years, Xavier Russell found that this wasn't sufficient to prevent his opinions falling foul of the censors at *Kerrang!* Although he recognised *Master of Puppets* as being 'a great album', Russell's commissioned review of the release found its way only to the spike and not the shelves of the country's newsagents. This would not be the last time that the magazine would take editorial decisions based on political calculations.

'Maybe *Kerrang!* thought, "We need to keep on the side of the band . . .",' reflects Russell. 'I was generally positive about it, but I think I gave it four Ks [out of a possible five], and Dante [Bonutto, then the magazine's deputy editor] was, like, "We can't run this, this is just too silly."'

The review of *Master of Puppets* was instead recommissioned in the direction of Mick Wall, who gladly accepted the chance not just to review the most significant release of that year so far but also to ease himself into the position of Metallica's British cheerleader-in-residence, a post he would occupy for the next several years. His first act on the job was to write a full five-K review of the release, which proclaimed that, with *Master of Puppets,* 'Metallica have grown up' and now 'stand taller than ever before'.

'The band are still travelling the same hungry roads but where they used to stomp and maul the senses like a bully out of control, now they dance and fly adding an animal grace to their sheet metal aggression,' Wall wrote, adding that, 'Metallica should be very pleased with themselves: *Master of Puppets* is their finest LP to date, finer I think than any of their so-called contemporaries are likely to record this year.'

What Wall was alluding to with his use of the phrase 'so-called contemporaries' were the other groups that populated the now bustling thrash metal genre. Revisiting the articles published about Metallica at the time of *Master of Puppets,* it is striking just how much ink was wasted not only on attempting to define 'thrash' as a musical form, but also to locate Metallica's place within this form. In point of fact, Wall's opinion that the LP under review would prove to be a work superior to anything 'their so-called contemporaries are likely to record this year' would prove to be inaccurate. In the autumn of 1986 Slayer would release their new LP, *Reign in Blood* in the United States. Produced by Rick Rubin and released on the hip hop label Def Jam, the Los Angeles quartet's third album was a body of work of such overwhelming speed and power, not to mention (in studio terms) technical perfection, that in no time at all its ten songs were recognised as being timeless. What was less immediately apparent, however, was that with the twenty-eight minutes that comprised *Reign in Blood*, Slayer's dominance of the form had effectively killed thrash metal for every band other than themselves.

Not that Ulrich himself would have had any truck with this development. Like any artist worthy of the name, the drummer had been attempting to negotiate an exit from the pigeon-hole into which his group had been placed from the very second that they'd been placed there. With the clarity afforded by hindsight, Metallica's place within the thrash metal movement seems so obvious that one wonders why at the time it was viewed as being a topic worthy of any kind of discussion at all. As with the Clash and punk and, later, Nirvana and grunge, Metallica came *from* thrash metal but were never quite *of* the genre. The group were desiring of the form's intensity, but were of no mind to pay heed to its many creative restrictions.

'From a musician's point of view, I don't really like that term,' the drummer stated at the time. 'It implies lack of arrangement, lack of ability, lack of songwriting, lack of any form of intelligence. There's a lot more to our songs than just thrashing.'

Ulrich's efforts to place clear water between his group and the gnashing and foaming of the chasing pack, and to shake loose the thrash metal tag that had been tied to the toe of his band, were as fully understandable as they were entirely boring. To his acute frustration, distinctions that to the drummer were piercingly apparent were often overlooked by magazine journalists who saw it as their job to contextualise the kind of groups who sang songs about Satan – Slayer – and those who did not, but who possessed an adolescent fascination with death (Metallica, Anthrax and Megadeth). As ridiculous as it seems today, such divisions were at the time viewed by otherwise sensible people as being entirely crucial.

'One of the reasons we've progressed the way we have is [is that we] realised that from working with a lot of different moods and dynamics that there are other ways of being heavy [other] than just playing fast,' says Ulrich. 'People always want to lock you into a little square and say, "Okay, this is what you do." They don't need to know if we're thrash, speed, heavy, slow, green, black. All those categories – I hate 'em. That's why we have a band name, so that people will know who we are. If you want to pinpoint one thing about us, the best thing you could say is that there's always some kind of power there. As long as you have some kind of intensity, it's fuckin' Metallica.'

Such was the perfect alignment of Metallica's fortunes as heard on *Master of Puppets* that to this day the album is viewed by a number – perhaps even the majority – of the group's audience as being its authors' creative high-water mark. Even if one does not subscribe to this point of view, it is difficult to deny the praise that still rains on this album's broadest of shoulders. From the opening acoustic strum that precedes the forensic flurry of opening number 'Battery' – to this day, one of Metallica's finest compositions – to the broken-glass staccato thrust that signals the end of closing track 'Damage, Inc.', the overall effect of the band's third release is to take lightning thrown from the sky of a perfect storm and capture it within the twelve-inch sleeve of a vinyl album.

As was inevitable, much has been made of the musical progression evident throughout the release. Anchored by a riff that is not so much a signature as it is a leitmotif, the album's title track manages to find the space to stretch its limbs from the kind of chorus that begs to be sung by an arena full of faces to an unhurried and even hushed middle section that is progressive to the point of seeming classically trained. In this vein, more impressive still is the defiantly restrained 'Orion', an eight-minute instrumental piece comprising an opening act that throbs like the banks of a swollen river and a middle section of such restrained and melodic beauty that its template is one that seems to have been set by Pink Floyd more than it does Black Sabbath.

Metallica's forward strides were not merely musical, either. In 1986 metal was a genre whose lyrical quality was rarely considered, often for good reason. But listeners minded to pay attention to the words being sung would have noticed James Hetfield's continued emergence as a lyricist. On occasion the subject-driven nature of the *Master of Puppets* lyric sheet did carry with it a note of convenience, or even of contrivance. As beloved of its audience as the album's title track quickly became, nonetheless as a lyric the portrait of an individual's free will broken on the wheel of drug addiction is not wholly convincing, not least because at the time Metallica were a band familiar with the smell of cocaine. The line 'chop your breakfast on a mirror' is in fact directly inspired by their old friend Rich Burch's morning routine on the many occasions he woke up on the floor of 3132 Carlson Boulevard. Elsewhere, themes such as the pernicious influence of TV evangelists ('Leper Messiah') and the futility of war ('Disposable Heroes') may have been shop-worn metal favourites, but at least in Hetfield's hands such topics were examined with bite and an uncommon degree of articulation. The same could be said of the feelings of entrapment and control inherent in 'Welcome Home (Sanitarium)', a song inspired by Ken Kesey's 1962 novel *One Flew over the Cuckoo's Nest*, which revisited many of the themes explored on *Ride the Lightning*. On the occasions when Hetfield's developing sense of wordplay is afforded free rein, the results are magnificent. The most impressive example of this is the lyric that accompanies 'Battery', an examination of a tsunami-like force the exact nature of which remains undefined. Taking as its starting point the not entirely promising premise of the sight of a Bay

Area Metallica concert – the title comes from the Old Waldorf club being situated on Battery Street – the subject is given flight by words that are both powerful and poetic. 'Smashing through the boundaries, lunacy has found me, cannot stop the battery,' sings Hetfield, over music that sounds like life being spirited away amid rapids of foaming water. Inevitably, the song quickly becomes a matter of life and death, with its narrator unable to 'kill the family battery is found in me'.

Master of Puppets stands comparison not just with albums of a similar genre released during the same period of time, but with any collection of music released in the Eighties. Gauged by such exacting standards however, it would be incorrect to describe the work in a musical sense as being flawless. For example, an attentive ear will identify the grinding gears that separate the middle sections of both the title track and 'Orion' as belonging to a band whose technical vocabulary was not yet fully equal to their artistic vision. But such criticisms are as nothing compared to the achievements to which Metallica's third album can lay claim. The release displays a strident forward propulsion, in its creators' ability not merely to write songs but also to balance these songs together in a collection that, as with all great albums, appears to be more than the sum of its parts. Alongside this, the group's 1986 release also carries with it a willingness to fly in the face of mainstream commercial wisdom that is more strenuous and far bolder than heard on its predecessor.

'*Master of Puppets* is definitely a more uncommercial album than *Ride the Lightning*,' believes Flemming Rasmussen. 'Definitely. *Master of Puppets* is Metallica celebrating that they've got a major label deal and that they no longer give a shit. It was them saying, "We're just going to do the stuff we like and if the record company doesn't like it, then fuck them." I think that was the attitude. And it worked too. There's not one bad song on the album, not a single one. It is just fabulous from start to finish.

'They had that youthful attitude of "We're better than everybody else in the whole world" and they were just out to kick some ass.'

For his part, Lars Ulrich merely adopts his best what-can-I-tell-you? voice, and says that '*Master of Puppets* is a motherfucker of a record.'

†

In the month that followed its release, *Master of Puppets* gatecrashed the US *Billboard* Top 200 album chart at no. 29. In a barbed dig both at radio programmers who had thus far ignored the band and also at the right-wing pro-censorship lobby, the Parents Music Resource Center (PMRC), who were starting to demand that albums be labelled for 'explicit material', second pressings of the now hit LP came bearing a sticker that read 'The only track you probably won't want to play is "Damage, Inc." due to multiple use of the infamous "F" word. Otherwise, there aren't any "shits", "fucks", "pisses", "c**ts", "motherfuckers" or "cocksuckers" anywhere on this record.' In subsequent years the ground broken by Metallica has allowed albums as uncommercially minded and even as extreme as Pantera's 1994 release *Far Beyond Driven* and Lamb of God's 2009 outing *Wrath* to appear not just in the US Top 30 but even in the top three, a state of affairs that attracts very little comment. But in 1986 Metallica's appearance on the lower rungs of the American Top 40 album chart represented the crossing of a Rubicon. Without doubt *Master of Puppets* was the heaviest album ever to have found itself in such a setting; the fact that it did so propelled by word of mouth rather than radio or television airplay served only to make the reality of Metallica's surroundings all the more remarkable.

'With the tour bus, the girls, the room service, the big halls,' wrote *Spin* magazine journalist Sue Cummings in a 1986 feature that can be remembered as being one of its subjects' first printed profiles in a mainstream magazine, 'it has just dawned on Metallica that they are making it in rock 'n' roll.'

The band's appearance in the *Billboard* Top 30 coincided with the Californians embarking on the most significant heavy metal tour of the American spring and summer. Beginning on March 27 at the Kansas Coliseum in Wichita, Kansas, Ozzy Osbourne's Ultimate Sin tour was the kind of caravan that travelled to the kind of cities to which other excursions of its size did not care to journey. Comprising no fewer than seventy-seven dates and with an itinerary that stretched into the dog days of August, as well as appearing at such established and prestigious rooms as the Long Beach Arena in Los Angeles, the Cow Palace in San Francisco and the Joe Louis Arena in Detroit, the tour also spent the night in such one-horse-or-fewer towns as Chattanooga, Binghampton and Bethlehem, to name just three: proof positive that when it came to heavy metal audiences were often to be found in towns of rust rather than cities of neon and chromium steel. Managed then as now by his wife Sharon Osbourne, Ozzy was the public face of an operation that had become shrewd when it came to ensuring that its figurehead continued to appear relevant amid the churn of modern rock music. One means by which this aim was realised was by associating the former Black Sabbath singer with younger, emerging groups. Two years previously, Sharon Osbourne had invited Mötley Crüe to join her husband as the support act on the tour in support of his *Bark at the Moon* album. Twenty-four months on it was Metallica whose name sprang from the lips of anyone in the know asked to nominate the genre's most vital new act. Hence the pairing of one of metal's original architects with the form's most strident young group seems not just logical but inevitable.

From the headliners' point of view, the mid-Eighties was not a golden age. Released in February 1986 *The Ultimate Sin* album saw its author's thin voice stretched over many a weak chorus presented within songs that had been overproduced to the point of being rendered sterile and impersonal. Propelled by the hit single 'Shot in the Dark', the parent album was not so much the work of an artist once so pioneering as to have provided heavy metal with its original voice but instead the sound of a man who was attempting to catch the flavour of the age with the minimum of risk. That said, Osbourne's less than grand design yielded a dividend: *The Ultimate Sin* found its way into the homes of a million listeners in the United States within two months of its release.

But if Ozzy Osbourne had reached the point in his artistic life where risk was to be averted – as these related to his music – the same could not be said for his decision to tour with Metallica. Each night for almost five months, the support act were permitted a generous fifty-five minutes' stage time, an allowance that exceeded the courtesy normally afforded a band whose name appears in the smallest print on a ticket stub. With the audience for the group occupying the 'special guest' slot multiplying like chromosomes in the womb, fans of the American band infiltrated each arena to such a degree that the tour quickly came to resemble a co-headline event. Illicit video footage shot by Metallica fans from various positions front of house – itself no mean feat when one considers that in 1986 hand-held camcorders resembled toilet cisterns with a camera lens stuck on the side – showcase a band whose efforts are greeted by the animalistic roar of an audience the energies of which seem both vibrant and raw. Such was the extent of this adoration that in numerous cities Metallica found themselves summoned back to the stage by an audience demanding not one but two encores.

'That's when it kicked in in terms of exposure,' remembers Lars Ulrich of his band's five months on tour with Ozzy Osbourne. 'It was the funnest [time] of my life. We only had [fifty-five] minutes a night – not like the two-plus hours we play as headliners today. That was the sex, drugs and rock 'n' roll tour – we were only twenty-two back then and drank a bottle of vodka a day. We've never hidden the fact that we like to indulge. We have this nickname "Alcoholica". But we can all control what we do.'

The same could not always be said for members of Metallica's audience. On April 21 at the Meadowlands in East Rutherford, New Jersey, the crowd in the two-tier arena found themselves sufficiently lost in the moment to cause $125,000 worth of damage to the venue's inner bowl, a level of destruction described by the room's president of operations, Bob Karney, as being 'entirely without precedent'. Worse yet, when Metallica arrived in Corpus Christi, Texas, on June 4, they were met by the camera lenses and questions of a local television news crew, on hand to revisit a grisly incident to which Metallica were unwittingly aligned. In 1984 eighteen-year-old Troy Albert Kunkle and three companions drove from San Antonio, Texas, to Corpus Christi. En route, the party offered a lift to Stephen Horton, a stranger the party encountered as he walked along the side of the road. Daylight soon fell on this apparent act of kindness when Kunkle demanded Horton's wallet; when he refused, Kunkle placed a gun to his victim's head and told him, 'We're going to take you back here and blow your brains out.' The car was driven behind an ice-skating rink, at which point Kunkle shot Horton in the back of the head. The dead man's wallet was stolen and his body pushed out of one of the car's doors. Subsequently arrested for this crime – a crime for which he would be executed by lethal injection some twenty-one years later – Kunkle quoted James Hetfield's nihilistic refrain from the song 'No Remorse', 'another day, another death, another sorrow, another breath'. For those naive enough to attempt to make narrative sense of just one of America's numerous random acts of senseless violence – as well as those seeking to demonise heavy metal – Metallica were judged guilty by association.

'We pulled into Corpus Christ, Texas, and woke up with a call from our manager who said, "There's some shit going on,"' remembers Lars Ulrich, with a not wholly reassuring handle on the facts of the story. '[We were told that] The local TV station is making a big deal because this kid apparently took some acid or other fucked-up drugs and went on a killing rampage, and the one thing that stuck in this witness's mind when he shot someone at point blank range was that he was quoting one of our lyrics – "No Remorse". He got sentenced to death and there was this big yahoo when he stood up in the courtroom and quoted the lyrics again.'

'On the news the next day they had the headlines that this guy got convicted while singing a Metallica song,' added Hetfield. 'They showed our *Kill 'Em All* album cover and they even interviewed me. It was weird. We do write about some sick stuff, but we're not trying to promote violence. It did give us some publicity, but the wrong kind.'

On tour with a man himself no stranger to being drawn into a dark drama over which he had no control – in Ozzy Osbourne's case, the 1985 suicide of John McCollum, an act allegedly informed by the lyrics to the song 'Suicide Solution' – Metallica found themselves unsure as to how to conduct themselves when in the presence of the tour's headline name. The quartet had been warned that the Englishman could be prone to bouts of unpredictable ill-temper, especially if the singer had been drinking and was out of sight of the watchful eye of his wife and manager. To this day Ozzy Osbourne divides his time between the roles of the world's most likeable man and its most overgrown and spoiled infant. He is the kind of person who has long since become accustomed to being asked questions, while at the same time has neglected to remember that conversation requires that questions be asked of the person to whom one is speaking. Possessed of a keen sense of humour, Osbourne is also a man known to be haunted by uncertainty; upon hearing Metallica playing the riffs to old Black Sabbath songs during sound checks, Osbourne's first instinct was to lunge toward the conclusion that the American group were viewing him as an object of mockery, rather than the correct inference that what he was hearing was a token of respect. Another potentially calamitous miscommunication occurred when Lars Ulrich presented the headliner with the impossibly banal question as to whether or not he washed his hair after performing in concert. With both men drunk, for reasons unknown the Englishman took sufficient offence to this line of enquiry that Metallica's continued presence on the Ultimate Sin tour was placed in jeopardy.

The San Franciscan band meanwhile devoured the food proffered by Ozzy's hand, all the while desiring to tear and taste the flesh that fed them. In 1986 the headliner was a man en route to becoming a brand that would be pinned beneath glass rather than an artist in the present tense, a transformation that was anathema to the younger band. In one revealing exchange Ulrich commented to a visiting journalist that she should be grateful to be backstage with Metallica rather than front of house watching Osbourne. The reason for this, the drummer explained with a roll of his eyes, was that the headliner 'has got his back to the audience [and is] humping the drum riser'. Suddenly alarmed by the unguarded nature of his words, Ulrich retracted this statement and replaced it with party-line boilerplate.

'We think Ozzy is great,' came the on-message message. 'He's been really good to us on this tour. We're honoured to play with him. He's one of the people who started this whole thing. Say that [in print].'

While on tour with Ozzy, each member of Metallica was allowed a per diem – the daily pocket money handed out by tour managers to the travelling musicians, yet another example of the state of perpetual adolescence in which musicians find themselves while on tour – of $30. Hammett spent this money on sushi when he could find it and on comic books. Hetfield meanwhile considered the idea of saving his stipend in order to finance the building of a half-pipe for skateboarding in the garden of 3132 Carlson Boulevard, a flight of fancy that would come to naught. Metallica, however, did ask their managers for the company line on the prospect of the band using skateboards on the summer afternoons of the Ultimate Sin tour, and received a reply from Q Prime that was some distance removed from the kind of passive-aggressive corporate double-speak typical of those that walk the American music industry's more powerful corridors.

'We told the management, "Hey, look, we're thinking about taking boards out on tour," recalls Hetfield. "I thought [Peter Mensch] was going to go, "Oh shit, no way, you can't." [Instead] he just said, "Well, you break something, you still play."'

'Yeah,' harmonises Hammett, adopting the voice of the man to whom the band devoted a percentage of its pay. 'You break a leg on your skateboard, you play onstage with a broken leg.'

On the Ultimate Sin tour no member of Metallica played onstage with a broken leg – though someone did with a broken arm. On July 26, in the hours that preceded Metallica's performance at the Mesker Theater, Hetfield was riding his Zorlac skateboard on the concrete terra firma of Evansville, Indiana, when his wheels slipped from beneath his feet. Extending his left arm to break his fall, the guitarist hit the ground with a force sufficient to fracture bone. That evening, with Hetfield being attended to by medical staff, his three band mates took the rather noble decision to inform the audience in person that their band would not be performing for them, and to offer their apologies. This news was not universally well received by the hardcore, to the extent that even during Ozzy Osbourne's set sections of the audience could be heard chanting the name 'Metallica'. For the remainder of the the Ultimate Sin tour the support act performed as a five-piece unit, with Hetfield singing onstage with his arm in a cast while his rhythm guitar parts were played by John Marshall. (The job had originally been offered to Anthrax's Scott Ian, a commission he reluctantly declined as his own band were due to commence pre-production on their third album with producer Eddie Kramer within weeks.) Mensch's warning that should a member of the group break a limb as a result of their skateboarding activities they would be compelled to perform onstage in this condition proved correct. For the benefit of the paying customers, James Hetfield wrote the phonetic insult 'Pha-Q' in black letters on his white plaster-cast.

Metallica would play a further six dates as support to Ozzy Osbourne. Following the final show – an appearance at the Coliseum in Hampton, Virginia, on August 3, James Hetfield's twenty-third birthday – the group were addressed in their dressing room by Cliff Burnstein. The band's co-manager had for his charges some good news, which he delivered in simple terms: Metallica had earned money in sufficient quantities that its members could now each afford to buy a house.

†

As the days began to cool in the summer of 1986, to outside eyes at least Metallica were beginning to take on the form of the year's unlikeliest success story. This was a role in which they excelled and revelled. As the group embarked upon their first headline tour of the United Kingdom in September that year, audience members in possession of a £6 programme were confronted with a headline splashed in bold yellow type across page three that read, baldly:

THEY'RE DIRTY, OBNOXIOUS, NOISY, UGLY
AND I HATE THEM . . .
BUT YOU CAN'T DENY THEIR SUCCESS

Beneath this quote – a sentiment attributed to journalist Dave
Roberts from the now defunct US magazine *Faces* – is a picture
of Metallica, each member dressed in a T-shirt and either jeans,
black canvas trousers or else sweat pants. As journalist Sue
Cummings had noted, with not quite perfect equanimity earlier
in the summer, this was a union in which 'no one [wears] platform
shoes, spandex pants, designer leather, hairspray or make-up.
Metallica are too proud to dress up; their uniform is the uniform
of their average fan, the teenage American slob: sneakers, ripped
jeans, T-shirts.'

It is difficult for fans of Metallica who do not adhere to a
stereotype not so much crudely drawn as finger-painted to view
Cummings's words with anything other than irritation. That
said, a glimpse at the group photograph that appeared on the
inner sleeve of *Master of Puppets* showcases four men who not
only fit the profile of the 'American slob' but do so with sufficient
relish that such an appearance is rendered not as a mark of shame
but rather a badge of honour. Photographed by Ross Halfin
in the living room of 3132 Carlson Boulevard on July 25, 1985,
Metallica are seated on a sofa beside a coffee table atop which are
strewn bottles of beer and that day's edition of the San Francisco
Examiner, the headline of which announces to its readers that
[film actor Rock] 'Hudson Has AIDS'. A copy of the Misfits'
twelve-inch single 'Die Die My Darling' and *Penthouse* publisher
Bob Guccione's latest skin trade magazine *New Look* also lie in
shot. The subjects of the image greet the watching eyes at the
other side of the lens with outstretched middle fingers and looks
of off-duty disdain.

Here Metallica resemble a gang at least as much as a band.
More than this, they resemble a gang that has just been in
a fight, and who hope that it will not be too long until they
find themselves in another fight. Not only was such an image
unusual when compared to the gloss lips and tinted highlights

of the 'hard rock' community of 1986, it was also some distance removed from even the kind of bands who at the time proudly represented heavy metal in all its blokeish glory. Few bands were as unreconstructed in their devotion to the 'full-English-breakfast' school of mainstream yet still (relatively) heavy metal as Iron Maiden, a band on whom a long-haired devotee could not only depend but even set his watch by. But a glimpse at the English quintet as pictured on the inner sleeve of their 1986 album *Somewhere in Time* offers a vision of a heavy metal band as imagined by the curators of London Fashion Week. Despite being no more attractive than a mouthful of cockles, the five pale men nonetheless stand stock-still in poses of studied neutrality, their hair cleansed to a shine, their sleeveless T-shirts and blue jeans crisp and box fresh. Even for those who believed that the advent of thrash metal meant that heavy music was going to the dogs, by comparison Iron Maiden had gone to a stylist. Set against Halfin's El Cerrito portrait, the result was the difference between five men who looked like brand-new waxworks on display at Madame Tussauds and a quartet that gave the appearance of rats in T-shirts living out their days in the squalor of an apocalyptic nightmare.

Such visual and sonic defiance was not to everyone's taste. Although readers of *Kerrang!* who took the trouble to nominate their choices in the magazine's end-of-year poll for 1986 were sufficiently swayed by the San Franciscans' charm to elect them to the position of the year's third-best group (behind Iron Maiden and Bon Jovi), a minority were sufficiently unimpressed to secure for the group the tenth rung in the category of Worst Band. More tellingly, thrash metal – the genre to which Metallica were at the time still inextricably linked – was decreed by the readership as being the year's second most boring subject.

But for the thousands of exclusively young people who bought tickets for Metallica's ten-date tour of the United

Kingdom and the Republic of Ireland, the emergence of a new breed of American metal played by bands who looked exactly the same as their audience was a cause for jubilation. Dispensing with Oscar Wilde's maxim that no good deed goes unpunished, the headliners returned the kindness shown by Anthrax in the borough of Queens three and a half years earlier by gifting the New York quintet the tour's support slot.

By the habits of today's emerging American rock bands, Metallica's 1986 tour of the United Kingdom is notable for two reasons. The first is that in the twenty-first century it is inconceivable that a group of an appeal sufficient to earn them a silver disc – as had been presented to Metallica almost two years earlier at the Lyceum – would wait until the advent of their third album before undertaking a full British tour. That said, when Metallica did finally decide to visit the parts of the British Isles often referred to by the London-based music industry as 'the regions', they did so with the kind of attention rarely seen from the overseas visitors of today. As well as performing to audiences in larger cities such as London, Birmingham and Manchester, the Damage Inc. tour also pulled up at the loading bays of venues situated in the rather more out of the way towns of Bradford and Newcastle. The group also performed in Belfast at a time when many American groups declined to visit this then conflicted city. But regardless of whether Metallica were working up a sweat in the megacity that is London or else in an historic and these days overlooked West Yorkshire mill town, night after night the words 'Sold Out' could be read on the frontage of venues and in letters placed upon the slates of front-of-house marquees.

For metal fans of advancing years, the tour was without question the event of season, if not the year. Within weeks of the Damage, Inc. tour having left British shores, Iron Maiden and Saxon would also tour the island; to younger adolescent eyes, both bands would suddenly appear part of an older and stuffier order. And while Metallica's position as the ringleaders of metal's new cutting edge was accepted by all, the presence of Anthrax on the Damage, Inc. tour's undercard lent the excursion an even greater sense of occasion. Such was the momentum now gathering behind the thrash metal movement that within seven months of Metallica's first UK tour, Anthrax, Megadeth and Slayer would each headline London' s 3,300-capacity Hammersmith Odeon.

Writing of the pairing of San Franciscan headliners and New York support act, in a review of the tour's appearance at Dublin's SFX Hall on September 14, *Kerrang!*'s Paul O'Mahoney observed that 'this one had all the makings of a First Division football league top of the table clash', a contest between 'two of the meanest, most hellraisin' rock 'n' roll bands on planet Earth'. Having filed his entry for the most cliché-sodden opening paragraph in the history of music journalism, O'Mahoney then reviewed against type by asserting that while Anthrax 'looked and sounded like a truly *great* band should', for their part Metallica 'didn't quite click into gear as their mighty reputation suggested'.

'The set was largely inconsistently balanced,' the reviewer went on to say, 'seeming to lag at times – oh, and the mere sight of an acoustic guitar onstage must have made many a Metallurgist throw up!' With regard to the evening as a whole, O'Mahoney concluded that 'My friends will be hearing about this because . . . Anthrax blew the Goddamn [Metallica] muthas away!'

If this was the case in Dublin, it was not a scene repeated on the final date of the United Kingdom and Ireland leg of the Damage, Inc. tour. On Sunday September 21 Metallica's tour bus pulled up at the stage door of the Hammersmith Odeon. Opened in 1932 as the Gaumont Palace Cinema, by the middle of the Eighties the balconied room had become an iconic venue for live metal due to its patronage by groups such as Iron Maiden and Saxon, the latter act having recorded their 1981 live album *The Eagle Has Landed* at the theatre. The Odeon's status as a folkloric setting was further enhanced by another live album, Motörhead's *No Sleep 'Til Hammersmith*, which despite not having been recorded in west London – the title actually referred to the final date of the band's Ace Up Your Sleeve tour of 1980 – became a landmark for its authors and ensured the same status for the venue to which its title referred.

The desire of young American metal bands to perform at the Hammersmith was so strong as to override the simple fact that the venue was entirely unsuited to music of the type. In 2003 the Odeon was renamed the Apollo – an occasion marked by an appearance from AC/DC – and the room renovated to the extent that its dance floor became an unreserved space free of seats. In 1986, however, the Hammersmith Odeon remained more or less unchanged from its days as a cinema, with rows of cramped raspberry velvet seats lining not just the balcony but also the space stretching from the back of the stalls to the lip of the stage. For fans wishing to express their passion for the sounds made by visiting thrash acts by partaking in the new pastime of 'moshing' – a phrase coined by Agnostic Front guitarist Vinnie Stigma and popularised by Scott Ian – a seat at the Hammersmith Odeon was no more suitable a location than the inside of a phone box.

Despite this, the sense of anticipation inside the venue in the minutes before an intro tape of the theme music from *The Blues Brothers* announced the arrival onstage of Anthrax was both amphetamined and intense. As a voice from the darkness asked the entirely full room to welcome 'the heaviest band in the world' – some claim given that the support act were not even the heaviest band on the bill – more than 3,000 pairs of adolescent eyes were greeted by the sight of a group that at the time were thrash metal's equivalent of *The Muppet Show*. Dressed in skateboard shorts and T-shirts, in 1986 Anthrax could lay a respectable claim to being American metal's most energetic live band. Although providers of heat rather than light, over the span of a forty-five-minute special guest slot the impression made by the East Coast quintet was sufficiently startling (and, for that matter, original) to find support in a room packed with people very much in the market for new kinds of thrills.

But to claim that Anthrax's hit and run transmission was sufficient to steal Metallica's evening is nonsense. Even with James Hetfield's onstage presence impaired by an arm that would remain in its cast for another six days – and with the answer to questions about how best to occupy himself during the lengthy instrumental sections of his band's songs never fully answered – the sight and sound of a band who were fast becoming the soundtrack to the lives of tens and even hundreds of thousands of people framed in such an iconic context was of proportions sufficient that many in attendance would remember moments of the sixteen-song set for decades to come.

'Onstage at Hammersmith Metallica looked like a big band,' remembers *Kerrang!*'s Malcolm Dome, his presence that night as inevitable as the following morning's dawn. 'They dwarfed the stage and they looked like they belonged. This wasn't some small young band who were trying to look tough while wondering, "Oh God, what are we doing here?" This was a band who grabbed the opportunity and said, "We belong here. It's taken us two years to get here. We should have been here earlier [in our career] but now we are here we've sold the place out. Not only that, but we sold out every other date on the UK tour as well."'

After Metallica had bid its audience goodnight with the peacenik-sentiment of the battle-hymn that is 'Fight Fire with Fire', hundreds upon hundreds of people surged to the wooden counter of the merchandise stand positioned by the exit doors of the Odeon's ground-floor foyer. There, in a flurry of activity that itself resembled a concert groaning on the precipice of becoming out of control, fans battled to purchase items such as the Pushead-designed Damage, Inc. T-shirt for £8. Others bought themselves a tour programme, the pages of which were perused as tube trains ferried concert-goers to other parts of London or to connections to outlying satellite towns. As the reader regarded the programme's back cover, their eyes would have been met by a strange image positioned at the bottom right corner of the page. It was a picture of Metallica, an image that all members of the group had liked aside from Cliff Burton, who disdained the shot for it having captured him striking a facially comic pose. In order that the picture not be seen by wider eyes, the bass player had torn the original print and blinded his eyes with a sharp instrument. In spite of this – or, perhaps, because of this – as the man who had supervised the design of his band's tour programme, Lars Ulrich decided to include the image anyway. The photograph's two pieces were reunited with Sellotape, and the bass player's disfigured face was hidden behind a black strip.

As one scans the back page of the twelve-page booklet, the image upon which the reader's eye finally falls is a picture of Metallica that shows Burton with his eyes redacted like the victim of a tragedy, like a corpse.

†

On Friday September 26, 1986, Metallica played their final show with Cliff Burton. On the afternoon of the group's appearance at a busy but not entirely full Solnahallen hall in Stockholm, the visiting musicians were introduced by their Swedish distributor, Alpha Records, to local music journalists that had abetted the group's cause. As was the case elsewhere in the world, Alpha employee Stuart Ward recalls that 'the mass media didn't put [in] much of an appearance. We had a big-selling album, but no one would touch Metallica. Most people thought the band's music was repulsive. You would see column inch after column inch written about artists who only had a fraction of Metallica's sales. It was hugely frustrating. I only remember someone being there from

[the] youth magazine *Okej*, which sometimes contained a lot of hard rock, and there were a few guys who wrote for fanzines.'

Following this formal pressing of the flesh, band and journalists were led into a room stocked with a healthy supply of food and alcohol and a round table around which the Americans and Europeans might sit. Not untypically, Lars Ulrich was noticeable by his absence, preferring to secrete himself away in yet another room, alone save for the voices at the far end of a telephone line. Unperturbed by this, Ulrich's band mates broke bread and raised glasses in the company of representatives of the lower orders of the Scandinavian music press.

It was in this company that Burton gave what was to be his final interview, an exchange with the Swedish music journalist Jörgen Holmstedt. The writer is honest enough to remember that his silent reaction upon discovering that he was seated alongside Burton was one of an 'annoyance' informed by the fact that 'in all honesty I was more interested in meeting Lars Ulrich'.

'Frankly, no one was very interested in talking to the normally taciturn Cliff when the other band members were around. In fact, I can't recall seeing more than a handful of major interviews with Cliff up to that point,' Holmstedt recalls.

It is an interesting quirk of the music journalist's mind that he or she usually desires to speak to the member of a group that enjoys the highest profile in the press, this despite the fact that such a strategy runs the risk that the quotes supplied by this subject will echo the words given to rival publications. True to this trait, Jorgen Holmstedt viewed Cliff Burton not as a untapped source of information, or of one potentially possessed of a fresh insight, but rather as the 'Quiet One' to whom journalists rarely spoke.

'He just sat there, sipping a beer,' recalls the writer. 'Close up he looked older than his twenty-four years. He had discoloured teeth, a slightly worn and wrinkled face, a tired gaze and the slow, deliberate speech pattern typical of someone who likes a smoke.

Cliff was as quiet offstage as he was wild on it. He was wearing a T-shirt with an unbuttoned shirt on top, a battered denim jacket and his legendary old flared jeans which he was alone in wearing during that poodle-head year of 1986, when ball-crushingly tight stretch jeans were de rigueur.'

Reading the transcribed exchange between Burton and Holmstedt, one is once again struck by the subject's inscrutable nature, as a canvas of sufficient size and tonal neutrality that listeners and fans are able to register upon it any impressions they choose. To an uncharitable eye, as interviewed on the afternoon of September 26, 1986, Burton appears disinterested and dull, his answers vague to the point of opacity. On his group's burgeoning level of success, the musician observes that Metallica 'haven't become stars overnight' and that 'the whole time we've just done what felt right' having 'never striven for rock-star status or anything like that'. Metallica, he explained, 'just do what [they] do' with a sense of insular purpose of sufficient authority that even a contract with a major label is seen as 'merely an opportunity to buy more equipment and to be able to spend more time in the studio' – this despite the fact that on *Master of Puppets* the bassist was of the opinion that his band had spent too *much* time in the recording studio, 'You know, to build the whole thing further.' Elsewhere in the interview Burton spoke of a group that 'can't be bothered to worry about the mass media' either in terms of 'what they say or what they write' and that instead improves its station by touring as extensively as possible because 'that's how a band like ours gets bigger. Because we don't get any radio play, we have to play [live] as much as possible.'

'Touring has become more pleasant now that we have a better [tour] bus,' the bassist observed.

In the smallest hours of Saturday 27 September, the component parts of the Damage, Inc. tour began the journey from Stockholm to Copenhagen. First to depart the loading doors of

Solnahallen was Metallica's tour bus, a vehicle inside which the four musicians and their road crew would watch a video before retiring to sleep in coffin-sized bunk beds. Forty-five minutes after this, a lorry containing Metallica's instruments and amplifiers left the Swedish capital en route to its Danish equivalent. Inside the first vehicle Kirk Hammett and Cliff Burton drew cards in order to determine which member of the band would that night sleep in the bunk fitted with a window.

'The first card that Cliff picked was the ace of spades and he looked at me and said, "I want your bunk,"' Hammett recalls. 'And I said, "Fine, take my bunk, I'll sleep up front, that's probably better anyway."'

Several hours later, at 6.30 on the morning of September 27, the vehicle was travelling along the E4, a road that passes between the Swedish towns of Ljungby and Värnamo. Two miles north of Ljungby, the tour bus began to drift to the right side of the road, an occurrence to which its driver responded by turning the vehicle's steering wheel in the opposite direction. This action caused the bus's back wheels to skid further to the right. At this point, the young men asleep in the vehicle's interior were woken by the sound of tyres screeching on cold concrete.

Metallica's tour bus was engaged in a skid that lasted for as long as twenty seconds, the inertia of which propelled the vehicle from an upright position to one where the bus was lying on its right-hand side in a ditch by the side of the road. In the pitch blackness of its interior, bunks containing startled and semi-naked men collapsed on top of each other. In the stunned confusion that followed, a number of the party were able to navigate their exit into the morning air through the bus's side door (the vehicle was provided by Len Wright Travel and was British made, which meant this door was on the left-hand side). Tour manager Bobby Schneider remained inside the bus until it appeared that its occupants had been led to safety.

'I got thrown out of my bunk and knocked unconscious for like three or four seconds,' recalls Hammett. 'When I came to, I heard everyone screaming, but I didn't hear Cliff. And I instantly knew something was wrong.'

Gathered by the roadside, the shocked party attempted to make sense of their situation. Hetfield and Hammett were shaken but had incurred only minor flesh wounds; Ulrich had suffered a broken toe. Quickly the three men's attention was captured by the sound of shouting from other people, their eyes trained and fingers pointing towards the tour bus's bottom edge. Like an horrific re-imagining of a scene from *The Wizard Of Oz*, protruding from beneath the stricken vehicle could be seen a pair of legs belonging to Cliff Burton.

'I saw the bus lying right on him,' recalls James Hetfield. 'I saw his legs sticking out. I freaked. The bus driver, I recall, was trying to yank [a] blanket out from under him to use for other people. I just went, "Don't fucking do that!" I already wanted to kill the guy. I don't know if he was drunk or if he hit some ice. All I knew was, he was driving and Cliff wasn't alive any more.'

In the minutes that followed, Hetfield learned from the driver that the bus had crashed as a result of losing traction due to ice on the road. As the party waited for the first of seven ambulances that would ferry the injured to hospital, Metallica's front man scoured the road for evidence of this claim, but found none.

'I recall, in my underwear and socks, walking for miles looking for this black ice, walking back going, "Where's this black ice? I don't see any black ice . . ."' says Hetfield. 'And I wanted to kill this guy. I was going to end him there.'

As a matter of routine, the bus driver was arrested as soon as Swedish police arrived at the site of the crash, while Burton's body was removed from the scene in order that it be examined for forensic evidence. His passport – numbered E 159240 – was cancelled and posted to his parents in Northern California.

Discharged from hospital, Metallica's three surviving members spent the night of September 27 at the Hotel Terraza in Ljungby. As news of the accident spread, a crowd began to gather at the hotel's front entrance. At the hospital a traumatised Hetfield had been sedated with medication that did little to anaesthetise his pain. Back in his hotel room raw grief gave way to blind rage as the front man began smashing whatever object came to hand. Later that night he found himself on the streets of Ljungby; as he walked without direction, guests in the Hotel Terraza could hear the American screaming 'Cliff? Where are you, Cliff?'

With typical efficiency, Peter Mensch immediately flew from New York to Denmark in an attempt to manage the situation. Hetfield and Hammett were dispatched home to the Bay Area while Ulrich remained in his country of birth in order to be with his family. While there Ulrich gave his first interview following the death of his friend and colleague. Speaking to Fia Persson from Sweden's *Expressen* newspaper, the drummer spoke of being woken in his bunk as the tour bus skidded and being 'thrown around in the [vehicle]'.

'It was completely dark and it seemed like it would never stop rolling,' he recalled. 'But it did stop eventually, and as soon as it did I scrambled out and started to run clear. I was afraid the bus would explode.

'After a while I heard cries of help from inside,' he continued. 'It was Flemming, our Danish drum roadie. I thought about climbing in and helping him, but it was only then I realised that I'd hurt myself so badly I could hardly walk.'

On the elephant in the room that was the pivotal question as to whether or not Metallica would live on after the death of their bass player, Ulrich was respectful but unequivocal, saying, 'I don't know anyone who can play bass like he did,' and adding, 'It's going to feel really strange the first time we stand onstage with a new bassist in the band.'

On the Monday morning following Burton's death, the regional Swedish newspaper *Smallanniggen* ran on its front page the headline 'Rock Star Killed'. The story beneath told its reader that 'the European tour of the American hard rock group Metallica ended in tragedy in a fatal accident in Dorarp on the E4 Road on Saturday morning'. The report went on to say that the driver of the bus 'thought that an ice spot was the reason why the [vehicle] slid off the road. But there were no ice spots on the road.'

'For that reason the investigation continues,' said Detective Inspector Arne Pettersson, as quoted in the same article. 'The accident's course of events, and the tracks at the accident location, are exactly like the pattern of asleep-at-the-wheel accidents.'

The piece then went on, 'The driver [swore] under oath that he had slept during the day and was thoroughly rested.' The following day the same publication told its readers that

> The driver of the tour bus . . . is now free from arrest. He is forbidden to travel and must contact the police once a week until the investigation is over. The driver was arrested after the accident, suspected of being careless in traffic and causing another person's death. He said that the bus drove off the way because there was ice on the road. But the technical investigation from the police said that the road was totally free from ice at the time of the accident. The driver is suspected of having fallen asleep at the steering wheel.

Nine days later the travel ban against the driver of the bus was lifted and no charges were ever brought against the man who will for ever be suspected of bringing to a premature close the life of one of his passengers. In his autopsy report Dr Anders Ottoson concluded that the cause of death of Cliff Burton was '*compressio thoracis cum contusio pulm.*' – or in layman's terms, a fatal compression of the chest cavity with correlating damage to the lungs. In even shorter terms, the bass player was crushed to death.

Were such a scenario to occur today, the events would be played out to the wider world only seconds behind real time. A tweet from one of the party would shine the first light into the morning gloom on the back roads of northern Europe. Calls from the scene would be placed to management, who in turn would field queries from the press and release online a prepared statement containing details of what had occurred. News of the event would echo over the rooftops of cyberspace from Aberdeen to Adelaide, propelled by the constant drumbeat that is social media.

But news of the death seeped out slowly, like blood into soil. To many who knew him, hearing about the bassist's death is an event that seems as if it happened only yesterday. But while this cliché carries with it a certain emotional resonance, the unfolding of the drama as it occurred at the time affords the story a quality that belongs squarely in a bygone age. First hours and then even a day passed by before even those professionally equipped to gather details managed to lay in place what journalists sometimes describe as 'the blood and guts' of the story.

Malcolm Dome recalls being in the *Kerrang!* office and of 'having heard a rumour that someone in Metallica had died in a tour-bus crash'. As startling as this unsourced and entirely unconfirmed Chinese whisper may have been, its very existence was typical of the kind of fanciful hot air that propelled music journalists through a working day in an age before the advent of the Internet. As Dome remembers, 'At the time there were always rumours going round, "Oh, such and such a person has just died," and stuff like that.'

Nonetheless then as now Dome's nose for a story was acute, and he placed a call to the Music For Nations office in Germany. From a voice on the other end of the line, he learned that Burton really was dead.

'I believe I was the first in the office to find out,' he recalls today. 'But in terms of the *Kerrang!* office as a whole, it was the most depressing day of our lives, because we'd all met Cliff and we all liked him very much. So we heard the news and then we all went to the pub, strangely enough with Scott Ian [whose band were attempting to navigate their way back to New York, via London]. But I remember it being such a strange day, because it was the first time we'd all been confronted with what it felt like to have someone that we all knew die.'

As news of Burton's death shifted from casual conjecture to concrete fact, those who had known him began to attempt to make sense of the ending of a life that seemed to have been robbed not only of so many years now destined to remain unlived but also of the rewards of success that the bass player had, along with his band mates, worked so hard to achieve. More than a generation on, the death of a musician in a rock band tends to excite the kind of theatrical emotion witnessed following the death of Diana Spencer, an odd state of affairs given that metal in particular spends so much of its time concerning itself with, and even glorying in, the subject of human mortality. With the death of Cliff Burton, however, matters were tastefully restrained. In the pages of *Kerrang!* a one-page memorial paid for by Music For Nations read, simply, 'Cliff Burton 1962–1986'. In the same issue, Johnny and Marsha Zazula had booked a double page spread, entirely black aside from the couple's names and the epitaph, 'The Ultimate Musician, The Ultimate Headbanger, The Ultimate Loss, A Friend Forever'.

Following the conclusion of the investigation by the Swedish authorities into the bus crash of September 27 – at least as it related to the remains of the one killed as a result of this event – Burton's body returned to the Bay Area, and was laid to rest on October 7, 1986, with a service at the Chapel of the Valley in his home region of Castro Valley. Having been informed by Cliff Burnstein on the morning of the crash that Burton was dead, Michael Alago subsequently travelled from his home in New York to California to attend the musician's funeral and cremation. He sat on a wooden pew and listened as the stirring, and by now piercingly poignant, 'Orion' was played through the chapel's stereo system. Burton's ashes were then scattered at the Maxwell Ranch, where along with his teenage friends the adolescent bass player had discovered his love of making music in concert with others. As the day drifted on, Alago found himself in the company of Hetfield, Ulrich and Hammett, musicians and Elektra executive united as nothing more than young men attempting to make sense of both grief and Metallica's suddenly obliterated circumstances.

'At one point [during the day], the band and myself made our way over to the Burton's home,' remembers Alago. 'When we got there, we all sat in Cliff's room and drank and cried and spoke about it.'

'It was', he recalls, 'really incredible.'

†

Just like that, everything changed. The remaining members of Metallica were robbed of their de facto father figure, while the group's audience were gifted a martyr rendered incorruptible and silent by the violent suddenness of his death. With time the memory of the bass player would inevitably fade; Metallica's music would change and the group's growing appeal would attract the attentions of an emerging audience for whom the name Cliff Burton had only ever been uttered in the past tense; and for some, not at all. For the never insignificant number of older fans who viewed not only increasing levels of success but any stylistic deviation from the blueprint laid down by *Master of Puppets* as signs of artistic betrayal, the questions often asked were, 'What would Cliff do?', or 'What would Cliff make of it all?' The answer, invariably, being that the dead musician would have agreed with members of the group's audience who viewed themselves as being 'defenders of the faith' and as such would have been suitably outraged by whatever actions had been taken by Metallica's surviving members.

'I think about Cliff all the time,' says Ulrich. 'It's not something that goes away, and it's not something that I want to go away. I'm the kind of person who doesn't look at a glass and see it as being half-empty or half-full, I see it as being overflowing. So when I think of Cliff, I think of the three albums we were able to make together, and the friend I was able to have in him. You could hear his influence on the band in songs like "Orion", and I suppose there is always the question of how that influence would have continued had we been able to make more music together, but I suppose that's something we'll never be sure of.'

A largely unheard response to the question 'What would Cliff do?', however, is, 'Conspire with James Hetfield to remove Lars Ulrich from Metallica's ranks.' In the years since the bass player's death, it has become something of a badge of honour for those associated with Metallica at the time to have been privy to the rumour that the group's Danish member was keeping a beat to borrowed time. The whisperers have it that Hetfield and Burton were tired of playing with the drummer, and that it was believed by both men that their colleague's uneven technical abilities were holding back their band. Offstage this still smouldering rumour asserts that front man and bass player had grown weary of their drummer's relentless energies with regard to the business aspects of Metallica's operation and had come to view their colleague's drive for matters other than the music itself as being characteristic of a calculating and career-minded rock star. As the story goes, such was the tinnitus-like insistence of the Dane's shtick that it had been decided that following the conclusion of the group's bookings for 1986 – the final date of which was originally scheduled to take place at Selina's in Sydney on November 27 –

Ulrich's position as a member of Metallica would be terminated.

Reviewed today such a plan seems fanciful, and for reasons that go beyond the simple truth that Ulrich owns the legal rights to the very name 'Metallica'. It may have been that prior to Burton's death both the bassist and Hetfield – and to an unspecified degree, presumably Hammett as well – were foolhardy enough to believe that the attentions of their audience could be attracted to a similar-sounding group with a different name, but had this folly been realised the musicians would quickly have had cause to consider their absent drummer with fondness. Ulrich had taken charge of Metallica's offstage operation to such a formidable degree not only because his temperament and outlook were suited to this role, but also because his band mates had allowed him to do so; in many cases Ulrich's partners could not be bothered to sully their hands with matters more routine than the writing, playing and recording of music. Such was the level of Hetfield's inattentiveness to such exterior details that the front man would often fall asleep during business meetings; this it was safe to do because elsewhere in the room sat another man possessed of such attention to detail that it is difficult to imagine him falling asleep at any point in his life.

Nonetheless this rumour had sufficient currency that it has been addressed publicly on more than one occasion (the first time by Xavier Russell in *Metallica: A Visual Documentary*, a 1992 band biography co-authored with his *Kerrang!* colleague Mark Putterford). Writing on the website for the magazine *Classic Rock*, former *Kerrang!* editor Geoff Barton recalls how 'in pre-*Classic Rock* days a few of us from *Kerrang!* went out for a drink with Scott Ian and [Anthrax drummer] Charlie Benante, circa 1986', an occasion where the author 'distinctly remembers Ian pretty much telling us that Metallica were thinking of changing drummers, although not blatantly'.

There is perhaps something of the dark art regarding the

circulation of this rumour at the time. Whether the group's stated aims were a plan of action, the details of which had been laid with meticulous attention to detail, or else a tactic driven by political intentions is at best unclear. But such careless talk was untypical of the Metallica operation. In 1983 such was the secrecy that surrounded the removal of Dave Mustaine that even those in close proximity to the group's corridors of power were astonished to learn that the errant guitarist had been dispatched home to San Francisco on a Greyhound bus from New York's Port Authority Bus Terminal. That three LPs and somewhere in the region of a million album sales later, discussions to unseat a founder member were being spoken of by lips so loose that the story had made its way to a pub full of English journalists seems unlikely. It should, then, at least be considered that the plan to sack Ulrich from Metallica amounted to little more than an indirect means of drawing the drummer's attention to the degree to which his behaviour was grating on the nerves of his band mates.

'I think that theory makes sense,' is the view of Malcolm Dome, a man who at the time was, of course, privy to this gossip. 'At that point Metallica were really on the rise, and you'd have to think they would have asked themselves, "Do we really want to go to the trouble of getting a new drummer?" But it would make more sense that [the rumour] was more the form of a wake-up call and a warning shot to Lars than it was a case of them being serious about getting rid of him.

'Because at the time,' he adds, 'Lars was a bit, shall we say, out of control.'

In a subject whose clarity is informed only by conjecture, just one thing can be said with any certainty: that the notion that Metallica might replace their drummer died at exactly the same moment as Cliff Burton. In the time it took for a bus to fall on its side, both the group's priorities and the dynamic between the surviving members changed. In the vacuum created by a dead friend, Hetfield and Ulrich's complicated relationship entered a period of unification. It would be a generation before the union between the two men would once more be threatened.

As was the case with AC/DC following the death of vocalist Bon Scott in 1980, Metallica wasted little time in finding a replacement for their fallen friend. Those who remarked that the group acted with undue haste in this pursuit were usually sufficiently bereft of sensitivity to understand that this was not their place to say. Predictably it was Ulrich who led the charm offensive in the search for Metallica's newest member. The first person the drummer telephoned was Joey Vera, who was offered the job sight unseen. This approach was the second time that Metallica had attempted to plunder the ranks of Armored Saint, and the second time such an entreaty had failed.

'Of course, I thought about it,' recalls Vera today. In 1986 the LA quintet were signed to a major label, Chrysalis, and despite their career having not experienced the same kind of vertical elevation as enjoyed by Metallica, were still a band the best days of which were perceived to stand before them. On receiving the telephone call from Ulrich, Vera addressed the drummer's request with the words, 'Let me think about this and I'll call you tomorrow.'

'So I slept on it,' he says, 'and, of course, I thought about it overnight. I had conversations with my girlfriend at the time, and I even spoke with my mom about it; and, of course, I spoke with the guys in the band. But mostly I think that my mind was pretty much made up in the first five minutes. I knew what it meant right away. It meant uprooting and making such a big change in my life; and at the time, I had to think about if this was something that I was really looking for. Was I looking for doing something completely different? And my answer was, "No." I just wasn't ready for it.'

Elsewhere Kirk Hammett suggested to his school friend Les Claypool that he audition for the job, a request the musician was happy to grant. Hearing Claypool play, Hetfield remarked that the candidate was 'too good' and should instead concentrate on 'doing his own thing'. The bassist followed Hetfield's advice and formed the group Primus, a trio that to this day remain one of the most berserk acts ever to gatecrash the *Billboard* Top 10 album chart. Hetfield's own candidate of choice was Willy Lange from the by now floundering Laaz Rockit; this nomination, however, found little traction with either Ulrich or Hammett. Another name positioned briefly in the frame but quickly forgotten was Mike Dean, bassist with South Carolina hardcore punks Corrosion of Conformity.

In order to cast the net properly over the full range of candidates that had applied to succeed Cliff Burton in the ranks of Metallica, the band held auditions in the Castro Valley neighbourhood of Hayward, with an open-house policy that attracted visitors from all over the United States. Over a period of three days up to forty-five musicians introduced themselves to the still-grieving trio, a number of whom were patently unsuited for the position to which they aspired. One hopeless hopeful arrived at the audition carrying a instrument upon which could be read the signature of Quiet Riot bass player Rudy Sarzo.

Metallica, however, did have their eyes on one musician scheduled to audition in October 1986. Following Burton's funeral earlier in the month, back at home in New York City Michael Alago received a phone call from Ulrich. The drummer told his friend, 'We are moving forward . . . We're going to need a bass player: can you help us out?' Three time zones west, in Los Angeles, Brian Slagel received a similar call, with the owner of Metal Blade at first nominating Joey Vera's as the name for the frame. Having learned of Vera's declination, the second name in Slagel's mental Rolodex concurred with the first in Alago's:

Jason Newsted, then both bassist and bandleader for the Phoenix speed metal quintet Flotsam and Jetsam. Alago had witnessed a sufficient number of this group's live shows to recognise that their bass player 'was this wild young character with lots of charm and personality'. With Flotsam and Jetsam signed to Metal Blade Records, however, Slagel knew Newsted not just as an onstage presence but as a human being. Equipped with this knowledge, the impresario was able to calculate in his mind how the young bass player's talents and character might be of a size and quality sufficient for the members of Metallica to begin to piece their professional lives into some kind of order. After mentioning the name, Slagel informed Ulrich that he would place a call to Newsted 'just to make sure that he's into [the idea]', a conversation which led to the bassist 'almost having a heart attack because Metallica were his favourite band'. Slagel himself 'had the feeling that Jason Newsted was the perfect match because he was a really smart guy' who was 'just the perfect guy for that band. He was a younger guy, he was totally into the music, could play really well – he's a phenomenal bass player – and a really smart guy too, which I think was really important. All those guys in [Metallica] are really intelligent. So it seemed like he would fit the bill . . .'

†

Jason Curtis Newsted was born on March 4, 1963, in Battle Creek, Michigan, to parents Bob and Jo Newsted. The third in a family of four children, the youngest son was raised on the family's horse farm in nearby Niles, Michigan. 'My parents were very hard workers,' recalls Newsted. 'They always set a real good example – you know, "go-getedness". My dad would always say, "Take the incentive and don't sit around waiting for something to come around. You gotta get to it and take advantage."'

When Jason was fourteen, the family home relocated from Niles to Kalamazoo, a medium-sized town at the southernmost tip of Michigan known by the unpromising sobriquet the 'Mall City'. To the outside eye the Newsted home appears to be the embodiment not just of the American dream but of also of this dream's unspoken corollaries of self-sufficiency and independence of spirit, not to mention faith. The Newsteds were sufficiently tethered to the notion of living as citizens of One Nation Under God to send the teenage Jason on a church field-trip to Chicago's Museum of Science and Industry in the neighbouring state of Illinois. This occasion proved to be an epiphanic experience for him. For a moment detached from the other members of his church group, the visitor found himself wandering the downtown streets stretching east and west from the Windy City's 'Miracle Mile'. As he did so, his ears were alerted to the sound of a bass guitar, and of one note being played repeatedly with a hypnotic rhythm. The muscle-swaying frequency was emanating from a record shop called Laurie's Planet of Sound, to whose entrance Jason was led like a child to water on the streets of Hamelin. In the shop's window was a small stand positioned beneath the words 'Now Playing'. On the stand rested the sleeve to Van Halen's self-titled 1978 debut album; the track that had attracted Newsted's attentions was this album's toweringly influential opening number, 'Running with the Devil'.

'It was like, "Oh my God, what the hell is happening?"' recalls Newsted. 'It changed everything, everything was different from that day on.'

As with most American teenage rock fans, Newsted was also obsessed with Kiss, an affiliation that informed his decision to learn to play the bass guitar. As would be the case with many musicians that would emerge in the Eighties playing a more muscular brand of rock and metal, Kiss served as a gateway through which Newsted found heavier treasures such as Rush, Blue Oyster Cult and Black Sabbath. At this point in his musical pilgrimage, the bassist recalls being 'sucked in completely'.

Newsted planted his feet on the boards of a stage for the first time as a member of Diamond, a group both long forgotten and entirely typical of the kind of union formed in small towns all over America. At the time his aspiration amounted to little more than playing cover versions of popular songs at local house parties and small town halls. The bassist's second band, Gangster, also performed numbers made famous by other musicians and as such would have also been unremarkable aside from the fact that the group's line-up featured guitarist Tim Hamlin, a man who can be said to have fulfilled the role of Newsted's first mentor. Such was the respect the bass player had for his colleague that when Hamlin decided to move to Los Angeles in order to pursue a life dedicated solely to rock 'n' roll, Newsted opted to move with him.

While the experience of many young men who travel to Hollywood in search of musical stardom results in a retreat from streets where, as Thin Lizzy's Phil Lynott once noted, 'nobody gives a damn when you're down on your luck', this could not be said for Hamlin and Newsted, who never made it as far as California. Instead the pair turned off the engine of their U-Haul truck on the streets of Phoenix, Arizona, and decided to call the desert city – a place crawling with snakes literal rather than figurative – home. The date was Hallowe'en, 1981; Jason Newsted was just eighteen years old.

As with many teenage promises sworn to be remembered, soon enough the new arrivals would drift apart. In the months that followed, Newsted moved from Phoenix to the exurban city of Scottsdale, Arizona. There he formed the band DOGZ, a union in which the bass player also assumed the duties of lead vocalist. Along with second guitarist Mark Vasquez, it was with this group that Newsted composed his first pieces of original music, in the form of the songs 'Dogs of War' and 'Screams in the Night'.

'We thought we were pretty big shit,' remembers the quartet's short-lived front man.

As with many bands without a record deal, DOGZ existed in a form of sufficient liquidity that Newsted was able to step away from the microphone stand in order to concentrate on playing bass guitar. In doing this he handed over the responsibility of singing and communicating to audiences to new recruit Eric A. Knutson, then known as Eric A. K. The band changed its name to Flotsam and Jetsam and recorded a four-song demo tape that appeared under the entirely unpromising title 'Metalshock'. By this point the Arizonian quintet – the line-up of which was completed by guitarists Edward Carlson and Michael Gilbert and drummer Kelly David-Smith – had become a regular presence in the clubs and halls of Phoenix and Scottsdale, and had tuned up the audiences of bands such as Armored Saint and Megadeth. As the group's confidence grew so too did their reputations, to the extent that soon enough the quintet's profile had spread across state lines to the offices of Metal Blade Records in Southern California. Sufficiently impressed by the group, Brian Slagel not only included the song 'I Live You Die' on the seventh instalment of his *Metal Massacre* series but he also signed them to a recording contract. The band's debut album, *Doomsday for the Deceiver*, was released by Metal Blade Records on July 4, American Independence Day.

Considered more than two decades later, the Arizonian band's full-length bow is remarkable for two reasons. The first is its cover artwork, which ranks among the worst, if not the worst, in the history of contemporary music. With quasi-religious implications, the image that appears beneath the band's name features a green lizard-cum-monster squatting atop a boiled-lobster-red Satan. This cack-handed concept is handicapped yet further by a stylistic execution so rudimentary as to make Metallica's idea for the original front of cover of 'Metal Up Your Ass' appear sophisticated. The music contained within was, however, superior to that suggested by the album's packaging. *Doomsday for the Deceiver* is a solid set of second-generation speed metal informed more by the hint of potential than by any particular mastery of execution. Despite this, *Kerrang!* writer 'Harry Headbanger' – the pseudonym of contributor Mark Putterford, a journalist who on the subject of thrash metal knew not a thing – afforded the album a review of such praise that for the first time the publication permitted a rating of six Ks, one more than the maximum usually allowed. With a tone that rang as hollow as the arguments upon which the review was based, Headbanger's notice served only to remind *Kerrang!*'s more discerning readers that a number of its journalists were no more aware of the difference between thrash metal and white noise than was the office cleaning lady, that and the fact that some of the title's commissioning editors could sometimes be heard snoring on the job.

For Newsted, however, Flotsam and Jetsam were about to live up to their name. Following Slagel's telephone call, the bassist focused his considerable energies on not just mastering Metallica's songbook but doing so to professional specifications. In the seven days that elapsed between first contact from Slagel and an audition at Castro Valley, Jason claims that he did not sleep once.

'I may have lain down a couple of times,' he says. '[But] For five days I stayed up and played as long as I could. Blisters on blisters broke [on his hands]. When I could feel the nerve inside [his finger] as I played the string, I stopped for a while. A couple of my friends got together some money to pay for a $140 plane ticket to go do my audition.'

With limbs as thin as the spokes of a television aerial and hair that was not just shoulder-length but also shoulder-width, as Newsted made his way from Arizona to Northern California he could take comfort in the notion that he at least looked the part. The young musician was also savvy enough to understand that on the day of his audition it mattered not at all how he was feeling

– inside he was nervous to the point of physical illness – all that mattered were how his actions registered in the eyes of those who would be watching, and judging, him.

Newsted was scheduled to play music for the first ever time with Hetfield, Ulrich and Hammett in a lunchtime slot during a day of auditions that saw at least sixteen other musicians plug their bass guitar into one of the amplifiers that made up Metallica's backline. Newsted arrived far earlier than was required and was able to see at close hand the operations of a group that had no time for social niceties. 'It was a little bit tense, I have to say,' recalls the bass player. '[The band] arrived and they were pretty much already drunk, and this was maybe midday. People were judged very much on the way they looked, the way they carried themselves. [Metallica] were very brutal. If someone's bass was pink, or if their bass was yellow with green stripes on it, James would be, like, "Next!"'

By the time Jason Newsted came to play with Metallica in the final week of October 1986, forces were beginning to coalesce in his favour, and quickly. An organisation that was as inherently fraternal as it was musical, the band understood that as well as musical compatibility, some order of social cohesion was also required. In pursuit of this, Metallica took their visitor out on the town in San Francisco.

On any other occasion, by the time the four young men rolled into the final watering shed of the night, Newsted would have been drunk beyond measure. But as the party took a table in one of the dimly lit back rooms of Tommy's Joynt on Geary and Van Ness, the bass player was kept sensate by a beehive of nerves busy with the sense of imminent expectation. Tommy's was an establishment popular with Metallica: not only did its quiet corners permit discreet misdemeanours, but its menu featured soul food selections that were both affordable and flavoursome, and pumps and fridges filled with beers of a variety sufficient to satiate the most discerning of palates.

As the evening found an unspoken and inevitable momentum, Hetfield, Ulrich and Hammett found themselves gathered in the toilet of Tommy's Joynt. The drummer has since asserted that the three men were urinating in a line, but given that the bar's smallest room features just two urinals and one toilet stall, this cannot have been the case. There are, of course, other reasons why three young rock musicians might gather together in the toilet of a city-centre pub at three o' clock in the morning. Either way, without making eye contact with his band mates, Ulrich asked, simply, 'That's him, right?'

The answer came back, 'Yeah, that's him.'

As the three men returned to the company of Newsted, Ulrich fixed the man whose life he was about to irreversibly change in his sight and asked a very simple question.

'So,' he said, 'do you want a job?'

8 – BLACKENED

Jason Newsted joined Metallica on October 28, 1986, three weeks to the day after the funeral of Cliff Burton and just thirty-one days after his predecessor's death. On the afternoon of his appointment Ray and Jan Burton travelled down from their home in Castro Valley to meet the young man who was to take their late son's place. After formal introductions had made been, Jan Burton clutched Newsted to her chest, held him tight and wished him luck.

'You must be the one,' she said quietly, 'because these guys know what they're doing.'

Metallica made their first public appearance with their new bass player at the 1,000-capacity Country Club in Reseda, California, on November 8. Fulfilling the role of support band for Metal Church – and thus handing their friends in the headline act a chalice brimming with a liquid of the highest toxicity – onstage at a venue which in 2013 plays host to an actual church, Iglesias De Restauracion, the quartet performed a thirteen-song set that contained the answer to the future pub rock-quiz question: 'Name the first composition Jason Newsted performed in concert as a member of Metallica.' (Answer: 'Battery')

'I was there for Jason's first show and it was fantastic,' recalls Doug Goodman, one of the Bay Area metal scene's original 'Trues'. 'Everyone in the audience knew who Jason was because we all knew him from Flotsam and Jetsam. I remember everyone there was looking forward to the show. You have to remember, it was a different situation from when Kirk joined the band. There were some people who didn't like Kirk when he joined Metallica because they were mad that Dave Mustaine had been thrown out of the band. I remember at one of Kirk's early shows in Palo Alto, someone pulled the power on his [equipment] rig. But when Jason joined the band there was no one that felt any animosity towards him. And why would they? It's obviously not his fault that there was a fucking bus crash that had caused someone to die. It has nothing to do with him that a position in Metallica had opened up in the first place. So Jason is coming in not as someone on hand to save the day, but just as a kid who finds himself in circumstances that neither he nor Metallica could have imagined. And everyone watching knew that, and that's why they were rooting for him.'

Following their appearance at the Country Club, Metallica retreated to the nearby Franklin Plaza Suites Hotel, a facility popular with travelling musicians. Doug Goodman remembers that on the evening of November 8, the hotel was 'party central', with members of Slayer, Anthrax and Overkill on hand to wet the head of the Bay Area band's newest member. By the time the party's heads hit cotton-covered pillows, Saturday night had long since blurred into Sunday morning.

For Jason Newsted, these days and nights must surely have sped by in a kind of blur. A month before, in Arizona, he played bass guitar and the role of bandleader in Flotsam and Jetsam; his position of authority was such that on the wall of the group's practice room he posted a piece of paper on which were written the seven qualities required for a group to succeed. Among these were featured 'consistency' and 'concentration'. Upon learning that his colleague was willing to abandon their union in favour of a job with Metallica, vocalist Eric A. K. defaced the poster, adding the words 'go try out for another band' in black marker.

'It was,' recalls Newsted, 'really a bitch.'

Just days removed from having crossed state lines in order to audition for the position of bass player in his favourite band, it was as a member of this band that Newsted was ferried across the dateline on an aeroplane bound for Narita Airport in Tokyo. Like author Robert A. Heinlein's fictional creation Valentine Michael Smith, the bass player found himself a stranger in a strange land. Metallica's first Japanese tour had been booked prior to the events of September 27 and although the death of Cliff Burton forced the cancellation of thirty-five concerts, their dates in the Orient were honoured.

Reviewing the speed at which these events occurred, one is struck by the force of Metallica's sheer bull-headedness as well as their refusal to permit even genuine tragedy – trauma, actually – to slow them down. It is tempting to wonder why the band's management did not intervene and encourage them to spend the remaining weeks of 1986 on the intermittently nightmarish but necessary process of mourning the loss of a loved one. But such a query operates on the assumption that had it even been offered, cautionary advice from older and presumably wiser heads would have made the slightest difference. That year the energy emanating from Metallica's core was sufficient to register the band by turns as both an unstoppable force *and* an immovable object. If Metallica desired to undertake a tour of Japan that began just weeks after the death of a member with whom the three remaining members were evidently besotted, then Metallica would do just that. The consequences of this course of action could go hang.

It is worth noting too, however, that the savvy Q Prime team must surely have been aware of the potential ramifications a decision not to undertake the five-date tour may have had for their charges in one of the world's most lucrative music markets. In the Japanese music industry, as in all other forms of business, the concept of honour is paramount, and to this day it's not unknown for western rock bands who choose to postpone or cancel Japanese tours to find themselves blackballed by promoters. In booking Metallica the legendary Mr Udo had placed his reputation on the line for the young San Franciscans. Even with the shadow of tragedy framing the band, to dishonour the venerable Japanese music business veteran's invitation to perform in the East, would have been a brave, perhaps even foolish, decision. At least aware of this, on the evening of November 14, 1986, the new-look Metallica touring party checked in to Tokyo's Pacific Meridien Hotel as originally planned.

Inevitably the next seven days would prove to be something of a baptism of fire for Jason Newsted. The bass player was immediately afforded the sobriquet 'New kid' – 'kid', you will notice, not 'member' or even 'recruit' – and subjected to a process of 'hazing' of a kind one might associate with fraternity houses at colleges some way south of the Ivy League, or of small-town Canadian ice-hockey teams, rather than young men who, while fast becoming rock stars, were also artists. Like the English football term 'banter' and the Afrikaans word 'klap', 'hazing' is a verb that obscures a multitude of sins. As visited upon Newsted, this 'hazing' took the form of initiation ceremonies that cast the bass player in a role to which he was not entirely suited: that of victim.

The pranks to which he fell prey in Japan were, however, informed more by high jinks than cold menace. At a sushi restaurant Newsted's new colleagues told him that the wasabi on his plate – a foodstuff made from Japanese horseradish, the potency of which is similar to English mustard – was green pickle, only to laugh themselves dizzy as the diner scorched his palate with a portion of a size sufficient to bring tears to his eyes. During the same week Hammett, Hetfield and Ulrich drank themselves to the point of disorder in the bar of their hotel and charged the bill to Newsted's room, an act not overburdened with consideration given that they were at the time paying him a salary of just $600 per month plus change. The party also took a childish delight in informing anyone who would listen that the new bass player was homosexual. As if this were not quite enough, photographer Ross Halfin, on hand to photograph Newsted's first international concerts as a member of Metallica on assignment for *Kerrang!*, maintains that within these seven days, Ulrich took such an intense dislike to the bassist that he unsuccessfully lobbied Peter Mensch for his instant dismissal from the group.

Despite these low-level hostilities and alleged illicit manoeuvrings, when asked if rather too much has been made of the bass player's initiation into the ranks of Metallica, the man in whose name such capers occurred answered that 'way too much has been made of it'.

'It was certainly fraternity stuff,' Newsted says. 'How much can you drink? Can we wake you up in the middle of the night and turn all the furniture in your room on top of you and run away laughing and everything's cool? It was just regular prankster stuff. We were all twenty-two or twenty-three years old. We were all the same age, we had the same heroes, the same drinking habits. It was really all in good fun.'

In autumn 1986 this 'fun' obscured the fact that the greenhorn with whom the other members of Metallica were playing merry hell was the group's most emotionally articulate member, and would be so for the duration of his tenure. In time, though, the attitude expressed by three-quarters of the band towards its newest recruit would harden into spite. But of all the things his colleagues would attempt to strip from him over the years, the one thing Newsted would refuse to surrender was his dignity. In turn the attitude and behaviour displayed by the other members of the band towards the man they would in many ways always regard as being the 'new kid' would cast them in a light that might generously be described as 'unflattering'. With their frequent insistence on striking the pose of big men, Hetfield, Ulrich and Hammett projected an image of small people.

'I remember we'd do these in-store appearances [to sign

autographs],' recalls Hetfield, nominating just one example of the casual cruelty visited upon his bassist. 'We'd sit in a line and we'd have him go first. So he'd write his name and in the beginning he'd write, "Jason, bass face.' That was his thing. And then as it got down to me I'd scratch the "b" off so it would look like "ass face".'

When asked to nominate a word to describe the treatment that over time would be meted out to Newsted, Michael Alago is of the opinion that 'torture isn't too strong a word at all'. But if Metallica intended truly to move forward as a band, Alago believed that they 'had to accept this new member', this despite the fact the effect of his band mates' action on the bass player 'didn't make things easy for him'.

'At the time it was very much a feeling of waiting for someone to wake me up and go, "Ha ha! Gotcha!",' says Newsted on suddenly finding himself in Metallica's ranks. 'My being the new guy was multiplied on them because they had to set the example while staying a step ahead of me. And I was all about [being the] first one in, last one out. It worked perfectly – they *had* to have someone who was that dedicated. There was no two ways about it. There were only three other people up for the gig, and if [any] one of them would have got [the job] it would not have been the same thing. I know those people and it's not a diss to them – it's just the facts. I mean, I knew all those Metallica songs before anything ever happened, before any of that horrific [bus crash] shit came about. I knew them through and through, so it was meant to be. I was already the biggest fan. I was the guy who was *supposed* to get it.

'In Metallica, the most important lesson I learned is that you should never be seen as the weak link.'

A less discussed topic of the union between Newsted and his band mates in Metallica is not what he had got himself into, but rather what he had got himself out of. At the time of his departure, Flotsam and Jetsam may have been the kind of act that few people would nominate as being their favourite band – a status that has remained unchanged for more than a quarter of a century – but it was a union in which the bassist's hands were responsible not just for the instrument he played but also for the control of the wheel that steered the group's course. With musical co-writing credits on every track featured on *Doomsday for the Deceiver* and sole authorship of all but three of the ten songs contained on the album, for better or worse Newsted was Flotsam and Jetsam's alpha male – a position he would in an instant swap for omega status in Metallica.

'See, that was kind of the big problem,' remembers Brian Slagel, a man who in that autumn acted not only as kingmaker but also as wise counsel. 'I remember having this three-and-a-half-hour conversation with Jason about this. He said to me, "Hey, you know I think I'm going to do this – what do you think?" And I replied, "Well, there are a couple of ground rules that you need to understand. You gotta remember that you're going from a band that you control, where you do everything to the point where it can be described as being *your* band, to Metallica, where you'll have zero say. You'll be joining a band that belongs to James and Lars. Every single decision about the writing of songs and everything else, for that matter, will be taken by them; you're going to have to be happy just to be a bass player, and that's it. You won't have the power to make any decisions – so can you deal with that?"

'At the time he said that he thought he could,' Slagel recalls, 'but I think ultimately, as time went on, I think he was more and more frustrated by the situation. In many ways, he was very similar to [his band mates in Metallica]. Like them, he started a band from nothing, which was very similar to their experience.'

While Slagel is no doubt correct in his assertion as it stands in principle, in practice in Japan in the declining months of 1986 it is reasonable to assume that Newsted had seen nothing of the like of his new band mates. While the new recruit's senses were being heightened by the neon-lit immediacy of Tokyo – 'the girls are nice . . . the girls are stylish . . . it's fun here,' were his rather sweet first impressions – the men with whom he now played music were occupied with the business of filling their boots. Following a visit to the Lexington Queen nightclub in the Japanese capital, Hetfield and Ulrich found themselves sharing a taxicab with what the drummer describes as being 'a Japanese woman of dubious morals'. For men whose own moral code did not always correlate to the standards of the Quakers' Religious Society of Friends, the brow is raised at the prospect of the kind of behaviour that would be viewed by the pair as lying beyond the limits of the acceptable. To their occidental eyes, however, their fellow passenger quickly revealed herself as being 'not exactly the kind of person we wished to share a cab with', leading to the musicians 'dumping her out at a stop light'. Despite this, the drummer reports that 'When we got back to the hotel [the woman] was already there waiting for us . . . a real mystery of the Orient.' Elsewhere, Hammett recalls the morning after a night before that saw him waking up in his hotel room to the sight of 'a pile of puke to my left, a pile of puke to my right, all the lights on and [me] still fully dressed. I also found a cup of tea with a tea bag still in it. I couldn't find my room key, then realised it was in the puke. When I checked out the receptionist asked for the key . . . and I did a runner.'

As Metallica's lead guitarist fled in the manner of someone fast growing accustomed to not being held responsible for the consequences of his actions, among his possessions was a letter from a fan whose words expressed the kind of attentiveness for which Japanese audiences have become known, if not famous. 'Dear Kirk,' the correspondence read, 'I will go to every [Metallica] show in Japan . . . The first show in Tokyo was fantastic, but the shows in Osaka and Nagoya were very bad.'

Such a subjective evaluation, however, was unlikely to dent

the undeniable momentum of Metallica's growing public profile, and little sleep would have been lost by the band as they flew east across the Pacific for Jason Newsted's first North American tour.

Such was the eventual extent of the group's dominance of the genre they represented that in retrospect their ascendancy seems inevitable to the point of being preordained. The moves made by the quartet and their representatives were so effective that viewed today it appears as if their route to success was plotted from the bowels of a volcano by a team of military strategists, corporate raiders, brand consultants and media tastemakers.

This impression, though, is deceptive. As with the group waiting until their third album to embark on their first tour of Britain and the Republic of Ireland, the twenty-date tour of North America that began at the mid-Hudson venue in Poughkeepsie on November 28, 1986, was Metallica's first tour of their home continent to feature themselves as the evening's sole headliners (even then just seven dates took place on US soil, with the remainder occurring north of the fifty-first parallel). But as the musicians boarded their single-decker tour bus, they could hardly have failed to once more recognise an appreciable improvement in their standing. In Ontario the quartet performed at Toronto's Maple Leaf Gardens, the most famous and storied venue of any city in Canada. Opened in 1931 and at the time home to the ice-hockey team the Toronto Maple Leafs, the 15,000-odd seat arena is noteworthy for being the first of scores of major league sports arena at which Metallica would play.

Another milestone performance came in the form of the band's second appearance on the island of Manhattan. On December 1 Metallica's equipment trucks pulled up at the loading doors of the Felt Forum, between 7th and 8th Avenues and 32nd and 34th Street amid the constant chaos of Midtown Manhattan. It is here that each day thousands of people every hour are disgorged on to the New York streets from the subway carriages, New Jersey Transit trains, Long Island Rail Road cars and Amtrak express trains that open their doors to the platforms of Pennsylvania Avenue Station situated a short escalator ride beneath street level. As if this subterranean labyrinth wasn't itself the epitome of cheek-by-jowl urbanity, directly above one of America's busiest transport hubs stands a circular, then nine-storey building into which as many as 23,000 people ascend on any given evening. Opened in 1968 and built to conform to the brutalist aesthetic of the age, in 1986 Madison Square Garden was not only the world's most famous arena but also the venue that attracted more bookings than any other on the planet. Operated by the Madison Square Garden Company, the facility houses a 5,600-seat theatre as well. Today known as the Theater at Madison Square Garden, until the mid-Nineties this smaller room was known to all as the Felt Forum, a name derived not from the material that covered seats that tier from the stage in the shape of a fan but rather in honour of the New York sports impresario Irving Mitchell Felt.

For a city populated by people that comprised audiences known for being difficult to impress, New York took quite the tumble not only for Metallica but also for other groups collated in the folder marked 'thrash metal'. Affording these bands the kind of reception that suggests that as with punk this militant musical movement was a fundamentally urban phenomenon, audiences in the five boroughs would respond to the ferocity emanating from the stage with behaviour that would strike even members of the San Franciscan underground as being unbridled. Thrash shows at the Ritz were often policed by the crouching figure of a densely proportioned skinhead known as Billy Psycho, a man who would calm the sea of limbs and skulls that made up the audience's front rows by stage diving on top of them. This, though, was as nothing compared to the events of the evening of August 31, 1988, when Slayer performed their own headline set at the Felt Forum. Touring in support of the pivotal if not entirely convincing *South of Heaven* album, the Californian quartet were forced to cut short their set as many in the audience tore the padding from their seats and used the cushions as missiles. Bootleg footage from the Forum that night shows a band who appear to be performing in the sightlines of a skeet (clay pigeon) shooting range. Standing helpless amid the mêlée, Tom Araya's exasperated admonishment to the crowd that 'You guys fucked up!' is no more effective than a peace sign on a battle field.

During this period, *Kerrang!* had as its New York correspondent a writer by the name of Don Kaye, a critic possessed of a style that combined both a passion and love for metal's noisiest sub-genre and a sense of critical perspective which meant that on the occasions that he did lunge toward hyperbole – at the time the default setting for the majority of writers that comprised the rock press – he did so with full conviction. Kaye was the kind of writer that not only appeared impossibly exotic to British readers too young to know that CBGB was an airless hell-hole in a sketchy neighbourhood, but he was also a correspondent whose dispatches carried with them a note of the authentic. Where other journalists would eye the coattails of emerging groups for rides suitable for a courtier, Don Kaye would check their rap sheet for charges against credibility, as was the case with his accusation that Anthrax were appropriating the hallmarks of the New York hardcore scene and passing them off as their own (a claim the group denied).

At the Felt Forum on the evening of December 1, 1986, *Kerrang!*'s man in New York was typically resolute. 'No doubt,' he wrote, 'that this [has been] the year of Metallica. No band in recent memory have had such extreme twists of fortune . . . while at the same time capturing the hearts and minds of a loyal following that has multiplied into a vast, planet-wide legion of fans . . . The monster that invaded the Felt Forum on this cold December night has been through both heaven and hell in the past eight months, but has ultimately emerged victorious, its hunger unabated, its power intact.'

If this kind of language appears uncommonly gargantuan, at least the subject about which Kaye was writing conformed to the specifications of his prose. Metallica's short tour of America and Canada in the weeks of North America's holiday season had about it the sense of both a lap of victory and a recognition of all the band had achieved and endured in the calendar year now drawing to a close. In this regard New York was no exception. Performing a fourteen-song set that also found space for both the bass solo Newsted had been performing onstage on all but his first two appearances as a member of the band, and a solo spot from Hammett, Metallica were afforded a reception of such enthusiasm that the group was summoned back to the stage for no fewer than three encores, and closed the show with a run through 'Blitzkrieg', a case not so much of giving the people what they want as handing to them something most of them did not know.

'I'll state right now that next year Metallica won't be playing the Felt Forum; they'll be upstairs, headlining [Madison Square Garden],' predicted Don Kaye, entirely incorrectly. 'For that's what being the Kings of the New Age of Metal entails. And the show I saw at the Felt Forum earns them my vote for that title . . . James, Lars, Jason and Kirk are unstoppable.'

†

An aspect of the Metallica story as it relates to the outlaw years of the Eighties that has proved indefatigable is that the group's ascendancy was propelled by their own steam rather than from support from the infrastructure of the entertainment industry. As 1986 ceded ground to a successive year, the majority of radio stations in the United States would sooner utter the word 'fuck' on the airwaves than play a track from *Master of Puppets*. As yet the group had declined to film music videos to accompany any of their songs. Had they done so, it is difficult to imagine a station such as MTV depositing a clip anywhere on the schedule outside the confines of the then recently launched and often entirely gormless *Headbangers Ball*. As such, as the sales of their third album marched towards the platinum landmark of a million, Metallica were still a group the appeal of which went entirely unnoticed by tens of millions of people who regarded music as something that was delivered rather than sourced.

But as Metallica finished the tour in support of *Master of Puppets*, the band were offered the opportunity to appear on what was at the time – and what in many ways, still is – the hippest and most influential TV show on American network television. Debuted as part of NBC's fall schedule in October 1976, *Saturday Night Live* quickly became a lightning rod for all that was hip and urbane. Filmed in studio 8H on the eighth and ninth floor of 30 Rockefeller Plaza in Midtown Manhattan, *SNL*, as it is more commonly known, distilled the energy of the city from which it broadcast into a comedic sketch show that launched the careers of John Belushi, Dan Ackroyd, Chevy Chase and, in subsequent years, Tina Fey and Adam Sandler. Married to its distinctive brand of hipster humour, *Saturday Night Live* also prided itself on placing onto the air groups unlikely to be granted floor space on the kind of late-night television fare offered by the likes of the more conservative Johnny Carson. With a booking policy that might reasonably be described as striking, the weekend sketch show has over the years featured acts as such as the LA punk band Fear – an appearance made on the insistence of John Belushi – Elvis Costello and the Attractions, the Beastie Boys and Nirvana. Over the course of its thirty-seven-year history, a number of the show's musical moments have proved to be worthy of note. It was on *Saturday Night Live* that in 1995 Dave Grohl became a member of Tom Petty's Heartbreakers, a tenure that lasted for two songs, with the drummer instead deciding to forge ahead with the then new Foo Fighters. Six years later, with New York concussed by the physical and psychological battering of the World Trade Center spectacular, SNL's creator Lorne Michaels requested his friend Paul Simon begin the first episode following the massacre with the Simon & Garfunkel song 'The Boxer'. In this, the performer was flanked by members of the city's beleaguered but unbowed emergency services.

In 1987 *Saturday Night Live* contacted Q Prime and requested Metallica's presence on the programme. By any measure this was a significant break for a band who up until this point had been forced to find their own luck and had become fittingly proud to have done so. From the point of view of the show's producers, the decision to approach Metallica was one informed by a sense of courage and conviction. At that time heavy metal's stock among trendsetters and opinion-formers – actually, among anyone other than the genre's core constituents – was so low as to have ceased trading. The previous year had seen the release of the cult film *Heavy Metal Parking Lot*, a documentary consisting of interviews with fans gathered to attend a Judas Priest and Dokken concert at the Capital Center in Landover, Maryland. Featuring a cast of characters of whom many are so stupid that the viewer can only presume they begin each day being milked, the film provides disheartening proof that a number of metal fans (at least at that time) lacked the cognitive skills required to walk and breathe at the same time.

Elsewhere, when it came to rock music, MTV opted for a policy that equated to an aural version of Chinese water torture. During 1987 the channel pumped out videos such as Def Leppard's 'Animal', Mötley Crüe's 'Girls Girls Girls' and Poison's 'Talk Dirty to Me' into the bedrooms of teenagers all over America. A corollary to this was the delivery of the subliminal notion that the heavier a band played – although in these cases, heavy was a relative term – the dumber and more clichéd their music should be. That Metallica were not just the antithesis of this but actually the antidote itself was a fact obvious to fans of the band who viewed their music as being the nuclear warhead in the battle against pop metal. But for the distinctions that separated Metallica from the worthless mush of most hard rock and metal of that time to be recognised by the coolest programme on American network television showed that the group were gaining traction and notice in the most notable of places. With this Metallica were presented an opportunity as golden as the disc for *Master of Puppets* that hung on the wall of Elektra's New York office.

But if this booking looked to some eyes like a thing that should not be, it was soon scuppered. On March 26 James Hetfield headed outdoors with his skateboard in hand and returned home with a broken arm – again. Until the fracture healed, the band were placed on hold; *Saturday Night Live* did not call back.

'I was skateboarding with some friends in El Cerrito and got going a little too fast, lost control and fell off: landing on my arm trying to break the fall instead I broke my arm,' Hetfield wrote in a note to his insurance company. 'I have since hung up my skateboard.'

There are, though, worse places than the Bay Area in which to find oneself with idle hands. To cries of anguish from every thrash metal musician from San Francisco to San Jose, equal in volume only to the cheers of the neighbours next door, Metallica had recently handed back the keys to the landlord of 3132 Carlson Boulevard and probably did not receive in return their cash deposit against fixtures and fittings. After having been told by Cliff Burnstein that the fruits of their union's labour were of a size sufficient to enable each member to buy a house, instead Lars Ulrich rented an apartment just 200 yards from the Metallica Mansion, and on the same street.

Surrendering their first home in the Bay Area presented

Metallica with a problem. In moving out of the place in which they had lived, the group had also lost the location at which they wrote and practised music. In literal terms Metallica were no longer a garage band.

This, though, would be a change of circumstances that would be as short-lived as it was keenly disliked. As befits upwardly mobile professional musicians, the group found for themselves a professional rehearsal space, one of a number of soundproofed cocoons housed in a multi-room facility in Marin County. The musicians moved in their equipment on March 23, and practised on this and the following day. Their neighbours during this period were local rockers Night Ranger and Starship, the latter act being the Eighties incarnation of Jefferson Airplane that had adapted to the Reagan era by switching from a policy of turning on, tuning in and dropping out to calming down, shutting up and cashing in. Suffice to say Metallica were not greatly enamoured of their surroundings; when Hetfield broke his arm on the fourth day of their tenancy, the decision was made to eschew the polished floors of the professional rehearsal studio. Instead Ulrich placed a phone call to his new landlady and asked if she might consent for him and a group of drunken long-haired males to convert the garage of her property in order that it might be used as a practice facility for one of the world's loudest and most unrelenting heavy metal bands. As any sane person would, the landlady replied with words to the effect of, 'Sure, what's the worst that can happen?'

Under the leadership of Jason Newsted, Metallica set about transforming the garage to their own specifications. This task mostly involved soundproofing the structure to an extent that would prevent the tenants from being shot to death by neighbours at the end of their wits. Despite being temporarily handicapped, Hetfield was also on hand to help.

'I remember trying to saw things with one arm and help

build the thing,' says the front man, painting a touchingly comic picture.

After experiencing the strange sensation of a buzz saw cutting a plaster cast away from a limb without violating the skin it covers (and for the second time in nine months, at that), Hetfield was once again ready to play with Metallica, while Metallica were once more a garage band. In returning to this state, the quartet had gone from a rehearsal facility with floors buffed to the extent that one could see one's face in them to a place where one could not always be guaranteed to see the floor at all.

'The term "garage" isn't something you can really define,' believes Ulrich. 'It's more to do with vibe and feeling around a project and a band in general. We've always considered ourselves to be kind of different to whatever else is out there at the moment, in so much as we do things for fun, and for ourselves; for our own enjoyment.'

As time marched on, membership of Metallica would be seen as exclusive to people whose behaviour was often self-centred to the point of dysfunctionality; the result of hearing the word 'no' fewer times than is good for them, combined with the nasty habit of taking gratification only in its instant form. As this selfishness relates to matters of creativity, however, Metallica had few traits in their collective make-up of such valuable currency. It is an irony of this group's magnetic appeal that the reason so many members of its audience believe the band speak for them is in fact because they do quite the opposite; Metallica speak only for themselves, and the music they make is made first to please the men who play it. At least as much as the abundance of talent to which the band can lay claim, it is this authenticity that listeners find so compelling. Representing a genre where rebellious poses were struck by groups whose music adhered to a blueprint that was conservative, in both in its thinking and its execution, in an artistic sense – as well as in a few other senses – Metallica were outlaws.

They were, though, outlaws who craved recognition. That this was the case could be gleaned from a glance at the back cover of *Master of Puppets*, which contained a picture of the band onstage at the Oakland–Alameda County Coliseum performing at an event they did not headline. Theirs was an appetite for adulation that was keen even by the standards of those who desired to write the words 'rock star' on their passport application form. The band, though, wanted the glittering prizes of success without the endless compromises normally associated with such pursuits. While other groups made merry idiots of themselves on video tape, for example, Metallica simply opened up a four-pack and merrily kicked the spent cans in the opposite direction.

The quartet's next stride towards the destination of world domination came with the decision to record an EP of cover versions the originals of which would be familiar to only the slimmest minority of their audience. The tracks would be recorded quickly by the band themselves, rather than slowly by Flemming Rasmussen. This do-it-yourself approach was born from the group's DIY work in renovating Ulrich's garage from a place where a car might park to a space in which it sounded as if a combustion engine was exploding. In this space the four musicians practised their way back to form by playing not their own songs but rather a selection of tracks composed by others. From this standing start, within a month the *$5.98 E.P.: Garage Days Re-Revisited* was conceived, recorded and mixed.

'We never had these huge group meetings planning just how we should come across or look, you know?' says Ulrich. 'It's just the way we are that people see, and the EP wasn't any major planned thing . . . We did it all in six days down in LA, which was very quick for us. We usually like to take our time on stuff, but we wanted this to be as spontaneous as possible . . . The time it took us to record the EP . . . was the [same] time it took us to set up the gear in the studio for the last album!'

But just as at the outset of their career Metallica neglected to point out to LA audiences that the songs they were hearing were New Wave of British Heavy Metal cover versions rather original tracks, so here Ulrich omitted to mention the fact that the original impetus behind his band's decision to record in this distinctly punk rock manner came out of conversations with a major international corporation.

In spring 1987 Q Prime negotiated a new European home for Metallica. *Master of Puppets* had marked the end of the quartet's licensing deal with Music For Nations and so, without waiting for MFN boss Martin Hooker to prepare an improved contract, Peter Mensch offered his group to Phonogram, the British record company which released Def Leppard's recordings. When Hooker approached Mensch with the offer of a new one-million-pound contract for the band, he was brusquely informed that their Phonogram deal was a fait accompli.

'The band actually wanted to stay at MFN,' maintains Hooker, 'but Q Prime wanted them to go to Phonogram so that they'd have all their eggs in the one basket and have more clout. And I could understand that at the time. But they ended up signing with Phonogram at a time when nobody at Phonogram liked heavy metal in the slightest. People at the label didn't get it, they just didn't understand the music. I remember talking to people at the label at the time and they admitted that they'd never even heard of [Metallica], despite the fact that they'd already got three gold albums.'

If Phonogram, whose roster in the mid-Eighties included Dire Straits, Soft Cell and Swing Out Sister, thought they were landing themselves the new Def Leppard they were swiftly disabused of the notion by Mensch, who with some bluntness told the label's departmental heads that he fully understood that they knew nothing of his band, and therefore would play no role in their creative development. Nonetheless the shrewd New

Yorker listened calmly as the cowed executives timidly enquired if perhaps they might be allowed to deliver a hit single for his band. Senior product manager Dave Thorne pointed out that with Metallica already booked to return to the United Kingdom that summer, their visit would provide an excellent marketing opportunity to sell the band afresh to British metal fans. The sole problem, as Thorne saw it, was that *Master of Puppets* was now almost eighteen months old, and the band had no spare material in their vaults. He politely enquired as to whether a solution might be found. At which point the idea of an EP of cover versions was first raised.

Despite its title, then, . . . *Garage Days Re-Revisited* was recorded at studios the specifications of which resided at the highest end of professional music making. While its creators never claimed that the five tracks they committed to what was at the time still tape were rough and ready to the extent of actually being *recorded* in a garage, nonetheless as regards the making of the *$5.98 E.P* . . ., while speed was of the essence the same could hardly be said for the cost. For a release that took less than a week to complete, Metallica utilised the services of two top-line recording facilities: A&M Studios in Santa Monica and Conway Studios in West Hollywood. At the latter establishment, Metallica were gifted recording time by Ted Nugent, where the 'Motor City Madman' had finished work early on his *If You Can't Lick 'Em . . . Lick 'Em* solo album, a set which would flop the following year on Atlantic Records.

Amid the hospital-white walls and small but verdant gardens of Conway Studios, Metallica attacked the task at hand like workmen on a makeover television programme. Recording at a rate that equated to a song a day, in less than a week the quartet had placed in the can the tracks 'Helpless' by Diamond Head, 'The Small Hours' by New Wave of British Heavy Metal tadpoles Holocaust, the exquisitely titled 'Crash Course in Brain Surgery' by Welsh rock act Budgie, a rendition of 'The Wait' by English post-punk cult Killing Joke, plus a cut 'n' shut melding of 'Last Caress' and 'Green Hell', two chalk-and-cheese selections from the Misfits (who, despite having disbanded four years earlier, were fast becoming the punk rock group most beloved of metal fans, owing mainly to the fact that Metallica wore the band's T-shirts with almost perfect ubiquity).

The $5.98 E.P.: Garage Days Re-Revisited sees Metallica showcased with a naked clarity that borders on the blinding. From the front cover showing four young men and three guitars framed in a communal shower stall – this at a time when it was most uncommon for metal releases to feature a photograph of the artists as a front sleeve – and represented by a logo that appears to have been written by the tip of a rollerball pen, to Hetfield's handwritten expositionary notes on the back sleeve, even before the listener had removed the twelve-inch single from its cover the effect was to present the image of a band that were clinking together beer bottles on a cloudless summer's day. For a group positioned at the high table of a genre most other representatives of which were photographed with facial expressions that appeared to betray the symptoms of irritable bowel syndrome – the high-water mark of which had been attained by a gurning Slayer as seen on the back cover of *Reign in Blood* – this change of approach was as appealing as it was refreshing.

Oddly, of all of Metallica's releases from the Eighties, it is this slight and carefree offering that has best weathered the passing of time. It may be that a collection as unvarnished as this has little to lose by way of lustre, but the urgency with which Ulrich's drumbeat propels itself from the speakers on 'Helpless' is as startling for listeners today as it was more than a quarter of a century earlier. Embedded by rhythm guitar parts that are drawn tighter than a high wire – the barely audible shriek that accompanies Hetfield's fingers as they adjust their position on the wholly unforgiving 'Green Hell' is a moment of intensity equal to anything in modern metal – underpinned by Newsted's relentless bass lines and resplendent from the attention of Hammett's dazzling yet rarely gratuitous guitar solos, with a panache that seems entirely effortless in just five tracks Metallica pummel home the point that it was by design rather than accident that theirs was the name first on the lips of metal's emergent fan base.

Not for the last time, with the release of *The $5.98 E.P: Garage Days Re-Revisited* Metallica desired not only to be successful but also to be seen to be successful. In pursuit of this end, in order to be deemed eligible for certification on the UK singles chart, *The $5.98 EP* . . . (which on CD was re-titled *The $9.98 CD* . . . , this despite the fact that compact discs are cheaper to produce than vinyl records), Metallica's debut single for Phonogram, emerged on British shores shorn of 'The Wait'. Six days on from its release on August 21, 1987, the band's name was duly heard on the official singles chart as announced each Sunday on BBC Radio 1 for the first time, as their late summer release gatecrashed the pop party at no. 27. And while Metallica could not lay claim to being the first group of their type to be rewarded with a British hit single – in this they were beaten by Anthrax's 'I Am the Law', released earlier that year – the quartet could with some certainty be sure of the fact that they had deposited the most offensive lyric in the then forty-seven-year history of the British singles chart. A decade after Johnny Rotten had excited and appalled the nation with his observation that the Queen 'ain't no human being' in 'God Save the Queen', virtually no one seemed even to notice Hetfield's announcement in 'Last Caress' that he had 'something to say', that he 'raped your mother today' and that 'it doesn't matter much to [him] as long as she spreads'.

The release of *The $5.98 E.P* . . . . coincided with its creators arriving on British soil for their second appearance at Donington

Park's Monsters of Rock festival, held that year on Saturday August 22. Positioned two slots from the top of the bill, Metallica were joined at the racetrack by headliners Bon Jovi, classic rockers Dio, old touring partners Anthrax and W.A.S.P. and raspy-voiced Philadelphian troubadours Cinderella.

For once that most unreliable of entities, the British summer, was playing against type. In the days that led up to August 22, much of the United Kingdom was basking in sunshine. As Metallica worked the jet lag from their eyes in the comfort of Peter Mensch's London flat, elsewhere preparations were being made so that the group might be fully prepared to face the largest audience yet to meet their eyes. As if the pressure associated with an appearance onstage in front of an audience of 97,000 people – at least 40,000 more than witnessed the San Franciscan group's first appearance at Donington Park – weren't quite enough, Metallica's appearance in the East Midlands was the quartet's first scheduled live engagement for more than six months.

For professional musicians there is a difference between being able to play and being able to perform live. Metallica needed to reawaken the muscle-memory required for the latter task. In pursuit of this aim, on a stifling Thursday afternoon customers browsing the epicurean selection of import metal and punk albums in the racks of the specialist Soho record shop Shades would have seen on the wall a handwritten poster that announced that later that evening a group by the name of 'Damage Inc.' would be performing in concert at the 100 Club on 100 Oxford Street, just half a mile away.

August 20, 1987, was the first occasion that Metallica appeared live under an assumed name, albeit one that even the dimmest member of their audience could decode. (For the record, one of this book's authors was in Shades that very afternoon and failed to place the pieces of the puzzle together.) Years before the advent of instant worldwide communication, the prospect of Metallica appearing onstage at a venue for which they were absurdly unsuited was a prospect sufficient to draw an expectant crowd.

'To be honest with you, I wasn't really that into Metallica at the time,' recalls Scarlet Borg, who on that Thursday afternoon queued at the doors of the subterranean club inside which eleven years previously Sid Vicious of the Sex Pistols had assaulted music journalist Nick Kent with a bicycle chain. At the time Borg worked as the receptionist for an advertising agency based in nearby Mayfair; today she is the photo editor of *Kerrang!*, and someone who might reasonably be described as the conscience of the magazine.

'At that time I preferred the bands with big hair, groups like Mötley Crüe and other more unmentionable "Hair Metal" acts. But one of my friends had talked me into going to see Metallica at Hammersmith on the ['Damage Inc.'] tour, and I'd loved it. So the prospect of seeing them perform a tiny gig just before Donington – and I wasn't able to attend the Monsters of Rock that year – seemed like a great idea.'

Phoning in sick at work – 'I was terrified that someone would see me,' she remembers – Scarlet positioned herself on the concrete of Oxford Street and passed the hours until the doors of the 100 Club opened by drinking cans of warm lager. As the minutes passed, so the crowd grew; soon enough this already congested street was pulsing with the energy of hundreds of people dressed in black T-shirts and white basketball boots. In order to avoid a scene, an executive decision was taken by the operators of the venue to open the doors of the 100 Club earlier than was usual, and so it was that at least 350 people descended two flights of stairs into a club the temperature of which would quickly rise to a level sufficient to glaze pottery.

'It was rammed to the rafters in there,' recalls Scarlet. 'By the time the band came on the walls and the ceiling were literally dripping with condensation. It really wasn't a scene for the faint-hearted. I spent quite a lot of the gig with my face squashed against one of the [support] pillars, which totally blocked my view, and I remember that at least twice the sound from the PA just gave out. Apart from that it was just a case of trying to stay on my feet in the sea of colliding bodies and stage-divers. It was so hot in there that even Jason Newsted fainted [although this is disputed by the bassist himself, who maintains that he merely had his guitar cable pulled out in the mêlée]. Scott Ian was also there, stage-diving. It was an amazing occasion, the kind of thing you remember in detail for years and years to come.'

Unfortunately, for both the musicians and their audience, Metallica's triumph at a club with the worst sight lines in the country was not to be repeated at Donington Park. For their flying visit to the United Kingdom, the visitors from the Bay Area saved the worst for last. While the occasion of the eighth Monsters of Rock festival can be said to have announced the changing tastes of audiences partial to hard rock and heavier metal, in practice it did so without particular reference to Metallica. It might have been the case that by playing a racetrack in the bellybutton of nowhere for the second time, the quartet had already made the point that theirs was a name on which eyes should be placed. But the most striking image from Donington Park in daylight hours that afternoon was provided by Scott Ian onstage wearing not just skateboard shorts – this at a time when performers were more likely to appear in a tutu – but also a Public Enemy T-shirt (an allegiance that led to the band being honoured by name on the lyrics to the Public Enemy song 'Bring the Noise' from the 1988 album *It Takes a Nation of Millions to Hold Us Back*). As Anthrax opened their set with 'Among the Living', an exodus began from the front of the crowd of teenage girls in Bon Jovi T-shirts, tears streaming down their faces, repelled by the crop-circle-sized mosh pits opening up across the uneven viewing area in front of the stage.

Much more than this, though, the 1987 Monsters of Rock festival belonged to its headliners. While Metallica had propelled themselves into the limelight by dint of talent and force of will alone, Bon Jovi had secured for themselves a stratospheric level of success by utilising and even mastering every trick available to modern music marketing of the time. In harnessing the choruses and melodies of pop music together with the heft of stadium rock, the New Jersey quintet's third album, *Slippery When Wet*, released the previous year, had pushed its creators to the highest positions of the world's charts, with singles and videos for the tracks 'Livin' on a Prayer' and 'Wanted Dead or Alive' appearing on radio and television with a ubiquity to rival that of Madonna.

Three hours before Bon Jovi bombarded 97,000 people at an East Midlands racetrack with Rat Pack showmanship and blinding smiles, Metallica were struggling to manoeuvre their own vehicle out of the garage. It is a seldom discussed matter, but the truth is that on occasion the union of Hetfield, Ulrich, Hammett and (at the time) Newsted was one well capable of delivering live sets the standards of which were some way beneath code; occasions where Hetfield's vocals droned flat, where Ulrich's timekeeping was (at best) flexible and where Hammett's inability to harmonise with the rhythm guitars on a song such as 'Master of Puppets' was more pronounced than usual. As a light summer breeze wafted the sound from the Donington Park PA on to the runway of the neighbouring East Midlands Airport, Metallica huffed and puffed their way through an eleven-song set that seemed to excite only one person, a member of the audience who had somehow evaded security and was busy climbing the rope ladder that led from the side of the stage to the lighting rig above (all the while banging his head as if attempting to free it from a beehive).

'We played "Phantom Lord" and "Leper Messiah" which we hadn't played in ages,' recalled Lars Ulrich. 'I remember looking over at Iron Maiden's Steve Harris on the side of the stage. He *winced*. I realised we shouldn't have played those songs.'

At the end of a performance which even at the time was dismissed with a shrug of disappointment, Ulrich was met in the wings of the stage by a member of the road crew who proceeded to wrap the drummer in the kind of heat-retaining foil used by endurance athletes at the end of a triathlon. For a band that had just delivered a set that possessed all the bite of a de-fanged grass snake, such a sight appeared ridiculous.

The abiding image of Metallica's afternoon, however, was one gatecrashed by Bon Jovi themselves. As Metallica failed in their attempts to project themselves to an audience that stretched as far as the eye could see – at the time, the organisers of the festival did not see fit to supply big screens – above their scalps circled a helicopter containing the band that would appear last on the Castle Donington stage. Rather than make a beeline directly to the landing pad close to the backstage area, instead the helicopter circled overhead as if taking its time to regard both the audience below and the little band that were presently attempting to entertain them. As the sound from the speakers darted around like a table-tennis ball caught in the draught of a hairdryer, the loudest sound heard by those thousands of people was the thumping whir of helicopter blades.

In photo shoots that followed Metallica's second appearance at the Monsters of Rock festival, the body of Hetfield's white Explorer guitar would feature the words 'Kill Bon Jovi'.

†

1987 can be seen as being the first of Metallica's many stopgap years, periods where decks were cleared and curiosities unveiled. In November, in the United Kingdom the group released their first retail video compilation. 'Cliff 'Em All' was both a visual epitaph for a dead friend and also yet another marker in the stylistic distinctions that could be drawn between this band and others with whom they shared concert and festival stages. Comprised mostly of bootleg footage shot by fans, the eighty-six-minute VHS tape offered the viewer various concert clips of Metallica from the time Cliff Burton was still alive, spanning a period from the bassist's second appearance with the group at The Stone, all the way to a clip filmed at Denmark's four-day Roskilde festival less than three months before the bus crash that would end the musician's life.

As ever Lars Ulrich was on hand to drum up business for 'Cliff 'Em All'. That the release was an innovative idea was a notion seized upon by the drummer, while the nagging corollary that the reason such an idea had so far been untried could be explained by the fact that no other band would ask their fan base to pay money – and the video tape was not released at any kind of discounted price – for footage of such inferior specifications went unacknowledged. 'To be honest, I don't think the quality of the footage is going to affect us adversely,' Ulrich reported, not the least concerned as to how this footage might affect the viewer. 'It's not as if this video is going to act as an introduction [to] Metallica to a kid in Stoke or Derby. It won't be the first time he's seen us so he'll know what the score is. He might well find some of the shit amusing though, like seeing James in '83 on the Kill 'Em All for One tour wearing a pair of spandex trousers.' (This from a drummer who in 1987 was still wearing spandex trousers.)

But if viewers sat before their television screens at home might have had cause to wonder quite what it was that Metallica were up to with 'Cliff 'Em All', greater cause for concern might have been harboured by Newsted. The group's current bassist had been stationed in his post for longer than a year, yet here came his predecessor, back from the dead as if it to remind him that his current circumstances came at the expense of another man's misfortune. For all its sensitivity to the group's newest member, 'Cliff 'Em All' may as well have been titled 'We Wish Jason Newsted Didn't Exist'. When this point was raised with Ulrich, the drummer's startled response spoke of a power base that was more suited to issuing diktats than it was to asking questions.

'Well, to be perfectly honest we haven't really talked about the video with Jason very much,' was the drummer's answer. 'Obviously he wasn't there when the pieces were filmed and he's not really said much about it. I'm not actually sure that I want to get into all this, but basically however Jason feels about the video is how he feels. What I do know is that Jason has always had a lot of respect for Cliff, both as a bass player and as a human being [this despite the fact that the two men had never met], and you can't ask for more than that!'

In a just and fair world Jason Newsted would have asked for more than that; the fact that he did not, and felt that he could not, offers further evidence that Metallica's centre of gravity was beginning to calcify around the duopoly of James Hetfield and Lars Ulrich. Occasionally, however, the careless cruelties visited upon the band's bass player were replaced with something resembling a more humane face. In autumn 1987 Metallica returned to the Bay Area in order to begin writing their fourth album. Unlike the preparations for *Master of Puppets*, the group began piecing together new material from individual riffs secreted on numerous demo cassette tapes rather than from pieces of music already structured in a manner that might be recognised as songs in even an embryonic sense of the word. As Hetfield and Ulrich started to construct the often creaking structures of the compositions that would comprise their next album, the pair held the equivalent of 'open mic' auditions where contributions from all members were considered with an open-mindedness and air, even, of democratic debate.

'I guess my best memory, when I break open those vaults, is [of] James and I sitting in the bedroom of my one-bedroom apartment in San Pablo, CA, with my four-track machine – the one I still do my stuff on – in front of us,' recalls Newsted. 'There's a Damage Inc. poster on the wall . . . and I had the riff to [the song] "Blackened". I showed James the fingering for it, and we just started working on the song. We both still had long hair, thought the same way and listened to the same music. When I went away, he'd babysit my cats; when he went away, I'd babysit his cats. We both had one-bedroom apartments, and they were both equidistant on either side from Lars's garage, where we made ". . . *Garage Days* . . ." We were all living in the El Cerrito area, and we had a very gang-oriented, Ramones-oriented thing happening. We had that mentality very intact. Everybody was pretty much a straight ahead metalhead. We were very determined to be that American band that brought this kind of music to [the] people.'

Newsted's role in Metallica has often been described in rather sniffy terms as being that of a 'fan boy'. The bassist's perspective took in not only the dynamic of the group of which he was a member but also its affinity with, and even responsibilities to, its audience.

'Blackened' was the first song the group worked on, and they did so as a quartet in a process Ulrich describes as 'the famous, you know, "Let's get everybody together and try to work on stuff." '

'But it never really went anywhere,' remembers the drummer. 'Over the course of Metallica's career, whenever we get too many people to be part of the writing thing, it always ends up being not so good.'

Instead Hetfield and Ulrich squirrelled themselves away in the drummer's garage, listening to riffs recorded on tapes and editing the notes and chord-progressions into place. Such was the complexity of the structure of each of the compositions that began to emerge that Hetfield resorted to making written charts in order to help him to commit each song's component parts to memory. 'Back then,' remembers Ulrich, 'we just tried to cram as much shit into the songs as possible. But it wasn't like we had to keep cramming until they were nine minutes long. It was more like, "Wow, this is pretty cool."'

The pieces of music were given names: in the slipstream of 'Blackened' came 'Harvester of Sorrow'. Elsewhere, inspired by a conversation Hetfield had once shared with Cliff Burton, regarding the horror of the notion of a soldier returning from war bereft not only of all four limbs but of the powers of sight, speech and hearing, the third song to emerge from the songwriting session was given the title 'One'. Later in the process, the front man partnered a lyric that addressed the fury of a childhood blighted by parental suffocation to music that was as frenetically paced as it was tightly controlled; this song was christened 'Dyers Eve'. Elsewhere, a patiently expansive composition featuring an eight-line poem written by Cliff Burton, titled 'To Live Is To Die', would battle the song '. . . And Justice for All' for the title of Metallica's longest composition to date, and at sixteen seconds shy of ten minutes would win by four seconds. As if by way of consolation, the latter song would be afforded title track status on Metallica's fourth album.

'The writing was pretty much me and James in the sweaty, stinking garage there on Carlson Boulevard,' remembers Ulrich.

This process inevitably locked itself into the classic Metallica form, where Hetfield would author many of the riffs while Ulrich would concern himself with the invariably undervalued task of placing these parts into an order that sometimes adhered to and occasionally subverted traditional notions of song structure. The pair showed a willingness to utilise sections written by Hammett – the lead guitarist's name appears on the writing credits of five of . . . And Justice for All's nine compositions – but only if such sections met the editorial standards the pair had set for the band. The lead guitarist's own estimation of the worth of his contributions was without consequence. As for Newsted, 'Blackened' is the only selection on the first Metallica album on which he appeared to feature his name as co-author.

'We were waiting for [Jason] to write some big, epic stuff, but it never really came,' recalls Hammett. 'It was kind of weird. It was a non-starter, in retrospect. It was great that he was there and was enthusiastic about it, but he didn't make any huge contributions. The only thing he really came up with was the riff in "Blackened", and in retrospect that was pretty much the biggest contribution he ever made to the band. I don't know why that is, but it's kind of just how the chips fell.'

'I knew my place,' reasoned Newsted, 'and I couldn't write songs better than James.'

With the blueprints laid out on demo tape, Metallica convened at Burt Bacharach's One On One Studios on Lankershim Boulevard in North Hollywood in the first week of January 1988 in order to begin the process of recording their fourth album. In pursuit of this aim, the quartet hired the services of Mike Clink, a producer who at the time was coming into season as the man who had harnessed the raw energy of Guns N' Roses and translated this into the multi-platinum form of that band's debut album *Appetite for Destruction*, released the previous summer.

Events, however, would not proceed smoothly. As had become tradition, Metallica chose to acclimatise to the studio environment by recording a pair of cover versions, in this case Diamond Head's 'The Prince' and Budgie's 'Breadfan'. While Clink may have been the 'hottest' producer in rock at that time, to the eyes and ears of Hetfield and Ulrich, it only took the completion of these two tracks to realise he wasn't up to this particular job.

'We realised that working with Clink wasn't working out,' says Ulrich, remembering that the producer 'was a super nice guy' but that the 'vibe' in the studio 'just wasn't happening'.

Viewed today, the marriage between Metallica and Mike Clink seems like a union fraught with potential difficulty, if not one certain to fail. As timeless and revered as *Appetite for Destruction* would prove to be – and with more than 40 million copies sold, the fifteen-song set outstrips Metallica's most commercially successful release by some distance – as with the Sex Pistols' *Never Mind the Bollocks* the collection is a textbook example of the classic debut album. Mike Clink did not so much produce Guns N' Roses as he did translate the quintet's sound as heard in the clubs of West Hollywood and replicate it authentically onto the unforgiving parameters of a five-inch compact disc. But as the producer found them in the first month of 1988, Metallica were an entirely different proposition from Guns N' Roses. Theirs was a union of greater complexity, both in terms of the music it played and of the relationship that existed between the band's two alpha males.

In order to salvage the situation, Lars Ulrich made a telephone call to a man to whom he could speak in Danish. Listening from his home in Copenhagen, Flemming Rasmussen was asked by his countryman if he might be both willing and able to fill the vacuum left by the departure of Mike Clink. The producer answered that he was, but that to fulfil this brief he would require that accommodation in Los Angeles be provided for his entire family (the Rasmussen household had expanded to four with the birth of a second child on December 10) and that, as was the case with *Master of Puppets*, part of the technician's fee be registered as a royalty against each copy of the album sold. With these terms agreed, on February 14, 1988, the Rasmussen family flew from the bitter winter of Copenhagen to the sunlit temperance of southern California. With the kind of timing more suited to the pen of a dramatist, the Dane made his entrance into One On One Studios as Clink was packing up his belongings and leaving.

'I remember him being in the studio as I arrived,' recalls Rasmussen. 'It was a bit awkward, obviously. But he seemed like a nice guy. He didn't hit me or anything.'

Between first entering the recording complex and returning to Copenhagen in May, Rasmussen enjoyed just three rest days, and for each of these he was placed on standby in case his charges decided to open the microphones at One On One at short, or no, notice. During the early days of the recording sessions, the parties – usually Hetfield and Ulrich together with their producer – would convene at 11 a.m. and work for between twelve and fourteen hours. As the time of departure stretched to a point where late at night changed shifts with early the next morning, so too the time of the next day's sessions would be punted back an hour. It is difficult to tell whether or not Rasmussen is joking when he says that towards the end of the making of . . . *And Justice for All* the recording sessions 'were starting at five o'clock in the morning', but there is no doubting the rictus smile that accompanies the revelation that during his time in Los Angeles the producer 'didn't get much sleep – not much sleep at all'.

As work progressed on the nine songs that would eventually comprise . . . *And Justice for All*, Metallica appointed their latest collection the humorous working title 'Wild Chicks and Fast Cars and Lots of Drugs'. As the proverb asserts, this was a case of many a true word being spoken in jest. Newsted has revealed that during this period Ulrich and Hammett were 'experimenting' with 'powders', although how one can differentiate between the drummer before and after a line of cocaine is a question that lacks a convincing answer. Elsewhere Ulrich plunged himself into the Hollywood night life like the twenty-something major-league rock star he was fast becoming. And in Hollywood in the late Eighties the drummer had found his *métier*. For while Metallica may have fled the City of Angels and placed much noisy distance between themselves and the kind of groups represented on

Sunset Boulevard, when it came to savouring the pleasures and trappings of permanent adolescence that attracted themselves to such groups, the returning exiles were not quite so sniffy.

'One time in LA, Lars was determined that I would go with him to Nikki Sixx's porno party,' remembers Ross Halfin, who at the time lived in Los Angeles with journalist Mick Wall. 'After drinking sake all night in a sushi bar we drove around Bel Air and Lars said to my date, who was speeding, "Why don't you go a bit faster?" As he said this we whacked the kerb, spun around in the road, hit the opposite kerb and somersaulted, landing upside down, half in the road and half in someone's garden. I remember it all seemed to happen in slow motion. I looked around the car and everyone was okay. We crawled out of the window with my date screaming "My car!" as it was going up in flames. Three police cars arrived. I'm thinking, "Oh shit . . . we're wasted . . ." They handcuffed and carted my date off to jail, and the sergeant looks at Lars and said, "I have scraped people off this corner. There is not a mark on any of you. Remember this, [because] God is watching you." He then ordered us a couple of cabs. Lars rang me at 6 a.m. saying, "Did that really happen?"'

During the recording Metallica and Rasmussen were staying at an apartment complex close to the then iconic and now closed Tower Records shop on Sunset Boulevard. Each day producer and band would travel in the same car to One On One Studios, pausing on the way to buy bottles of pop and snacks. Rasmussen remembers that Hetfield and Ulrich were present in the studio 'pretty much all the time'. 'Look, here's a picture of Lars doing his favourite thing,' says the producer, showing the authors a photograph of the drummer in the mixing room speaking on the phone – and that Hammett and Newsted were on hand only for the purposes of the recording of each musician's individual contributions.

'The . . . *Justice* . . . album was probably the epitome of the Lars and James show, in terms of the writing, the recording, the mixing, the whole thing,' remembers Ulrich. (Interesting that the drummer should choose to refer to the union with Hetfield by placing his colleague's name second in relation to his own.) 'It was', he says, 'me and James running everything with an iron fist.'

However, when it came to the soon to be widely discussed contributions of Metallica's newest member, neither Hetfield, Ulrich *or* Rasmussen regarded the event as being an occasion worthy of their presence.

'We made [Jason] do all the bass tracks on his own, actually, so he could do his thing,' says the producer, in a tone of voice that suggests this memory is nothing more than an afterthought. For the bass player himself though, the recollection is as telling as it was troubling.

'For . . . *Justice* . . . , my situation was very awkward,' recalls the musician. 'I had nothing to do with any of the other guys in the band when they recorded their parts and they had nothing to do with me on the actual day – notice I said "day", singular – that I went into the studio to record my bass parts . . . I was put in a room with Toby Wright, who at the time was second or third engineer at One On One. He was more like the guy who got coffee, the guy we'd [smoke joints] with and stuff.' Wright would go on to further his name with bands such as Slayer and next-generation metal innovators Korn, but in the first months of 1988 the technician's seniority of position paled even when placed alongside that of the musician he was commissioned to record. Like the last two drinkers at a singles bar, the pair made the best of it.

'I walked in, Toby rolled the tape and I played the songs,' remembers the bassist. 'We started with "Blackened" because that's the one I knew the best. The rest of the songs were like a double-black diamond level of difficulty in terms of technical demands. I wasn't used to having fourteen or eighteen parts in a song, but I was ready for it. I can't remember exactly how much we played the songs together [as a band] before I went in there – I just remember learning the songs myself off the tapes that I had of the drums and the guitars. So I played the tape, recorded my parts, loaded up my shit [at the end of the session] and that was it.'

As events would transpire, when listeners first heard . . . *And Justice for All* on its release, the question they would unite in asking was whether Newsted had played on the album at all, but that was a shock the bassist still had in store.

Elsewhere the job of Rasmussen was to divine a path along which Hetfield – a man whose creativity is fuelled by the conflicting elements of a personality that is both progressive and reactionary – was comfortable traversing. The producer attempted to convince the front man to sing rather than merely to bark in key, only to be told that singing 'is for fags'.

'He was,' recalls Rasmussen, 'a very angry young man.'

Along with the rest of the band, Hetfield was a young man under increasing pressure. This came in the form of an imposing deadline: a place on the bill of that summer's most prestigious stadium rock tour. The Monsters of Rock tour would be headlined by Van Halen. It would also feature Scorpions, Los Angeles power rockers Dokken (who, much to the astonishment of all, appeared on the bill in the slot immediately above Metallica) and German–American Led Zeppelin clones Kingdom Come. The caravan would begin its twenty-six-date run through the largest venues in America on May 27, with the first of three performances at the 37,000-seat Alpine Valley in East Troy, Wisconsin. In order to shake off the studio dust and re-engage their stage chops for a tour that would be witnessed by more than a million people, Metallica booked themselves into the Troubadour as Frayed Ends for a pair of performance on May 23 and 24. That they also chose to schedule interview time with Jon Pareles of the *New York Times* on the same days signifies that even in the pressurised environment in which they found themselves, Metallica had their eyes firmly fixed upon expanding their constituency further.

'It's gotten so safe,' determined Ulrich, speaking to Pareles about the state of metal. 'You put on some make-up, you spike your hair, you go out and sing about sex and driving fast cars and off you go, two million records.'

This from a man who had recently been involved in a high speed car crash en route to a party populated by porn stars.

With their noses pressed against a tour itinerary that stretched until the end of July, the group could also feel on the back of their necks the breath from another pressing concern. Rasmussen was contractually obligated to return to Sweet Silence Studios in the first week of May. As days drifted by, Metallica's workload increased in a manner in inverse proportion to the time the group had left in which to record.

With just ten days before the end of the studio sessions for . . . *And Justice for All*, the nine songs that had been committed to tape were complete save for one detail: not a single note of music had yet been played by Hammett. In spring 1988 modern metal was a genre defined in large part by the dexterity of a group's lead guitarist, a definition by which Metallica rated highly. Along with Hetfield's forensic rhythm playing, the talents which lay at the fingers of Hammett were one aspect of the group's sound that could plausibly be described as being world class. Despite this, the manner in which lead solos were enticed from the strings of Hammett's guitars was yet another example of the Metallica operation defying convention, if not logic itself. Each note the musician played was subject to the scrutiny of Ulrich, a man viewed by many as being deficient on the one instrument he himself played.

With the drummer's eyes upon him, and to Hammett's dismay, the seconds on the clock sped by faster than the notes he was trying to place together on top of . . . *And Justice for All*'s most frenetic songs. Towards the end of his time at the plate, the guitarist found himself eschewing sleep in order to meet the approaching deadline. Fatigue was such that it became increasingly difficult to physically bend the strings in the manner required to access the notes the musician could hear in his head. The frustration from this process led to exasperation and ill-temper, ingredients that lent Hammett's contributions an emotional intensity that negated any suggestion of the kind of glib flamboyance often associated with the trade of the heavy metal lead guitarist. With an invention born of necessity, Hammett's contributions on . . . *And Justice for All* can be said to resonate with the one ingredient least often associated with the kind of music played by a band such as Metallica: soul. Nowhere is this more apparent than on the lacerating solo that accompanies 'To Live Is To Die'.

'It was very, very hard work,' remembers Rasmussen today. 'It was long hours and a great deal of intensity. But although we worked hard I've got to say that I always enjoyed working with Metallica. The reason for that is because you could always see a progression. A much more difficult thing to do is work hard with a band and not see anything happening at all. When that happens, it's hell. But with Metallica you can see the progression and you could see that if you just kept going then soon enough you would be finished. And even though some of the tracking took days to complete, some of the bits were played in just one take. For example, Lars's machine-gun double bass runs in [the middle section of] "One" were done in one take. He just nailed it.'

The recording sessions for . . . *And Justice for All* ran so close to the producer's deadline that on the day before his flight to Copenhagen departed, Rasmussen entered One On One Studios and did not leave for more than twenty-four hours, his shift ending only as a taxi carrying his wife and their two children arrived to ferry the family to LA in time for their plane journey home.

Once fastened in his seat aboard the aeroplane, Flemming Rasmussen closed his eyes and did not open them again until he was awoken by the sound of rubber wheels screeching on the concrete surface of a Danish runway. At the time he did not, and could not, know that his association with Metallica had come to an end.

9 – THE FRAYED ENDS OF SANITY

Metallica had a name for them: tub tarts. The description wasn't of their own invention, but had been supplied to the band by their tour manager, Ian Jeffrey. Prior to joining the Bay Area quartet for the start of the Van Halen-headlined Monsters of Rock tour in May 1988, Jeffrey had been employed in the same capacity by Def Leppard. As the Sheffield band conquered America not once but twice in the Eighties with 1983's *Pyromania* album and its expensive successor, 1987's *Hysteria*, a trail rampaged across the country that befitted a working-class band with red-blooded appetites and a blue-chip profile. One of the road crew's non-contractual daily tasks was to find audience members of the opposite sex who were willing to express their appreciation for the Yorkshire band in ways that went beyond a round of applause.

In the years that preceded rock music shedding its skin and changing at least its outward appearance at the start of the Nineties, the culture of 'the groupie' was one that was often celebrated in the most gratuitous manner. This culture took the *Zeitgeist* of the age and distilled it down to its most carnal and logical elements. Success and celebrity were seen as forces deserving of physical rewards; for both the boys in the bands and the girls in their company, humanity counted for little.

The premise of the 'tub tart' was simple: each night on tour members of the road crew were sent out to find attractive women in the audience who might enjoy the company of the members of the band after the show had finished. The exact nature of such encounters would not be stated explicitly; instead, euphemistic propositions such as 'Would you like to come back and party?'

were used. But as imprecise as the language employed may have been, for the most part the invitee understood that the provision of a laminated backstage pass was a privilege that came with clearly defined, if not loudly spoken, responsibilities.

So it was that following the first date of the Monsters of Rock tour, Metallica bid good day to the thirty-odd thousand people gathered to see them at Alpine Valley in East Troy, Wisconsin, returned to their dressing area and were greeted by the sight of a room full of naked strangers.

'We came offstage and there were ten girls in the shower with soap and shampoo, ready to wash us,' recalls Lars Ulrich. 'It was like, we could probably get used to this and do it every night.' This the band tried to do. 'Let's cut to the chase, once they're naked in the shower getting their hair wet you don't have to go very far to [take] the next step – "a home run", as the Americans call it. That was good fun.' In answer to the question, 'Were any of the young women standing around fully clothed?', the drummer replies, 'Not for long. They were either asked to vacate [the area] or get busy.'

In the twenty-first century the first two components of the Ian Dury-coined phrase 'sex and drugs and rock 'n' roll' have shrunk from view. The last mainstream rock band to embrace this most giddily hedonistic of philosophies were Muse, who did so with a gusto that was more cheeky than chauvinistic in intention. Elsewhere the tone that greets the kind of behaviour celebrated a generation ago (at least in the rock press) is one of prissiness. In an age that is at once more accessible and more suspicious than those of the penultimate decade of the twentieth century, few journalists would dream of asking a modern metal band the last time they were fellated by a stranger while wearing the clothes in which they had just performed onstage.

But while in 1988 Metallica made music that stood in diametric opposition to the kind of rock fare otherwise beloved of mainstream audiences, only one member of the union saw fit to demur at the kind of activities indulged in by groups who looked like girls.

'Jason Newsted might have been slightly less involved . . . than the other band members,' is Ulrich's recollection.

For his part, the bassist is of the rather sweet belief that 'people aren't going to like' the fact that, when it came such pleasures of the flesh, he was 'a little too righteous, maybe'.

'Those guys really went for it, James and Lars especially,' is Newsted's memory. 'Lars would probably be the king as far as that crazy promiscuity [went]; blow jobs under the stage during the bass solo, kind of stuff. That's definitely Lars' territory. I definitely had some beautiful models and wonderful relationships with actresses. I remember their names and still talk to them.'

That Newsted believes the fact that he can recall the name of someone with whom he has kept intimate company to be a measure of virtue does not speak highly of the standards of the age. But perhaps this is understandable, given that each evening while on tour the bassist would stand onstage and play to the beat kept by a drummer of whom it was said would not leave the venue until he had received oral sex from a stranger in the audience.

'No, that's not true,' says Ulrich, while at the same time admitting, 'It was rare that [this] didn't happen.'

'It was amazing,' he says, 'this American thing with blow jobs. It was a cultural phenomenon. I don't know what it is about a tour bus that makes a girl want to suck a guy off, but apparently tour buses had that effect on a certain part of the population of America in the mid-Eighties. When you're twenty-one years old and full of spunk, that's okay.'

Not that Ulrich could really be blamed for allowing success to go to his head in more than one sense of the term. Despite a position on the bill that underestimated his group's standing to the point of being negligent, the heaviest and most uncompromising group on the Monsters of Rock roster were busy making friends in large places. Despite a shift that began at the not exactly rocking hour of 2 p.m. and which lasted for a mere sixty minutes, Metallica's appearance underneath the punishing sun of the American summer was proving a huge financial success. As scores of thousands of fans were permitted entry through the turnstiles of such venues as New Jersey's Giants Stadium, the Silverdome in Detroit and the Coliseum in Los Angeles – the latter being the centrepiece of the Olympic Games four years earlier – the second band on the bill made a mockery of the conventional wisdom that the larger a crowd the more simple the music being played must be in order to keep its members entertained. At the merchandise stands, the only item of apparel to sell in quantities greater than Metallica's own garments was the official Monsters of Rock T-shirt, a fact that did not go unnoticed further up the event's supposed chain of command.

Such was the demand for the band's apparel that Hetfield was moved to tell an acquaintance, 'Dude, we made a million dollars today – in cotton.'

'[Metallica will be] the new kings of rock, just you wait and see,' commented Van Halen front man Sammy Hagar, apparently oblivious to the fact that for an increasingly large number of people this wait was already over.

Of course, Ulrich knew the truth of Hagar's prediction long before 'The Red Rocker' (or anyone else, for that matter) had ever heard his band's name. Aside from a handful of concert dates in the north-eastern states of the United States, this was Metallica's first US tour since the group opened and then stole the show from Ozzy Osbourne two summers previously. While on the road with Van Halen, the Bay Area quartet were once more partaking variously in sex and drugs and rock 'n' roll and the evidence before their eyes from the stages of the country's largest stadia suggested yet another Ian Dury-authored idiom: reasons to be cheerful.

'Obviously there's some kind of buzz on us and from Van Halen's point of view I guess it seemed like a good idea to take us out [on tour] because we're different from the other bands,' was Ulrich's opinion, sounding only slightly too big for his basketball boots. Elsewhere, though, with his working day finished just sixty minutes after it began, the drummer had the rest of each day in which to join his band mates in the pursuit of getting as drunk as was humanly possible.

'Basically, at that time, we used to start drinking when we woke up,' he remembers (which, on the Monsters of Rock tour was eleven o'clock in the morning). 'We'd get the gig over by three o'clock, and then we'd have eight or nine hours [in which] to drink. It was awesome. That was our first exposure to big crowds, like 50,000 people every day. We were just drunk basically all the time. The not-giving-a-fuck meter was peaking.'

Ulrich's memories of Metallica's summer as part of the Monsters of Rock caravan concur with those of Hetfield, who recalls that his band 'were drunk the whole time'.

'We were very much into drinking and having a good fucking time,' reveals the front man. 'That was the pinnacle of all the debauchery, drinking, fucking and general insanity.' Elsewhere, the front man would recall that 'after that tour, I went back to a lot of cities, when we went out on our own, and people, uh, kind of didn't like me, and I didn't know why. People would come up [and say], "Yeah, you don't remember grabbing my girlfriend's tits?" or something really rude I'd done when I was really fucked up and basically didn't remember what was going on. You'd come back into town [and say], "Hey, how's it goin'?" and people would give you the evil eye.'

As ever, though, Metallica's energies as they were applied to the business of bending the elbow, or someone's else's waist, were equalled by their creative energies. Given that the culmination of the recording sessions for . . . *And Justice for All* had buffeted

so tightly against their two warm-up concerts for the Monsters
of Rock tour that the four musicians might as well have caught
a cab straight from the studio to the nightclub's stage door, at
the start of the Monsters of Rock tour this was a unit that was
sorely under-rehearsed. This state of affairs, though, escaped
mention amid the fervour that surrounded the group's return to
the live arena. But even the rapture of this most compelling of
groups appearing before a most committed of audiences could
not obscure the fact that Metallica were caught in the headlights
of yet another fast-approaching deadline.

With a release date scheduled for August, as spring became
summer . . . *And Justice for All*'s nine songs were as yet unmixed.
Despite his exceptional work on *Master of Puppets*, the services of
Michael Wagener were deemed surplus to requirements. Instead,
the task of setting the levels for Metallica's latest recording
was handed to Steve Thompson and Michael Barbiero, who
had worked on material as varied as Guns N' Roses *Appetite
for Destruction* and Whitney Houston's 'I Wanna Dance with
Somebody'. Yet despite engaging these two expensive studio
technicians, Hetfield and Ulrich once again proved unwilling
to delegate and instead occupied much of their time attempting
to impose their own vision upon the two men. Whenever the
Monsters of Rock tour rested in order that the vast bulk of its
equipment might be transported across city and state lines,
Metallica's front man and drummer would journey to the studio
at which their forthcoming album was being mixed with the aim
of retaining absolute control of the proceedings.

For the vast majority of bands, this workload would have
proved intolerable. For Hetfield and Ulrich, however, such an
intense schedule was a fair price for men intent on having their
beer and drinking it, en route to demanding a double vodka.

'You have to keep in mind that we were continuously
inebriated from '87 through '89,' remembers Newsted. 'It was

mostly drinking – I know that Kirk and Lars got into some powders and stuff like that, and I used to smoke some herb back then, but mostly [it was just] drink. And that was part of the deal – we were pretty wasted and [Hetfield and Ulrich] were trying to burn the candles at both ends, mixing the record and doing the shows at the same time.'

. . . *And Justice for All* was mixed at Bearsville Studios in Bearsville, a picturesque town situated amid the postcard vistas of the Catskill Mountains in Upstate New York. Opened in 1969 by Albert Grossman, the manager of Bob Dylan, Janis Joplin and the Band, in the intervening years the studio has been the site for music recorded by such artists as the Rolling Stones, REM and Patti Smith. With its high ceilings and wooden beams the facility is well-suited to the aesthetic of rural Upstate New York; what it is not, however, is easily accessible.

In order to reach Bearsville Hetfield and Ulrich were required to fly in to one of the three airports serving New York City and then drive for two hours towards the Catskills. With time as an enemy, the only plausible reason for situating themselves in such a remote location – and by doing so eschewing the facilities provided by the dozens of recording studios in both New York City and Los Angeles – was the belief that Bearsville Studios would enable the group to release an album the sound of which would be unlike any other album of its kind. In this they were right: it sounded worse.

In the years that have elapsed since the recording and release of what was for the longest time Metallica's most divisive collection, few topics have been as widely discussed as to the nature of the sound heard on . . . *And Justice for All*. Many have glared in the direction of producer Flemming Rasmussen. The journalist Xavier Russell is not alone in his opinion that 'the production on that record really let them down' to the point where the writer believes the release amounts to nothing more than 'one of the worst-produced records I've ever heard – I just didn't understand what they were trying to do. They lost me on [that album].'

When such a point of view is presented to Rasmussen himself, however, his response is unequivocal even by the standards of the plain-speaking Scandinavian.

'The reason the album sounds like it does is down to the mix, not the production,' he says. 'But because of the way it was supposed to be set up with Mike Clink as producer, Steve Thompson and Mike Barbiero had already been hired as the people who were going to mix the record. The idea was to have the same team that did *Appetite for Destruction*. But it didn't work out like that.'

In summer 1988 Hetfield and Ulrich were artists incapable of taking direction. Worse yet, at this point in the group's development each man's opinion as to what would best serve Metallica's creative whole was so self-fulfilling as to be self-defeating. Hetfield wanted his guitars be the album's focal point, while Ulrich (for reasons that can only be described as 'perverse') desired that his drums stand front and centre stage.

The first time the pair arrived at Bearsville Studios, Thompson and Barbiero handed the musicians a tape of a rough mix of the album that they themselves were pleased with. Believing that their work would act as the starting point from which a finished mix might emanate, instead the technicians were instructed that their efforts were unsatisfactory. In a manner suggesting a forearm transferring the pieces of a chess set from board to floor, Thompson and Barbiero were advised that, for a start, the bass guitar should be faded down by no fewer than three decibels. So determined were Metallica to revolutionise heavy metal that they were putting their name to an album that might as well have been titled 'Small Bottom'.

'I heard the mix and thought, "Where the fuck is the bass?"' says Rasmussen, echoing a question that would resonate for more than a quarter of a century. 'And it's a shame as well because Jason was more than up to the job. His playing on that album is really, really good. The bass tracks he recorded are fabulous.' He pauses for a second, considers something in the middle distance and laughs as if confronted by the sight of gallows. 'I just wish that someone could have heard them,' he says.

Since that summer it has often been said that the lack of bass guitar evident on . . . *And Justice for All* is a personal slight to Newsted. At the time Ulrich was keen to assert that it could be explained by the fact that the tone of Hetfield's rhythm guitar occupied the same frequency as that of his group's newest member, thus eclipsing his contribution. While such reasoning amounts to more than mere obfuscation on the drummer's part, at the same time such a sentiment serves to articulate the symptoms of a condition rather than its cause. At the time Hetfield and Ulrich treated its newest member as the manner they did for no more significant a reason than the fact that they could.

'To answer [the] question about the intentional thing, maybe they were still exorcising that thing that they were still trying to deal with,' says Newsted, once more confronted by the spectre of a ghost in flared denim jeans. 'That was still present, absolutely. They didn't know how to channel those feelings and those emotions at that time. It wasn't something they had the capacity for. When you get young guys together and they all become millionaires by the age [of] twenty-five, you miss a few developmental stages that everyone else – people who live a less-accelerated lifestyle – go through. So the developmental things could've played a part in them just keeping the bass down rather than going through and listening to what was played good and what wasn't played good.'

Ulrich himself maintains that the slight visited upon Newsted 'wasn't intentional'.

'It wasn't [a case of] "Fuck this guy – let's turn his bass

down,"' he says. 'It was more like, "We're mixing, so let's pat ourselves on the back and turn the rhythms and the drums up." But we basically kept turning everything else up until the bass disappeared.'

Newsted regarded the decisions made during the mixing of . . . *And Justice for All* as lacking both clarity and a defined sense of purpose. But like the butler who sees all yet says nothing, at the time he kept his thoughts and ideas within his station.

In retrospect Newsted would publicly question the wisdom of Hetfield and Ulrich 'being drunk at three o' clock in the afternoon' at the same time as heading to work in 'some studio in Upstate New York with a couple of cats [Thompson and Barbiero] who are getting paid real good and [couldn't] really give a shit about being there or not at some times . . . guys who were assigned to make a certain product sound a certain way. This was a chance for Metallica to get on the radio, so they're mixing with that kind of thing in mind – those were the kind of people who were hired to mix the record. Look at the credits – those were people who mixed radio songs. Those weren't the guys who mixed Sepultura records.'

One wonders just what kind of madness possessed either Metallica or their advisors into thinking that their presence would be permitted to grace the playlist of any American FM rock station. As Hetfield and Ulrich fumbled their way towards completing the mix on an album the sound of which would at the time leave some at Elektra Records keenly displeased, the realisation that the chances of anyone outside a handful of DJs putting any of these songs onto the air was vanishingly small must have crossed their minds.

An album that would occupy two vinyl discs yet would not once be referred to as a 'double album', . . . *And Justice for All* is both a *folie à deux* shared by Hetfield and Ulrich as well as a logical interpretation of its authors' sound as heard by the band themselves. Unlike virtually any other group, in the studio Metallica recorded the bass lines to their songs *after* those of the rhythm guitar, meaning that in a conventional sense the band had no rhythm section. Elsewhere, in concert Ulrich would beat his drums surrounded by monitors that carried only the sound of Hetfield's guitars, a decision that contravened the conventional rock wisdom that the union between a drummer and a bass player provided the foundations upon which great bands are built. That Metallica could set their face against a principle as fundamentally held as this goes some way to explaining why in a period when the group's bootstraps were tightening and where guidance went unsought, the sound of the music being recorded should contort to such an unbalanced degree.

'It's the only record of ours that I'm not entirely comfortable with,' Ulrich would reflect fourteen years later. 'It became about ability and almost athletics, rather than music.' Elsewhere, the drummer would observe that with their fourth album 'we'd taken that side of Metallica to the end – there was no place else to go with it.'

†

Preceded by the twelve-inch single 'Harvester of Sorrow', . . . *And Justice for All* met its waiting public on September 5, 1988 (with the release coming a day later in the United States). Despite claiming afterwards that the length of the songs and the sound of the album left him feeling alienated, writing in *Kerrang!* in the dog days of August Xavier Russell appeared to have no such qualms regarding the quality and significance of the music he was hearing. 'Here it is folks,' began his review, 'Metallika's [*sic*] finest album since *Kill 'Em All*. Yeah, I kan't [*sic*] believe it either, even though Lars himself recently told me that people have already been saying that . . . *And Justice for All* is THE METAL ALBUM OF THE '80s!' Clearly unconcerned that such a grandiose opening sentence might one day come to back to haunt him, Russell does go on to say that 'the first thing you notice when you hear the album is Lars' drum sound, which is really odd, and I kan't [*sic*] quite put my finger on it.' More than this, the critic admits that the production and mix of . . . *And Justice for All* combine to leave him feeling 'baffled', before quickly dismissing this bamboozlement with the shrug of a sentence, 'It's all part of the METALLISOUND – just listen to [the] opening snare beats on "Blackened" and you'll see what I mean.'

To the ears of many of Metallica's core constituents, . . . *And Justice for* All is the third instalment in what has come to be viewed as a Holy Trinity. A number of adherents go further than this, however, and regard the album as being the last of the group's releases to be worthy of credit or attention; a last hurrah before the well was poisoned by compromise and betrayal. To those who hold – actually, cling – to such an opinion, the nine songs that comprise Metallica's final album of the Eighties would represent both the high-water mark and the calling of time on its creators' position as being the standard-bearers for those who plied their trade on the front line of modern heavy metal.

That an army of listeners should clutch so tightly to this notion is odd, not least because as an album . . . *And Justice for All* really isn't very heavy at all. Anchored by a drum sound no more emphatic than the click of a playing card struck repeatedly by the spokes of a child's bicycle, Metallica as represented here are a band the sound of which is dry and nagging rather than emboldened and emphatic. The preference of rhythm guitar parts over bass notes serves to inform a tonal range that is sufficiently airless as to seem vacuum-packed. With Hetfield's dry (if largely effective) vocals and Hammett's piercingly pronounced lead guitar solos, . . . *And Justice for All*'s preference for treble at the expense of bass is so pronounced as to make the theme for 'Looney Tunes' sound like the chimes of Big Ben.

As befits an album as naggingly insistent as a car alarm, Metallica's first album following the death of Cliff Burton is an often gruelling exercise. Taking the notion that 'less is more' and throwing it into the bins at the back of One On One Studios, the convolutions in the middle section of a song such 'The Frayed Ends of Sanity' – a composition the quality of which would be improved greatly were its duration trimmed by two or three minutes – are so complex that it comes as a surprise that the track ever finds its conclusion.

Elsewhere, the band's relentless meanderings become first numbing and then boring. There is something noble and persistent about Metallica's refusal to conform to many of the conventions of modern rock music as it was heard in 1988, but such was the insistence of this mindset that often the group's idiosyncrasies became arch and fussy. This tendency is particularly pronounced as it relates to Lars Ulrich. With the drums already egomaniacally loud in the mix, the Dane's declination to locate and engage with any kind of a groove suggests that the man tasked with keeping time for Metallica is often is doing so while attempting to calm a bout of delirium tremens. As Ulrich leads the way into the sprawling middle section of the album's title track, the listener is left wondering if the band to which he or she – at the time, almost invariably a 'he' – is listening have stolen an earth-shifter only to fall asleep at the wheel.

There are many moments, however, when even their best efforts cannot obscure the brilliance of the material contained within . . . *And Justice for All*. Taking as its blueprint both 'Fade to Black' and 'Welcome Home (Sanitarium)', 'One' provides a master class in the execution of dynamic possibilities, its authors guiding the listener from a hauntingly tranquil opening to a denouement the relentless precision of which suggests a sky filled with strafing bullets. This, though, seems as nothing when placed alongside the harnessed fury of 'Dyers Eve', a song that while adhering to thrash metal's beats-per-minute ratio – and then some – also qualifies as one of Metallica's most progressive compositions, with the music's jagged rocks providing the perfect foil for a searing lyric narrated from a standpoint equidistant between violent rage and perfect vulnerability. Better still is the barracking tempo of the never fully unleashed 'The Shortest Straw', the musical arrangement of which suggests a rat careering through the walls of a maze that offers no chance of either reward or escape.

This latter song had as its lyrical inspiration Victor S. Navasky's masterful 1980 book, *Naming Names*, recommended to Hetfield by Cliff Burnstein; the track takes as its subject matter the ideological and intellectual civil war into which America descended in the post-war era with the House of Un-American Activities, the work of Senator Joe McCarthy and the blacklisting of artists as well of swathes of people working in Hollywood suspected of being communists (or of having socialistic sympathies), without due process and often without any foundation in truth. But 'The Shortest Straw' is not a song *about* such topics, rather one which takes this period of American history and shapes it into a lyric that somehow manages to distil the sense of paranoia and dread prevalent during this period and place it in a context the authors can claim to be their own. A knowledge of the activities of such characters as J. Edgar Hoover or Joe McCarthy is not a prerequisite for appreciating or 'understanding' Hetfield's words. In this, the song is not driven by its subject but is rather merely informed by the universal emotions inherent in the tale, as with perfect economy the front man speaks of a 'witch-hunt riding through', and of 'channels red, one word said, blacklisted, with vertigo make you dead'.

One key distinction between Metallica and even the heaviest of metal bands plying a trade in 1988 was the gravitas of the group's lyrics. For most acts of the type in the late 1980s, the words printed on a lyric sheet were merely an afterthought. Whether it be Iron Maiden spinning yarns of prophets peering into crystal balls in 'Can I Play with Madness' or Slayer revelling in the topic of abortion – 'extraction, termination, pain's agonising stain' – on 'Silent Scream', the words sung were tailored to the bespoke specification of the music rather than from any kind of personal investment on the part of the lyricists themselves. For James Hetfield, though, the more words he wrote the more he revealed of his complex and troubled inner self. As these primal screams were hurled into the darkness, a sea of restless and disenfranchised listeners stirred with an attentiveness unreserved for other groups of their type.

There were, though, exceptions to this rule. With a body of work featuring songs about such topics as the desire to escape from a mental hospital and a toll placed upon Egyptians levied in the form of a first-born son, it would be folly to suggest that Hetfield was not above dirtying his hands with heavy metal clichés. Worse yet, on some parts of . . . *And Justice for All* the writer appears to be suffering from a tin ear. Not for one moment of the nine minutes and forty-four seconds it takes for its authors to slog their way through the album's title track does one believe that Hetfield is ever fully engaged with the subject about which he is singing. With its title cribbed from Norman Jewison's 1979 film of the same name, as a sentiment expressed in song '. . . And Justice for All' is as compelling as a legal argument filibustering its way from the floor of the House of Representatives. Brittle and artless, Hetfield sings of the 'halls of justice [being] painted green' and of 'money talking' before concluding that 'justice is lost, justice is raped, justice is gone', a ruling that fails to examine the plight of those who suffer from this state of affairs, or how. 'It was,' remembers Xavier Russell, 'like Ross Halfin used to say: "Justice is this, Justice is that, Justice is nine and a half minutes long."'

'I call [. . . *And Justice for All*] the complaining album,' recalls Hetfield. 'Lyrically, we were really into social things, watching CNN and the news all the time, and realising that other people really do kinda control your life. The movie . . . *And Justice For All* turned our heads a little bit. We discovered how much money influences certain things, and discovered how things work in the United States. How things might seem okay on the outside, but internally, they're corrupt.'

Elsewhere, though, the front man's recollections regarding his thoughts as expressed on . . . *And Justice for All* take a different form. 'It's not me sitting and reading the paper, going, "Oh, I have to write about terrorists; it's a good subject, real popular now," he says, before identifying 'drinking' as being the muse from which the album's many bitter fruits would blossom.

'Really [it was] drinking and thinking, [just] seeing what's going on around me,' Hetfield recalls.

What is most striking, however, is not that Metallica chose to author songs concerning the environmental plight of the planet, or against those who should choose to attack one's personal liberty, but how such topics should be articulated by a lyricist whose point of view was grim and tenaciously pessimistic. By the time the album's opening song, 'Blackened', has drawn to a close, Hetfield has had cause to employ the words 'death', 'dead' and 'dying' no fewer than ten times.

Despite all this, or because of it, . . . *And Justice for All* flew out of the world's record shops in numbers normally associated with albums propelled by hit singles. A week after its release, Metallica's latest album debuted at no. 6 in the US *Billboard* Hot 200 and at no. 4 on the UK album chart. By the end of the year, the nine-song set would have found its way into the homes of 1.7 million listeners in the United States alone.

'I can remember being pretty shocked when I was talking to a record company person after [. . . *And Justice For All*] was finished, right before it was actually released,' remembers Kirk Hammett. 'He was like, "Yeah man, it's probably going to sell a million [copies] in the first couple of weeks." And I was like, "No way." And he was like, "Yes, way." I thought it was too heavy and too progressive and there was no way it would sell that much. But you know what? It sold more in those first two weeks than he even talked about. We were [touring in] Europe when it was released, and it charted really high – the highest we'd ever charted in the States. It was insane. We just couldn't believe it . . . it all just came together. All the right things happened at the right time. It was just our time, I guess.'

Elsewhere, one of Hetfield's most vivid memories of his group's first million-selling album came when 'some friends of mine called me up and went, "Hey man – I hear you went platinum!" [They said] "Just quit and come home, give up and start a new thing. The new thing is to quit." Can you imagine [the headline]? "Metallica goes platinum and quits!"'

Metallica, of course, were about to do no such thing. Propelled by unflinching music and the attentions of a fan base that was already beginning to take on the appearance of one of the most dedicated in modern music, the quartet merrily kicked and punched their way through walls with an ease that suggested no obstacle was sufficient to detain them. On September 24 the quartet arrived in Scotland for the first of two appearances at the Playhouse Theatre in Edinburgh in what would be the opening night of a fourteen-date tour of Great Britain and the Republic of Ireland. Supported by the muscular yet ominous thud of Danzig – the titular group founded by former Misfits and Samhain front man Glenn Danzig – the excursion saw the headliners improve their station by performing their first arena show on English soil (a date at Birmingham's National Exhibition Centre on September 29) as well as finding themselves embedded beneath the Westway in London for a three-night stand at the Hammersmith Odeon, a venue no better suited to a band of Metallica's hue than it had been two years earlier.

With . . . *And Justice for All*'s place as the most gruelling and unlikely platinum rock album of the Eighties secure, its creators found that their uncooperative approach was fast approaching its logical conclusion. The group now faced a choice. They could continue upon the path they had trod since the release of *Master of Puppets*, a proposition which promised a significant level of success but not of a kind that could be described as being 'mainstream'. Were the group to choose such a course, Metallica could lay claim to being the ideological heir-apparent to another of the Bay Area's most significant and outstanding acts, the Grateful Dead. The second option, however, required that the quartet permit themselves to be presented in a manner that had to date been viewed as being anathema to their spirit. In order for the commercial momentum of . . . *And Justice for All* to continue to prosper, they would be required to make a promotional music video.

Given that in the Eighties virtually all hard rock and metal videos aired on MTV were facile and interchangeable, Metallica's decision to eschew the form was entirely sensible. Furthermore, the group consisted of a union of musicians, not film-makers; in order to make a promotional clip the band would be forced to collaborate with directors and editors, a process which by definition amounted to a surrender of control. Yet, despite this resistance, the fact that it took the band until their fourth album – three of which had emerged in the United States on a major label – to even consider the notion that the qualities inherent in their music might be translated to film is something of a curiosity. If Metallica were so fearful of the kind of cliché and stupidity associated with a certain kind of music, the group's members would surely never have united to form a heavy metal band in the first place.

'We never said that we wouldn't do [a music video],' recalls Hammett. 'That's often misperceived. Our attitude was that videos sucked and we weren't going to make some fuckin' thing with a bunch of chicks dancing around and us driving Ferraris down Sunset Strip. There was a lot of [those kind of clips] at that time. But it came to the point where we could either make a video that *wasn't* that, or we could not make one at all. So we ended up making a video that was just so much *not* that.'

The song Metallica chose to accompany their first music video was 'One'. Despite being some distance from the prototypical hit single, the track at least began in a manner sufficiently tranquil as to suggest the possibility of it remaining in the VHS recorders of TV executives long enough for James Hetfield to sing the song's opening line. This too seemed innocuous enough, with the narrator revealing 'I can't remember anything, can't tell if this is true or dream.' From here, though, the horror of the subject's surroundings begins to unfold in the story of a man whose experiences at the front line of human conflict have rendered him a 'war-time novelty' condemned to spend the rest of his life wishing for death.

Within weeks of the news that this was to be the song to which Metallica would marry their first music video, 'One' became the most widely discussed of all of the authors' creations. Tellingly, the topic of discussion concerned an aspect of the song most commonly overlooked by fans of modern metal: the lyrics. By the winter of 1989 no Metallica fan worthy of the name was ignorant of the fact that the composition took as its inspiration the 1939 Dalton Trumbo book and 1971 film *Johnny Got His Gun*, the centrepiece of which featured a soldier who had returned from the First World War a hospital-bed-ridden quadruple amputee with no sense of sight, taste, hearing or smell. Along with this, the band's audience were also informed that Trumbo had himself been a victim of the kind of blacklisting profiled in 'The Shortest

Straw', a fact that was giddily repeated by English teenagers who days before had never heard of people hunting communists as if they were witches.

It may have taken Metallica more than five years to consent to making a music video, but once the group had decided upon this course of action they were quick to marshal their forces. Keen to the point of obsession to avoid the kind of clichés common at the time, Q Prime were instructed by their charges to buy the rights to the film version of *Johnny Got His Gun*, a brilliant and unconventional idea. Licence secured, the group turned their attentions towards finding a film-maker capable of marrying the images from the motion picture with yet-to-be-shot footage of Metallica performing as live musicians.

The group opted to hire the services of directors Michael Salomon and Bill Pope, the latter of whom would go on to work as the cinematographer on pictures by *Evil Dead* director Sam Raimi as well as *The Matrix* film trilogy. This choice of collaborators, though, was informed not so much by the lofty ideals of a unified creative 'vision' but rather by the need to secure someone, anyone, willing to accept a commission from the band.

'At the time there wasn't much interest among big directors to get involved with Metallica,' recalls Michael Salomon. 'They were thought of as a fringe group. They brought me in to give the whole thing shape. They realised the project was an editorial job because they wanted to use so much of the movie. They probably saw it as a logistical nightmare that they could just dump in my lap.'

A clip was needed that would be as much a trailer for a film as a promotional tool in the conventional sense of the term. Metallica therefore consented to the idea that part of the video for 'One' would show the group performing the track live, playing their instruments together as for a live performance. With MTV at the time lousy with long-haired Americans playing loud guitars and beating drums in a manner befitting Captain Caveman, it would be this aspect of the video's production which would require the most careful navigation in order that its subjects avoid comparison with the kind of groups they otherwise wished to destroy. In order that this aim might be realised, Metallica chose to be filmed performing not on a sound stage dolled up to resemble the stage of an American 'enormodome' but rather on the concrete floor of a disused warehouse in the Long Beach area of Greater Los Angeles. As the group convened at this location, the men responsible for operating the cameras were told that their subjects would be playing 'One' live rather than simply miming to an audio track, a trick that was to prove harder than it looked.

One of the remarkable aspects of the video that accompanies 'One' is just how well the footage of Metallica themselves has aged. Captured in a gentle monochromatic wash rather than the soda-pop Technicolor preferred at the time, the band perform their composition dressed in street clothes that whether by luck or design have stood the test of time. Yet despite their 'everyman' appearance, the quartet perform with an aplomb that belies the fact that this was the first time any of the musicians had been asked to play for the attentions of a film crew rather than a live audience. Aside from being occasionally met by Hetfield's baleful gaze, the camera is at best tolerated and often ignored by the musicians upon whom its lens is trained. Instead Metallica set about their business with a grim determination. The players' eyes decline to make contact with other figures in the frame, choosing instead to fixate on some point in the middle distance. With seemingly little in the form of human emotion to command its attention, the camera shifts its focus from the musicians to the instruments the men are playing. Such is the combined unity of purpose on display that when a member of the group does deviate from the norm of collective determination – as when Hetfield angrily twitches his head in order to shift errant hairs from his face – the effect is like lightning fracturing the calm of a midnight sky.

The clip, though, is set apart not by Metallica but by the carefully appointed segments seconded from *Johnny Got His Gun*, moments which are deposited so as to slowly heighten the sense of horror regarding the plight of the song's subject. Attended to in his hospital bed by representatives of the armed forces and the medical profession, the torso of soldier Joe Bonham is seen on film with his disfigured face obscured by a crude mask, his head moving only to tap out on the pillow on which it rests a request in Morse code that his life be ended. The video's final scene sees the forcible removal from the hospital room of a nurse who had attempted but failed to comply with this request. As if this were not all quite grim enough, the short film also features fragments of an 'inner monologue' from the stricken patient, his voice pitched to a level of pathetic hopelessness that is as persistent and discomforting as white noise.

On being shown the finished video for 'One', however, Metallica were worried about putting their name to a music video that did not feature much music. Michael Salomon remembers that the band were 'taken aback by how much of the movie I put in there'.

'It's a complicated story and to do it with just one or two sound bites here and there really wouldn't have made it,' says the film-maker. 'Basically every time there was an extended intro or solo I covered the whole thing up. The musician side of them said, 'That's not cool, we don't get to hear the music.' I think they realised, though, that the story element was more important.'

'We managed to avoid the bright-lights shit,' recalls Lars Ulrich. 'The focus was to have something with a strong storyline running through it as opposed to us running around with lights and ramps and shit. It just seemed that we had to do something radically different. We decided that if [the video clip] was not what we wanted we'd throw it in the garbage can. [But] Pretty early on we felt we had something special on our hands; whether it was great or shit, it meant something.'

After viewing the clip MTV were of a mind to bury the thing under a rock. Speaking to Cliff Burnstein – the man who had introduced Hetfield to the book *Johnny Got His Gun* in the first instance – a representative of the then all-conquering music channel told the band's co-manager that the only way the clip would be viewed on television was on the news, whatever that meant.

Metallica would eventually edit the video clip for 'One' to a length more manageable than its original eight-minute duration (in fact ultimately the clip would be cut into three different versions). The film in its original (and best) form, though, made its world première on MTV's *Headbangers Ball* on January 22 1989, an appearance which, despite the forewarnings of the representative that had spoken to Cliff Burnstein, had been heavily trailed so as to attract the attentions of the band's ever-growing fan base. Once aired, the video quickly became the most heavily requested item on the programme's roster. This allowed Metallica to escape the confines of the weekly two-hour slot occupied by *Headbangers Ball* and to make their break for the wider waters of MTV's evening playlist. Within weeks, the song found itself occupying the no. 1 slot on MTV's weekly video countdown, the first time such a feat had been achieved by a metal band.

'I remember watching the video for the first time and thinking, "Wow, this is like nothing else that's on MTV right now. I can't believe they're actually playing it,"' recalls Kirk Hammett. 'That was mind-blowing to me. I remember sitting there one night, watching MTV and all this crap they were playing, and then our video came on. When it was over the VJ [Video Jockey] came on and said, "Wow, that's depressing. On a happier note, here's Huey Lewis and the News!"'

†

With a Top 10 album and a promotional music video that was both a creative and commercial smash, Metallica were beginning to take on the appearance of a band that belonged in the mainstream. Yet if this were the case, the quartet occupied a space *in* the mainstream without remotely conforming to the tides emanating from it.

But if the band did not think much of the esteemed company with whom they now brushed shoulders, the feeling was mutual. In a manner that would exceed the flourishes of the pen of even the most daring of dramatists, this impasse of mistrust was given full expression live on American network television. The occasion was the 31st Grammy Awards, held on February 22, 1989 at the Shrine Auditorium in Los Angeles. A gathering of the music industry's most (commercially) successful acts as well as the power-brokers and kingmakers in operation away from the spotlight, 'the Grammys' was the Super Bowl of the record business, the evening when the National Academy of Recording Arts and Sciences handed out sashes and gongs to what it believed to be its most deserving of subjects. 1989 was the first year this body recognised the genres of heavy metal and rap, and it was in the former category that Metallica were nominated. Along with this, the quartet were invited to perform 'One' live from the stage of the Shrine Auditorium.

That Metallica were offered such a berth was a remarkable concession on the part of a body that had certainly never before given house-room to a group of this kind. The quartet's place in the running order was as unlikely as the Sex Pistols being offered the chance to perform at the Royal Variety Performance a decade or so earlier. As with the English group, the Bay Area band were in large part defined by the things against which they stood in opposition. The invitation from the National Academy of Recording Arts and Sciences offered the first hint that Metallica were soon to run out of avenues for rebellion.

'It was a new thing for us,' recalls Hetfield. 'I remember our manager coming and saying, 'They want you to play the Grammys.

I thought, "Oh man, I don't wanna fuckin' be a part of this crap."
But then [again] it was, like, hey, this is an opportunity. You don't
get to do this every day, a chance to get on national TV and
show all these boring fucks what we're all about. So we kinda
turned the whole thing round to our advantage, instead of kinda
running away and hiding from it.'

It was in this spirit of open-armed embrace that Metallica
arrived at the Shrine Auditorium in order to sound check in
preparation for their first ever appearance on network television.
Amid the flurry of runners with clipboards and producers with
schedules buffeted by the countless commercial breaks seen on
American TV, the band were issued with a list of things prohibited
by the live broadcast. This news warily digested, the musicians
proceeded to position themselves on the stage and in front of
6,300 empty seats began to play 'One'. Thirty-three seconds into
the song, as Ulrich's drums punctured the tranquil soundscape
established by Hetfield and Hammett's guitars, Metallica were
forced to abandon their efforts as a functionary stormed their
stage and told the band that there was no way they would be
permitted to make that kind of racket on a prime-time television
show.

Come the evening of the performance itself, Metallica
proved willing to cut their cloth to the demands of the occasion.
Appearing on a stage designed as if to resemble an alleyway
behind the kind of hotel to which the police are called on a regular
basis, the group performed a number truncated by more than
two minutes from its original length. Neither the sight nor the
sound of the performance is particularly edifying. Throughout
the song's two verses and three choruses, Hetfield's vocals drift in
and out of tune, while behind him, illuminated only by gloomy
back-lighting, a topless Ulrich flails around like something that
lives in a bin on Sesame Street. Most striking of all though is
the impression that the musicians are playing for the benefit of

a brick wall. Throughout the performance, the camera declines to transfer its attentions from the people onstage to those in the audience, an editorial decision that lends the clip a functional quality shorn of human emotion.

'Looking out there and seeing people's faces, and all these black and white tuxes [was strange],' remembers James Hetfield. In words dismissive even by his own standards, the front man recalls how 'everyone had rented their nice fuckin' suit, and were sitting down and were expecting some nice little awards show. It was like, "Oh, we'll have a cocktail," all this kinda crap. "Ahhhh, terrific, let's do lunch!" All that crap. Then we got up there and just started bashing away. [The audience] basically had to clap. I'm sure if they were sitting there by themselves, there's no way they would have clapped. They would have got up and left!'

When it came time for Metallica to leave, they did so empty-handed. Nominated alongside AC/DC, emerging alternative rock pioneers Jane's Addiction, English folk-rock eccentrics Jethro Tull and Ann Arbor proto-punk icon Iggy Pop, the award for Best Hard Rock [and] Metal Performance (Vocal or Instrumental) was presented by veteran Michigan shock-rocker Alice Cooper and former Runaway-turned-power rock bombshell Lita Ford. As Cooper opens a cream-coloured envelope inside which is written the winner's name, even years performing to the unflappable standards of vaudeville cannot fully prevent the briefest look of shock from troubling his face. Immediately, though, the showbiz troubadour gathers himself and speaks to the audience.

'And the winner is . . . Jethro Tull.'

Moments before, as the nominees were listed by the presenters, the camera fell upon Metallica. With just two acts present at the Shrine Auditorium – Iggy Pop being the other artist in the category that deemed the ceremony worthy of his time – the viewer's attention is captured by a manic Lars Ulrich, grinning expectantly like a child at the first light of Christmas morning.

As the winner is announced from the stage, the camera remains fixed on the podium rather than returning to afford the audience at home the chance to pity or savour the reaction on Ulrich's face. As for Jethro Tull, neither they nor their label Chrysalis accepted the Academy's invitation to attend that year's ceremony, convinced that they would not win.

Yet Metallica took defeat with the kind of grace befitting men who have been snubbed by a body the opinion of which they respected not at all. So certain were Elektra Records that their charges would emerge victorious from the Shrine Auditorium that the company had taken the trouble to have printed up stickers announcing the group as 'Grammy winners'. With a chutzpah that was fully irresistible, Metallica insisted that this notice be affixed to the packaging of . . . *And Justice for All* with the word 'winner' replaced by the word 'loser'. Just as delectable was Jethro Tull front man Ian Anderson's verdict on his band's unlikely coronation as kings of metal. Following the anointment, the group's record company, Chrysalis, paid for a full-page advert to run in the subsequent issue of the trade publication *Billboard*. Accompanying a picture of Anderson's flute lying atop a pile of iron bars was a statement from the front man which read, 'The flute is a heavy, metal instrument.' Elsewhere, when asked for his thoughts regarding the Shrine Auditorium rhubarb, the Englishman answered that Jethro Tull 'do sometimes play [their] mandolins very loudly'.

Rather than grieve over a snub made by a body of men and women – mostly men – that saw fit to award Bobby McFerrin's grandly irritating 'Don't Worry, Be Happy' the accolade 'Song of the Year', Metallica once more turned their attention to ploughing their own furrow. This they did with an eye for detail attentive even by the standards of the hardest-working of showbusiness troubadours. Despite having blossomed into the kind of act who could fill any indoor arena in North America, the band continued to hustle as if its members were unsure of the source of their next meal. The difference now was that they had swapped their chromium steel tour bus for a sleek private jet.

'It's nice to be able to make your own schedules and not be at the mercy of a timetable for travel,' explains Lars Ulrich. 'That freedom allows you to have time to do what you do in a day [and] without the plane it couldn't happen. Plus on this tour, we're not just doing the sixty-date arena circuit, we're also doing the secondary towns and then a bunch of places that no fucker's ever heard of.'

Propelled by jet fuel and a work ethic befitting men long used to making their own luck, the Damaged Justice tour saw Metallica stare into the mirrors of dressing rooms of such minor-league venues as the Cumberland County Auditorium in Fayetteville, North Carolina, the Buckeye Lake Music Center in Hebron, Ohio, and the Center Georges Vezine in the town of Chicoutimi (population, 60,008) in the Canadian province of Quebec. As if to prove to people who required no convincing that this was a union willing to exert itself to exhaustive lengths, each night the group would convene onstage for sets that would last in excess of two and a half hours. Offstage Ulrich would bibble into the recording devices of no fewer than eight different music journalists each and every day. If by this point the drummer was growing tired of the sound of his own voice, it was one of the few things he kept to himself.

'The theory behind [Metallica's work ethic] is that we didn't want to rely on radio or video to keep us going,' he revealed. 'So in true European style we decided to play every town that has an arena and [which] wants us. By the time this tour is over in the US we'll have done nearly 200 shows, so you're effectively letting people know all over [the country] what you do.' As for the toll such an approach might take on the members of the touring party, Ulrich was nonchalant, saying that 'I have to be honest about this and say that I think the whole "mega-tour" thing has been blown gloriously out of proportion. Iron Maiden – who are one of the bands that I respect the most and one of the bands that opened more doors than they [are] ever [given] credit for – are a prime example of taking a tour and going overboard about what a pain in the ass it is to play for a long time . . . You obviously have to take breathers here and there, a few days off here and there to keep it from getting too monotonous and to allow you to clear your head. But I haven't found anything objectionable about these mega-tour things as long as you take the right precautions . . . [But] we've shown once again that I think we can do this whole thing without depending on the radio [and] video medium, which to us is very, very important.'

This may have been so, but to those less indefatigable than Ulrich, the tour was tough. As Hetfield himself would confess, there were evenings where 'after all the hoopla-bullshit after a gig and everything' the front man would 'go back and sit in [his] hotel room listening to [his] ears ring'.

'I dunno, you sometimes wonder to yourself, "Just what the fuck am I doing this shit for?" When [the touring has been] going on a long time, you think, "Fuck, we could just go home right now." But there's always something the next day that spurs you on and keeps you goin'.'

Almost eighteen months after it had begun, Metallica's Damaged Justice tour drew to a close on October 7, 1989, with the second of two appearances at the Projeto SP in Sao Paulo. Returning home to the Bay Area, the quartet afforded themselves the time needed both to draw breath and to cast their gaze over the remarkable successes of the preceding months. As the sun set on the commercial cycle for . . . *And Justice for All* (at least for the time being), its creators were able to look upon not one but two framed platinum discs equating to sales in the United States alone of more than two million copies, plaques which Ulrich chose to hang on the walls of his home and which Hetfield did not. The pair also shared different opinions with regard to the amount of time their band would require in terms of shore leave: Hetfield believed that a period of six months' rest was needed, while Ulrich thought three weeks should do the trick. Unusually, the two men compromised: Metallica stalled their engines for three months.

As a new decade dawned, the band once more began to stir themselves awake. In a move that spoke of hastily convened meetings in corporate boardrooms, on February 21, 1990, the National Academy of Recording Arts and Sciences awarded the quartet a Grammy in the category of Best Metal Performance, for 'One'. This time, the band declined to attend the ceremony. Instead Hetfield and Ulrich busied themselves preparing the ground for what would eventually become Metallica's fifth album. As if upending a box featuring the pieces of a vast and complex and jigsaw puzzle, the pair began to listen to riffs recorded on cassette tapes in hotel rooms and backstage utility rooms since the first days of the Monsters of Rock tour.

With no album to promote, in the spring the group took the unusual decision to head back out on the road, thus beginning what has become a long-standing Metallica tradition, that of touring for reasons other than simply to sell what some in the music industry call 'product'. But with just eleven concerts on the docket for the whole of 1990, in terms of live appearances this was the quartet's quietest year since the days before its members had ferried themselves and their belongings north on Interstate 5 in order to make a new home in Northern California.

In May Metallica arrived once more on British soil in order to embark on a tour that officially comprised just three dates. But in order to tune their engine in preparation for a European excursion that would include appearances at London's Wembley Arena, Birmingham's National Exhibition Centre and the

Scottish Exhibition and Conference Centre in Glasgow – on May 23, 25 and 26 respectively – the group once again performed in the English capital under an assumed identity. On a balmy spring evening on May 11, those waiting in line outside the Marquee club (at this point no longer situated on Wardour Street but on nearby Charing Cross Road) to see a performance by Metal Church learned that the support that night would be provided by a group named Vertigo. Unlike Metallica's appearance at the 100 Club in 1987, the quartet's set at the Marquee remained a closely guarded secret. This, combined with the fact that Metal Church were hardly a household name, meant that the support band's nine-song set was witnessed by a venue barely half full.

The same, however, could not be said for Metallica's triumvirate of billed appearances in England and Scotland's only three arena venues at the time. And while in 1988 the quartet's show at the National Exhibition Centre had attracted a crowd of 6,000 people, by May 1990 an audience of double this number arrived to fill the venue to capacity. In suburban north-west London, Wembley Arena also placed a 'Sold Out' sign above its front doors.

For anyone gathered in these vast rooms, the sight was of a powerful, muscular rock band that looked and sounded entirely at home. Whereas on the main body of the Damaged Justice tour Metallica had shared their stage with a towering 'Lady Justice' – a physical representation of the image from the front cover of . . . And Justice for All (nicknamed, inevitably, 'Edna') – that would collapse at the end of each set, for the handful of dates commissioned in 1990 the band performed without recourse to any visual embellishments. On a stage adorned only with a symmetrical backline of amplifiers and the centrepiece of Ulrich's drumkit, the performers no longer appeared to be 'hairballs strapped with guitars' or boys with 'teeth in need of a good dental plan' – as had been the opinion of the St Petersburg Times, following the quartet's Monsters of Rock appearance at the Tampa Stadium – but were instead men who had learned to harness their collective power in a manner both efficient and economical.

As Metallica bid Britain farewell in 1990, a new process of simplification had already begun.

10 – NOTHING ELSE MATTERS

It was in an anonymous hotel room that Metallica's fifth album first flickered into life. On the road as part of the Damaged Justice tour, Kirk Hammett found himself occupying the dreaded hours between curtain call and sleep by loudly playing his guitar in yet another identikit bedroom – 'I was,' he recalls, 'all fired up.' To help while away the time, Hammett regarded the instrument in his hands and decided to try 'to write the heaviest thing I could think of'. In doing so, and in committing the result of this endeavour to tape, Hammett placed his fingers on the chords and notes of what would become the spine of Metallica's most widely recognised song, 'Enter Sandman'.

Lars Ulrich first heard these building blocks following his band's appearance at the Scottish Exhibition and Conference Centre in Glasgow on May 26, 1990. The chord sequence was just one of scores contained on a cassette known as the 'Riff Tape'. Fortunately for the drummer listening to this tape, the riff that caught his ear just happened to occupy pride of place as the first recording on 'Side A' of the home-made cassette. This first impression was not one that Ulrich would quickly forget.

As the drummer listened to Hammett's riff, his mind went to work. He was the one responsible for placing the component parts of Metallica's music into structural form, and he recognised not only the fact that a song equated to more than its central riff – a point of view not universally shared by metal acts of the time – but that these riffs themselves could amount to more than a sequence of chords repeated as many times as was required before giving way to a chorus. The piece of music submitted by Hammett, however, differed significantly from the song that would be presented to listeners as the curtain raiser for Metallica's fifth album some fourteen months later. Instead of a riff that was repeated three times and then completed by what is known in songwriting circles as 'a tail' – in the case of 'Enter Sandman', a sequence of power chords the crunch of which was accentuated by the palm of Hetfield's right hand – Hammett's original submission took the more symmetrical form of one rendition of the first part of the riff – *der ner, der ner ner* – followed by the tail. To Ulrich his band mate's idea sounded great. What it did not equate to, however, was the door-smashing hit single cum statement-of-intent that the drummer envisaged by the time he had pressed the 'Pause' button on his tape deck. But with an ear for song structure that was both pronounced and sophisticated, Ulrich knew just how to transform a fine idea into a song that would be worth its weight in platinum.

'There was something about this record [even] from the days that we started writing "[Enter] Sandman" that sounded like a motherfucker,' recalls the drummer.

Rather than pretend that the group was some kind of working democracy, in preparation for the recording of their next studio album, Metallica divided itself into two halves. Jason Newsted and Kirk Hammett formed one camp, and were placed on shore leave; James Hetfield and Lars Ulrich comprised the other, and this pair went to work. Flush with the fruits of success from . . . *And Justice for All*, Ulrich had finally bid farewell to suburban Carlson Boulevard and had relocated to a home amid the vibrant boulevards and suspension bridges of San Francisco proper. As befitted a wealthy musician, the drummer's new address included as part of its facilities an eight-track recording studio the space for which was carved into the rock of one of the city's many vertiginous hills. Metallica's days of soundproofing garages with pieces of two by four and rows of empty egg cartons were officially now behind them.

Each day Hetfield and Ulrich would convene in this home studio and knit together pieces of music. Whereas this job of work as it related to . . . *And Justice for All* was a process as complicated as locating 'the God particle', in the summer of 1990 the pair's approach to making music had undergone a deliberate transformation. In place of musical wanderings the technical specifications of which were, as Jason Newsted memorably put it, 'double-black diamond', the guitarist and drummer concentrated on two qualities largely unheard on their band's previous album: simplicity and groove.

'By the end of the last tour "Seek & Destroy" had practically become my favourite song in the set,' recalls Ulrich. 'It had so much bounce and groove [that I] could really just sit there and play it without worrying about when the next quadruple-backwards-sideways paraddidle came in.' Conversely, the drummer remembers that 'about halfway through the [Damaged] Justice tour I was sitting there playing these nine-minute songs thinking, "Why am I sitting here worrying about how perfect these nine-minute songs have to be when we play stuff like 'Seek & Destroy' and 'For Whom the Bell Tolls' and [both songs] have such a great fucking vibe?"'

One aspect regarding the material heard on . . . *And Justice for All* that has largely gone unexamined, is the physical and mental toll of playing these songs live. Throughout the sixty-five minutes of the group's fourth album, Metallica had gone to extraordinary lengths to make life difficult for themselves. Even by the standards of modern metal, passages of music such as those heard prior to the final chorus of 'Harvester of Sorrow' or at any point in the bewildering 'Dyers Eve' pushed the group towards the limits of each member's technical abilities. In addition this music then had to be performed to vast numbers of people gathered together not so much to hear a concert as to see a show. At the time the band embarked on the Damaged Justice tour, Metallica were known for live performances that were interactive rather than passive experiences, demanding connections both emotional and physical. The group onstage were more than performers, they were ringleaders. For the quartet to have appeared before their audience only to then stare fixedly at the fretboards of their guitars while playing ' . . . And Justice for All' or 'One' would have seen energy levels in the room fall to an unacceptably low wattage. That Metallica learned to project themselves to those in the cheapest seats of North America's largest indoor arenas while playing songs of fiendish complexity is an achievement for which the group has never quite received adequate credit.

'Halfway through the [Damaged] Justice tour, we came offstage one night,' recalls Ulrich. 'We'd just played "Blackened", "One", "Eye of the Beholder", ". . . And Justice for All' and "Harvester [of Sorrow]" – and we were, like, "This shit is fucked up to play." It was really difficult. Every night became an exercise in not fucking up – our whole purpose was not to fuck up. We just decided it was stupid. It was our first go-round in the arenas, and we were playing with our minds, not with our bodies or our guts. It wasn't physical; it was mental . . . So we were, like, "Enough of this." We'd taken that side of Metallica to the end – there was no place else to go with it . . . When me and James started writing [material for the group's fifth album] we listened to the Misfits, the Rolling Stones, AC/DC – all these bands that wrote three-minute songs.'

For Metallica such thinking amounted to a root and branch reform of the group's entire modus operandi. Everything in which the quartet had previously believed was placed under scrutiny. Musicians whose talents had previously been dismissed – in Ulrich's case, economical drummers such as Charlie Watts from the Rolling Stones and Phil Rudd from AC/DC – were re-evaluated, this time correctly. Whereas previously Ulrich had been so keen to establish a style that was different from other players of his type as to become the world's fussiest musician, in 1990 the Dane relaxed his grip and learned to place himself at the service of a song. In the drummer's new home studio, Hetfield proved willing to do the same, authoring a fresh batch of riffs more aerated and thus even more powerful than any to which he had attached his name before. Things that had previously seemed important were suddenly rendered impossibly insignificant. For all four of his band's previous albums Ulrich had taken a keen interest in the duration of each song – the implication being that the greater a composition's length, the better – to the extent that the running time of each track was featured on the back cover of every release.

'I used to be really proud of it,' explains the drummer. 'In the past we'd do a rough version of a song and I'd go home and time it and go, "It's only seven and a half minutes!" I'd think, "Fuck, we've got to put another couple of riffs in there." Now I'm not bothered either way.'

In time a number of those who would hear the results of Metallica's re-imagined approach to songwriting would conclude that the results had become corrupted by compromise and contrivance. What is odd, however, is that few of these people seem to recognise the contrivance inherent in the desire to write a song of as great a length as possible simply for its own sake. Within the strictly codified metal world, when a band states in an interview that their latest album is the result of their attempts to write the heaviest music possible, overwhelmingly their audience will regard this as artistically honourable. Conversely, were a group to announce that their latest LP showcases their efforts to write the catchiest collection of songs ever heard, noses will concertina with distaste. In eschewing convolution and seeking to focus upon simplicity of purpose, Metallica were viewed by many as being guided by commercial expediency for the first time in their career. But while it was the case that the new aerodynamic sound the band was set to unveil did play more easily on the ear than much of the material of the past, such a circumstance did not render the enterprise inherently dishonest. In fact the manner in which Metallica manoeuvred themselves from the corner into which . . . *And Justice for All* had painted them was as artful as it was natural.

In the late summer of 1990 Hetfield and Ulrich's new instincts guided them to assemble a fresh collection of songs with incredible speed. On September 13 the pair convened at the drummer's home and recorded rough demo versions of four of these new tracks. Joining 'Enter Sandman' on cassette were the compositions 'Sad But True', 'Wherever I May Roam' and 'Nothing Else Matters'. Just three weeks later a rough version of 'The Unforgiven' was committed to tape.

As the music on which Hetfield and Ulrich were collaborating began to coalesce into form, the search began to find a technician capable of assuming production duties. As was their initial intention in regards to the recording of . . . *And Justice for All*, the quartet desired to enter the studio under the guidance of a producer other than Flemming Rasmussen, but following the failure of their union with Mike Clink, lessons had been learned. Minded not to make the same mistake twice, Metallica instructed Q Prime to place the producer on a retainer while the group sought his replacement, just in case the Dane's services might once more be required to undertake a second salvage operation.

Oddly for a man who held in his mind's eye a resonant vision concerning every aspect of his band's next album, Ulrich initially miscast the man who would step into the role of Metallica's producer. Having been impressed by the crisp sound and low-end heft of two of 1989's biggest hard rock releases, Mötley Crüe's

fifth album *Dr. Feelgood* and *Sonic Temple,* the fourth LP from
the Cult, Ulrich discovered that the studio sessions for both
recordings had been overseen by the fabulously named Bob Rock.
Ulrich decided that this was a man who could be trusted to mix
the next Metallica record. Rock responded to this proposition by
saying that he would be more interested in producing the group
from scratch than entering the process at the mixing stage.

'Peter [Mensch] called up and said, "He wants to produce
you, too",' Ulrich recalled. 'I'm like, "Yeah, sure, we're Metallica,
nobody produces us, nobody tells us what to do." And then after
a while, like, we kinda got the guard down a little bit and said,
"Well, maybe we should go hang with this guy."'

So in the summer of 1990 Hetfield and Ulrich flew to the
Canadian producer's home in Vancouver to break bread with
Rock for the first time.

'We were sitting there saying, "Well, Bob, we think that we've
made some good albums, but this is three years later and we want
to make a record that is really bouncy, really lively, [and which]
just has a lot of groove to it,"' recalls Ulrich. 'We told him that
live we have this great vibe, and that's what we wanted to do in
the studio. He was brutally honest with us. He said he'd seen us
play live a bunch of times and [then told us that] "You guys have
not captured what's live on record yet." We were, like, "*Excuse*
me? Who the fuck are you?"'

†

Born in Winnipeg, Manitoba, on April 19, 1954, Robert Jens
Rock began his musical life as a member of the Canadian group
the Payola$, who scored a minor-league hit with the 1982 song
'Eyes of a Stranger' – nominated for a Juno award as 'Single of the
Year' by the Canadian Academy of Recording Arts & Sciences – a
track which also appeared in the Nicolas Cage film *Valley Girl*,
released the following year. With the group's commercial fortunes

on the decline, the Payola$ would first change their name to Paul
Hyde & the Payola$ – Hyde being the stage name of Paul Nelson,
the group's front man – and then, latterly, to Rock and Hyde, a
titular pairing of the outfit's two permanent members. But while
an accomplished musician and a capable songwriter, it was away
from the limelight that Rock's talents truly began to take off.
Employed at Little Mountain Sound studios in Vancouver, Rock
began learning his trade as a recording studio technician with a
position as assistant engineer. Following his promotion to chief
engineer, in 1986 the Canadian joined forces with his countryman and fellow Little Mountain alumnus Bruce Fairbairn to
record Bon Jovi's blockbusting third album *Slippery When Wet*
with Fairbairn as producer and Rock as engineer. Propelled by the
emphatic clarity of that album's lead-off single, 'You Give Love
a Bad Name', *Slippery When Wet* would smash its way across the
divide that separated rock and pop and make its way into the record
collections of 28 million people. And although in the Eighties Bon
Jovi were the subject of much derision from audiences partial to
rock music of a heavier mettle, no detractor was quite deranged
enough to suggest that the sound of the New Jersey quintet's third
album – as opposed to the songs contained therein – was less than
sparkling.

But it was with his promotion to the producer's chair that
Rock's most valuable asset became apparent – an ability to identify
each band's strengths and the capacity to harness these to create
the most successful recordings of their careers. The producer
was the perfect person to transport Metallica to the airwaves of
American radio – and from indoor arenas to outdoor venues. The
only obstacle that stood in the way of this elevation was whether
Metallica themselves possessed the courage to embark upon such
a journey.

Rock was no one's fool, least of all the fool of presumptuous
and self-satisfied rock musicians. The producer had been known

to listen to demo tapes presented to him by bands with whom it was proposed he might collaborate, and in the company of the songs' authors to press the 'Stop' button on the tape machine and bluntly ask the musicians if they truly thought their music to be of any genuine worth. A producer who believed that great albums were born of hard work, Rock was also notorious as a man who possessed not only a keen musical ear but also an equally industrious whip hand. Speaking to Metallica ahead of their proposed union with the Canadian, Nikki Sixx warned the quartet that under Rock's tutelage his own group had been worked 'like galley slaves'.

But as the producer met the most recalcitrant rock band since Led Zeppelin and instantly disarmed his guests with his matter-of-fact analysis of the disparity between their sterile studio recordings and their visceral live shows – an observation that no doubt stung Hetfield and Ulrich to the quick simply because they themselves recognised its truth – elsewhere Rock appeared uncommonly effusive. As the three men listened to the demo of 'Sad But True', Rock found himself unable to contain the kind of excitement he was normally well used to keeping under the counter. As Ulrich recalls, the producer exclaimed, 'Wow! This could be the "Kashmir" of the Nineties,' a reference to Zeppelin's 1975 masterpiece, the main riff of which is regarded by some as being the greatest ever recorded. 'He's saying all this stuff,' the drummer remembers, 'and me and James are looking at him and thinking, "He's listening to one guitar and one set of drums and a vocal melody that goes na-na-na-na-na . . .?"' (Hetfield's unusual habit of establishing vocal melodies on his and Ulrich's demo tapes by singing 'na-na-na' and adding lyrics at a later date explains fully the perfect balance of syllables in Metallica's music.)

As Ulrich and Hetfield flew out of Vancouver International Airport the following morning, the drummer reminded his friend of a conversation the pair had held with Cliff Burnstein in Canada earlier that same summer. Following Metallica's early evening support set to Aerosmith at Toronto's CNE stadium on June 29, the three men had settled down in the grandstand to watch the New England quintet's performance, just as Hetfield had done back in the summer of 1978. On this particular evening, looking out at a crowd of 60,000 people, Burnstein turned to his companions and noted, 'If we want to really go for it, we can take this to a lot more people. But that will mean we have to do certain things that on the surface seem like the same games other people play.'

'They had broken through to one level, but they still weren't on mainstream radio,' says Rock. 'When they came to me, they were ready to make that leap to the big, big leagues. A lot of people think that I changed the band. I didn't. In their heads, they were already changed when I met them.

'They were two determined individuals. They wanted to be the biggest band in the world and they were driven by that. That was the goal.'

'The idea,' admits Ulrich, 'was to cram Metallica down everybody's fucking throat all over the fucking world.

'We went all out because there was nowhere else to go.'

†

The Eighties and the early years of the following decade were a period that gave birth to the cult of personality of the record producer. In the Sixties fans of such fabled groups as The Who and the Rolling Stones would struggle to identify the names of the men who had recorded those acts' earliest vinyl outings. Even the pairing of George Martin with The Beatles was a union recognised most clearly in hindsight. In the Seventies the identities of the technicians who plotted the studio course of such albums as Pink Floyd's *Dark Side of the Moon* and Led Zeppelin's *Physical Graffiti* were unknown to young men who studied with

care each album's artwork on bus journeys home from the local
record shop. By the Eighties, however, teenagers who had no real
clue as to the actual role of the record producer – as has been
examined, often much of the credit afforded to this task should
be directed towards an album's engineer – were fully cognisant of
the fact that Rick Rubin had taken the helm of Slayer's pivotal
Reign in Blood album and Mutt Lange was the architect of Def
Leppard's expansive sound. In the case of Flemming Rasmussen,
as unassuming a presence and (in the days before the advent of
the Internet, at least) as remote a figure as could be imagined, he
was for the period of *Master of Puppets* and . . . *And Justice for All*
seen as being nothing less than the group's fifth member.

Despite there being little sonic correlation between the three
albums to which the Danish producer lent his talents, the notion
that Metallica might move their forces against Rasmussen struck
many of the group's supporters as being anathema. When word
broke in the news section of *Kerrang!* that not only had the group
done just this but they had replaced their erstwhile collaborator
with Rock, it caused a minor scandal. Great umbrage was taken
that Metallica were working with 'Bon Jovi's producer' (that
Rock had served time as Bon Jovi's engineer rather than producer
was a fact disregarded amid the clamour of angry voices) and not
for the first time – and certainly not for the last – the inference
in the statement being passed around in pubs and noisy rock
clubs, at places of work and at colleges and schools was that once
again Metallica were embarking on an adventure which would
ruin their music for those who purported to love it the most:
the fans. The most striking thing about this position is its tribal
nature: those who were most opposed to the union between Rock
and Metallica viewed themselves as owning the moral copyright
on the music the group had recorded to date. As with the owners
of a football club, Metallica were cast in the odd position of being
mere custodians of the art to which they put their name. More

than this, they were custodians the judgement of whom was not universally trusted. For those who bristled with suspicion at anything the group attempted that deviated from a norm the boundaries of which they themselves defined, Metallica were seen as being their own worst enemies. Even without having heard a single recorded note a sea of listeners feared that in choosing to work with Rock the group had taken all that was good about their music and had put it to the sword.

Such concerns naturally filtered through to the members of the fourth estate.

Each music journalist to whom Ulrich deigned to speak would ask, 'So, what is the deal with working with Bob Rock?' They would do so in tones that suggested that while the rest of the world were privy to this folly, the only ones sitting behind a stanchion were Metallica themselves. It was, if nothing else, an ungracious line of questioning. Though Ulrich has surely sat for more interviews than any other musician of his kind, and in doing so shows a willingness to talk about his band until every glass eye in the world has fallen asleep – even he appeared to be a little exasperated by the limited imagination of those to whom he was speaking.

'It's funny because everyone I talk to goes, "What's the big deal about Bob Rock?"' the drummer revealed. 'But it just seems like everybody sits around and works each other into a frenzy or something. Everyone in England's really freaking out over it. It's like, put some fucking valium in the drinking water or something. What's the big fucking deal? Don't people realise that this guy wouldn't be doing this record if it wasn't because we fucking wanted him to? What's the big deal? I don't get it.'

'Where does all this big fuss come from?' wondered the drummer in a rare rhetorical flourish. 'It comes from all the people who take three key phrases like "Bob Rock", "shorter songs" and "mid-tempo" and conjure up all these horrific images.

It seems like one guy says something to somebody who relays it themselves. It's the snowball effect. By the time it comes out, everything is distorted beyond belief. I should be used to the fact that Metallica and rumour always go hand in hand, but it never ceases to amaze me.'

'The fact of the matter is, Bob Rock's got an incredible ear for attitude and feeling. Now that we've worked with him on pre-production, he's got us kicking ourselves for not doing certain things sooner. Bob's convinced that the four of us playing together had a certain magic.'

While the heavy metal community agonised over the potential ramifications of the collaboration between band and producer, sessions for Metallica's fifth album began in earnest at One On One Studios on October 6, 1990.

'We knew that the parameters had changed for us,' says Jason Newsted. 'We had a big studio, big money and a new producer. We all felt expectations that we hadn't felt before. But no one knew exactly how things would work out.'

Whereas two years previously the quartet had gathered at the same North Hollywood facility to record . . . *And Justice for All* and named their work-in-progress 'Wild Chicks and Fast Cars and Lots of Drugs', their fifth album was given the working title 'Married to Metal'. As befits men living lives the details of which were not always subject to the highest specifications of moral scrutiny, three-quarters of the group found themselves thrown together in the studio at a juncture when their marriages were falling apart almost as quickly as they had been put together.

†

Lars Ulrich first met Debbie Jones, a young lady from Diamond Head's home town of Stourbridge, in a London rock club in August 1986. The pair had become 'good friends', the drummer revealed and had started 'hanging out'. He added that after the death of Cliff Burton the following month, his new friend 'came to [his] side' and had 'stayed by [his] side through some difficult times'. The pair were married in the spring of 1987 but divorce proceedings were initiated in the summer of 1990, just as songwriting sessions for Metallica album number five began.

Kirk Hammett had married fellow San Franciscan Rebecca Kestelyn in December 1987. In Bay Area metal circles of the early to mid-Eighties, Rebecca was almost as well known as her future husband, the reason for this being that she was one of the few female devotees of the nascent thrash scene. Their union also lasted no more than three years.

'I remember going to the studio [during the making of *Metallica*], sitting down in the lounge and thinking, "I'm fucked,"' recalls the guitarist. 'Lars walked in, same face. Then Jason came in and I'm, like, "What's wrong with you?" He just shook his head. I said, "Uh-oh, well for me, my marriage is on the rocks." Lars said, "You too?" Jason said, "I'm there also!" [Newsted would divorce Judy, his wife of two years, during the same period.] We all realised that we were going through the same thing, all within that five-minute window. Working so hard, partying a lot. We were all really young too, all in our mid-twenties. I think it's all right for women to get married in their mid-twenties because they're a bit more psychologically mature. Men in their mid-twenties might as well be sixteen.'

The only member of Metallica not yet wed was Hetfield. At the time that he and his band mates were compiling the songs that would comprise their fifth album, the guitarist was, though, keeping company with a young woman by the name of Kristen Martinez. It was Martinez who would become the muse for Metallica's first conventional love song, the opening notes of which landed literally in the author's lap. Absent-mindedly plucking at a guitar laid on his lap during a phone conversation with a friend, Hetfield realised that the sound emanating from his guitar held greater possibilities than the voice on the other end of the line, and hung up on his caller. As the sequence of notes coalesced into the now instantly recognisable form of 'Nothing Else Matters', its author declined to believe that this was a piece of music suited to Metallica's cause, a certain indication that his group's fearless sense of artistic open-mindedness often appeared a good deal more convincing to outside eyes than it did the members of its inner core. But certain in the knowledge that it matters not how one feels, but rather how one acts, Hetfield married this delicate new piece of music to lyrics the like of which he had never previously written. A sentiment such as 'Never opened myself this way, life is ours, we live it our way' may not dazzle with flirtatious brio or pulsate with sexual tension, but the words are nonetheless remarkable as representing a strident leap from Hetfield's natural habitat. More remarkable still is the duality of purpose of 'Nothing Else Matters' as a song that can be read in two different ways. The most commonly accepted interpretation is that its lyric is a paean delivered to a lover. The song, though, works equally well if one imagines that its sentiment is intended for the men with whom Hetfield shares the name Metallica. If such a subtext was intentional, however, it went unnoticed by the rest of the band.

'All I could think of at the time was, "James wrote a fucking love song to his girlfriend?" That's just weird,' Kirk Hammett recalled. 'James always wants to be perceived as this guy who is very confident and strong. And for him to write lyrics like that – showing a sensitive side – took a lot of balls. Lars, Jason and I were going through divorces. I was an emotional wreck. I was trying to take those feeling of guilt and failure and channel them into the music, to get something positive out of it. Jason and Lars were too, and I think that has a lot to do with why [the album] sounds the way it does.'

'When I went to write lyrics, I didn't know what the fuck

to write about,' Hetfield admitted. 'I was trying to write lyrics that the band could stand behind – but we are four completely different individuals. So the only way to go was in.'

If Metallica were changing the way they wrote songs, the same could also be said for the manner in which these songs were recorded. Whereas previously the emphasis had been on precision and technical proficiency, now the onus was placed upon such intangible qualities as 'vibe' and 'groove'. In search of this, the band had AC/DC's indefatigable and timeless *Back in Black* album as their creative template, a body of songs of such authority as to appear to have been made entirely without effort. Metallica would soon enough learn that this appearance was a trick, and the truth could barely lie further away.

Each day at One On One Studios the band would gather to practise together the songs they were set to record. Bob Rock desired that the quartet coalesce into a fluid and supple band rather than the mechanised juggernaut featured on the group's previous works. Seated together in the studio's sound room, the quartet would trudge through their new compositions, time and time again. Tempers flared as dog days became dog nights. On one occasion Hetfield was nursing a sore throat, Lars Ulrich continued to nag the front man to sing the song the group were playing ('The Unforgiven'). With a terseness some way north of irritation, Hetfield told his band mate that if he desired to hear the vocal line to the track he should 'go sing' it himself.

Watching Metallica stretch their limbs over the first few weeks of what would be a nine-month recording schedule, Rock might have wondered what kind of fresh hell he'd wandered into. In order to record this stubborn and sometimes fractious group of musicians, he had declined to produce a solo album by his friend, and Bon Jovi lead guitarist, Richie Sambora. Along with this, and against his better judgement, the Canadian had agreed for the first time to relocate himself from Little Rock Studios in

Vancouver to North Hollywood for as long as the recording of
Metallica's fifth album might take. Rock had originally decided
to sign up for the job when during a visit to the Grand Canyon
he had in the same day heard one of the group's tracks on the
radio (itself a rare enough occurrence) and seen a native American
teenager wearing one of the band's T-shirts – these two events
equating, presumably, to some kind of divine providence. But as
he surveyed the task at hand in the windowless rooms of One On
One the Canadian must have wondered what he had done. It was
not even as if the band that had hired him seemed particularly
grateful for, or even respectful of, his services.

'We really put him through the ringer,' recalls Hetfield, a man
that Rock quickly dubbed 'Dr. No', given the guitarist's refusal
to entertain almost all of the producer's suggestions. '[But] he
survived. We were testing [him] and shit, making sure that this
guy can drive the Metallica train.'

'It was the first time an outsider had been allowed into the
inner circle and there was some butting of heads,' recalls Jason
Newsted. 'The first weeks were filled with posturing – people
wanted to get respect and show their integrity – but when we saw
that Bob's ideas flowed there was more trust.'

Metallica, though, did not just have one new pupil on to
whom they might project their pointed but never pointless
brand of hazing – they had two. As work began on the album,
the group permitted inner-circle access to a second outsider,
this one armed with a film camera. In mid-October, with band
and producer still tentatively attempting to broker an entente
cordiale, Q Prime extended an invitation to twenty-six-year-old
Adam Dubin to meet with Hetfield and Ulrich to discuss the
possibility of documenting the recording sessions for a possible
long-form video release (a revenue stream often bafflingly
bountiful during the Eighties and Nineties). At this point in
the young film-maker's career, Dubin had co-directed just two

music videos. But despite a film-reel shorter than ten minutes in length, the two promotional clips to which Dubin had placed his name – the Beastie Boys' '(You Gotta) Fight For Your Right (To Party)' and 'No Sleep 'Til Brooklyn' (the latter track featuring an impromptu appearance from Slayer's Kerry King, who also played lead guitar on the track) – were among the two most requested videos in MTV's then nine-year history. As if this were not quite enough, the director came with a spotless reference from his former New York University film school room-mate, one Rick Rubin.

'My manager was Juliana Roberts,' explains Dubin, 'a very well-connected music video producer, and she and Peter Mensch had been talking: everybody knew Metallica was going back into the studio to record and the idea came up, from Peter Mensch, like, "We should put a camera in there with them" and Juliana said, "Well, I've got the guy." So then I got a phone call in October 1990 where Juliana said, "How would you like to film Metallica in the studio?" I said, "Yes, of course" and she said, "Okay, great, can you be in California to meet the band?" I said, "Sure, when?" and she said, "Tomorrow." So then I get a flight and Juliana drives me directly to One On One Studios, and on the way she said, "By the way, the band is not really sure they want to do this film." And I was like, "But I'm here to talk to them!" She said, "Yeah, you have to convince them that filming is a good idea." And I'm like, "Oh my God!"'

Before Adam Dubin could ask, 'What kind of merry hell is this, and how do I get out of it?', the young director found himself in a room with Lars Ulrich. Innately charming – especially to those he suspects might be capable of doing his band a solid favour – Ulrich chatted happily to Dubin about films and about Rubin, whom Ulrich (of course) also knew. The sense of security into which the film-maker had fallen lasted until the arrival in the room of Hetfield, who on this day had decided to wear his awkward hat. For a man whose sense of inner conflict and often glowering disgruntlement is of a size sufficient to be visible from space, Hetfield also carries with him an aura of quiet patience that, while begging never to be tested, is rarely discarded in the face of those he feels undeserving of his scorn. In the presence of fans who have placed food upon his table, the front man is almost without exception gracious and kind, even gentle; he understands that for such strangers the image of him as a man of worth is not something that should be regarded lightly. Even in the face of music journalists armed with a notebook filled with questions the inanity and repetitiveness of which would test the patience of a tour guide, Hetfield presents himself with an air that is as unflappable as it is laconic. These character traits, however, are qualities that have been learned rather than accepted as instinct, and have been positioned in order to cover his essential shyness. When the mood took him, or when circumstances required nothing else from him, Hetfield could be as disagreeable as the worst drunk in the worst bar in the sketchiest part of town. This was the sight that greeted Dubin.

'James is a great guy once you get to know him,' Dubin insists, 'but then, and now, he has this wall of defence up. If I was just a fan, he probably would have been really, really nice, but I'm not a fan. I'm somebody coming in here possibly to film, so I'm a working person now. I represent business. So he has his game face on, which is not necessarily a friendly one. It's a guarded face. And so he just kinda grunts a "Hello" and sits down in this chair that looks like a throne when he sits on it – kinda like the statue of Abraham Lincoln at the Lincoln Memorial – and he's looking down at me and I'm becoming microscopic as I'm sitting there. And it's just becoming more and more terrifying.'

'So now I realise it's game time. So we start to talk about film and documentary film and I go through explaining the process, how, like, we'd use 16 mm for the classic documentary look. And

I say, "What kind of lighting do you have in there?" And James goes, "Candles." And I go, "Okay, well, that doesn't sound like enough light" and he just grunts. I realised, at a certain point, that he's messing with me – like later I came to know that they do this, they haze people, they want to see what you got – so he was kinda being difficult to see if I could keep up. And I said, "I'm going to need a sound man, because if we shoot film you need somebody running sound, because film and sound are separate, not like a video camera where they're together", and he's like, "You need *another* guy?"

'The whole thing they keep talking about is the vibe: you can't disturb the vibe in the recording studio. Which, as a documentarian, I completely agree with. And I made a promise that I'd be like the fly-on-the-wall, that they wouldn't see me or hear me. But to James it still sounded like interference, it sounded like two extra guys in their recording studio. So James said, "Let me get this straight: you want to record us as we are, but you want to come in here with lights and recording equipment and cameras and you're going to have all this stuff, and that's supposed to capture the way we are without all this stuff." And I said, "Er, well, yeah, kinda." And at that point I just felt like the size of an ant, like, "Boy, I am not getting my point across here." '

It was with a certain amount of surprise, then, that two weeks later, Dubin received word that consent had been given. Thus began a period in his life that the young director is unlikely to forget. Instructed to pack his bags for a four-month residency in LA, it would in fact be eight months before Dubin was granted leave to return to his native New York. Despite being on hand only to film the often dysfunctional workings of the group's inner circle, Dubin's presence was greeted as if he were an inductee at boot camp – which in a sense, was precisely the case. At one point during his time within the confines of One On One the director recalls that someone in the band or their inner circle had brought to the studio a stun gun or Taser – 'one of those things that if you hit somebody with it they're going to go down into a pile of human jelly' – the purpose of which was not apparent. Not immediately, at least.

'One day I'm filming in the studio and I hear this electrical crackling behind me and the guys are cracking up,' continues Dubin. 'And I turn around and James was behind me with this stun gun. I mean it's within, just, an *inch* of me, and it's crackling away and [they] were just laughing. He *so* badly wanted to hit me with that thing. He just wanted to see me go down with my camera on my head. That would have been a big joke, and probably would have wound me up in the hospital for a week.'

For a band who in time would become celebrated for washing their linen on public thoroughfares, even in the early years of the Nineties this was a collective that did not cower from the scrutiny to which they were now being subjected. Neither, for that matter, did Bob Rock, a man whose counsel was not sought on the wisdom of bringing a film crew into the studio. Throughout filming, Rock exudes a quiet charisma and a sense of stoic humour capable of withstanding the mockery of the men he was attempting to shepherd. At an early stage of the recording process, the producer incurs the disdain of Hetfield and Ulrich following the discovery by the pair of an old twelve-inch vinyl record by the Payola$. As the members of Metallica regard the item, their attention becomes focused on a picture of Rock on the release's inner sleeve. Tousled and groomed in a manner entirely typical of a band performing the kind of radio-friendly pop-rock fare common in the early Eighties, Hetfield surmises the image of his producer as a younger man with the put-down (and stay-down) 'Bob used to be a woman.' Such is the clamour of both guitarist and drummer to mock their new producer that the line is barely allowed to breathe before it is smothered by fresh insult.

'The whole first three months of pre-production were very difficult,' recalls Rock with a equilibrium worthy of a statesman. 'They were very suspicious.'

'Our reaction to [the producer's] proposals was initially negative,' admits Ulrich. Elsewhere the drummer noted that the union between band and producer was an occasion where 'all hell broke loose', the reason for this being that Rock 'really started challenging us and pushing us and arguing with us and he didn't take any of our bullshit. It was tough.'

For Rock the process of recording Metallica took the form of a war of attrition. As happens in politics, he had been given the role of realising the art of the possible. The producer understood immediately that he would gain no traction in the field of musical arrangements. Rock, though, was no pushover, and even in matters where his opinion seemed certain to be ignored the Canadian still proffered his point of view. Occasionally the force and sense of the outsider's outlook was sufficient to knock holes in Metallica's brick wall, as was the case when the producer wondered aloud why 'Sad But True' was written in the key of E. Rock's recollection of the answer to this question proves that while he regarded Metallica as often bullet-headed in their sense of self-assurance, in his eyes they could also be loveably naive.

'They said, "Well isn't E the lowest note?" ' recalls Rock. 'So I told them that on Mötley Crüe's *Dr. Feelgood*, which I produced and Metallica loved, the band had tuned down to D. Metallica then tuned down to D, and that's when the riff really became huge. It was just this force that you just couldn't stop, no matter what.'

It is possible, however, that the producer may have mis-remembered this exchange. Metallica had already experimented with down-tuning their guitars at Sweet Silence five years previously, in order to create the lurching, dread-drenched guitar tones of 'The Thing That Should Not Be' on *Master of Puppets*.

Given Hetfield's technical proficiency, it seems unlikely that the musicians would have forgotten such a detail. One thing upon which all parties were agreed, however, was that the task of recording their new album was a gruelling job of work. While the demands placed upon each participant were significant, none felt the strain quite as acutely as Bob Rock. It was the Canadian's job to orchestrate the band's schedule, the movements of which often resembled ships passing in the night. Following years of living his life on the far side of midnight, Hetfield was discovering a taste for working during daylight hours and for sleeping during periods of darkness. In this, as in much else, Ulrich was his band mate's exact opposite. On occasion the drummer would treat himself to a power nap and emerge in One On One's recording room at two o'clock in the morning, ready for his working day to begin.

'James was pretty diplomatic about it at the time,' recalls Jason Newsted, 'but it was difficult. James was the most frustrated, and Kirk and I had to be there as a kind of support system.'

For anyone that has witnessed a band at work in a recording studio, the level of commitment and attention to detail required in such surroundings is revealing. Nonetheless, many albums released fail to reach the level of their own potential, and too often those involved in the making of such albums are aware at the time that this is the case. For Bob Rock, however, the squandering of opportunity and talent in the face of hard work was an act of sacrilege. For those whose efforts failed to match this standard, the producer was capable of scalding scorn. During the recording of the guitar solos, the producer's opprobrium fell on the bewildered head of Kirk Hammett. One song in particular demanded a contribution from the group's lead guitarist that required the unification of two often incompatible bedfellows: grandiosity and tastefulness. This song was the epic 'The Unforgiven'. To give the musician his due, Hammett had invested much energy in composing a guitar solo he believed would suit the ebbs and swells of the track's middle section, the only problem being that everyone who heard the solo hated it. As the guitarist fumbled and dallied in his efforts to conceive a suitable replacement, Rock lost his temper – if not his sense of control. 'Cut to the chase and fucking play, man,' snapped the producer. 'Now that you've warmed up, let's hear the fucking *Guitar Player* [magazine] guitarist of the year play.' Appearing both alarmed and not a little wounded, Hammett replies, 'All right', and with hurt at his fingertips performs in just one take a guitar solo the magnificence of which would be heard by more than 20 million listeners.

In making an album that sounded like a million dollars – and for reasons other than the fact that it cost a million dollars – Bob Rock bullied, probed and seduced Metallica into realising a version of themselves that swelled to its fullest parameters. In order to achieve this aim, the producer first had to plunge the detonator on years of bad habits. Surveying the rubble, he then replaced this construct with a more unified and purposeful whole. Nowhere was this task more evident than on the performance coaxed from the larynx of James Hetfield. With the exception of the uncommonly carefree 'Enter Sandman', Hetfield's lyrical contribution to his group's fifth album took the form of unvarnished truths concerning the human condition. The words written were not so much subject-led as they were driven by the kind of emotion its author would surely struggle to express in conversational form. Because these words did not come without cost to the man who had authored them, the producer understood that in recorded form such sentiments required from their singer a performance of authority, nuance and depth.

'The word "Bob" strikes fear into all metalheads,' was Hetfield's opinion, a case of many a true word being spoken in jest. 'But a producer isn't meant to make you sound like him, he's meant to make you sound like the best version of yourself that you can possibly be.'

This Bob Rock did with both patience and determination. With the emotional skill-set of a behavioural psychologist, in relation to recording the sound of Hetfield's voice the producer assumed the role of nurturer and surrogate father. In this the producer was aided by a blessing that arrived cloaked in heavy disguise. Following years of barking into microphones positioned both in recording studios and the stages of clubs, theatres and arenas, Hetfield had wreaked havoc upon his throat.

'I went to [a vocal coach] who was a cantor,' recalls Hetfield. 'I walked in and I was so scared. He was sat there with a piano. [But] I looked up on the wall and saw gold records for a bunch of other bands and I thought, "Okay, I'll give it a go." And he got my voice into shape. He gave me a lot of confidence.

'I didn't end up singing like an opera singer, which I couldn't do even if I wanted to,' the front man is quick to add, before concluding, 'I still sing like a sailor.'

With Hetfield's mind opened following his encounters with a professional singer, Rock expertly positioned himself in the thoroughfare of this slipstream and coaxed from the front man a vocal performance far in advance of what had gone before. Equipped with the natural capacity to carry a tune, the producer built the singer's confidence to such a degree that by the end of their sessions what had been recorded amounted to as commanding and assured a performance as any in modern metal. While managing to accentuate Hetfield's bite and snarl (at least when required), in the vocal booth of One On One Studios the vocalist had journeyed from angry young man to complex and multi-dimensional narrator. At least as far as the recording of Metallica's upcoming album was concerned, it was Hetfield and Rock's finest hour.

'I wouldn't be where I am today without [the producer's]

willingness to open my mind and push me further into different singing styles and moods,' is the front man's recollection of his long hours spent standing level with a studio microphone.

Slowly, exhaustingly, the album began to take form. Pieces of tape were cut and spliced together; yet despite these technical sleights-of-hand, the songs recorded carried with them both an organic quality and a volcanic force. Cleared of clutter, the recordings swaggered with a gun-slinger's groove and the bite of a rattlesnake.

Away from One On One – and Little Mountain Sound, the studio in British Columbia at which finishing flourishes were added – Q Prime were beginning to marshal their forces in Metallica's name. The organisation knew that the music industry at large held the band in patronisingly low regard as a niche group that had no commercial crossover appeal; Cliff Burnstein and Peter Mensch intended to fix this misconception in their cross-hairs and blow it to pieces. This emphatic repositioning would take place (poetically enough) in San Francisco, at a convention of America's regional FM radio stations. It was at this event that record companies would present to the nation's broadcasters their 'product' for the forthcoming season, a smorgasbord of sound from which each station would determine the order and nature of its playlists. Determined to prove to this gathering of programmers that in radio terms Metallica were about to become more than a faint blip on the edges of the radar, Burnstein and Mensch instructed Rock to prepare a snippet from the group's as yet unheard album that could be played at the convention. This trailer would last just sixty seconds, and would be comprised of the opening minute of 'Enter Sandman'. Prior to this, arguments had taken place between Ulrich and Rock as to which of the batch of new Metallica songs should be presented to the public as the album's lead-off single. The producer believed this nomination should go to the wholly unsuitable 'Holier than Thou', while Ulrich – who held in his head a vision of his group's fifth album before even a second of music had been recorded – understood as if by instinct that this honour should be presented to 'Enter Sandman'. It took just one minute for the drummer to be proved correct.

'Imagine the first sixty seconds of "Enter Sandman",' instructs Adam Dubin, who recalls the decision with resonant clarity. 'You have the booming drums and the riff building up and building up and each instrument comes in and it builds up into that first vocal, and it's *huge*. [The track] has one of the greatest [slow] building openings of maybe any song in the whole of rock. So Bob Rock spent a day or two setting the thing up and mixing it and then we sat there and listened to it. Just as a fan, as a person who loves music, I was hugely excited. I just knew it was dynamite. Whatever somebody's conception of Metallica was before that, this song was about to shatter that preconception. So they took that song away and a few days later we heard back that it blew the doors off the room when they played it: everyone went nuts. You just had to know you had a hit on your hands. So that was a very key moment when that happened. I remember that as a very significant day.'

Over nine arduous months in Los Angeles and Vancouver, as the band and their producer squabbled over single seconds of music, the two parties were united in just one detail: a shared desire to achieve greatness. In a space as shorn of natural light as a Las Vegas gaming room, Metallica had finally showcased the full extent of their sound and talent on a record capable of seizing the attention of the mainstream and leading it astray. But as the sessions finally drew to a close, creative harmony and personal enmity did not unite in anything resembling a Hollywood ending.

'It wasn't a fun, easy record to make,' recalls Rock. 'Sure, we had some laughs, but things were difficult. I told the guys when we were done that I'd never work with them again. They felt the same way about me.'

'In retrospect,' concedes Ulrich, 'the nine months we spent in [One On One] were pure hell.'

†

Elsewhere in the summer of 1991 the American public were being presented with a touring package that had all the subtlety of swinging jackboot. Featuring co-headliners Anthrax, Megadeth and Slayer, the forty-eight-date Clash of the Titans tour was the most punishing metal bill ever assembled. With its three main attractions rotating their position on the bill on a nightly basis – although in truth neither Anthrax nor Megadeth relished following the God-in-tap-shoes thunder of Slayer – the tour drew audiences of up to 17,000 people a night in cities from Seattle to Miami.

On July 14 the Clash of the Titans caravan arrived in New York City for an appearance at Madison Square Garden. The location was significant, for if the touring bands could be viewed as conquering revolutionaries, their presence within the walls of the Garden represented the storming of an Imperial Palace. Originally designed to stage boxing matches, since being opened in 1968 Madison Square Garden had become the site of a bewildering variety of events. For up to eight months each year the venue's floor comprised an ice rink upon which the National Hockey League team the New York Rangers skated on up to fifty-seven occasions. The same number of fixtures could be played by the Garden's other sporting tenants, the National Basketball Association's New York Knicks. On other nights the arena was host to a wide variety of concerts, with its most frequent visitors being the Grateful Dead and Elton John. Perhaps most spectacularly of all, each April Madison Square Garden is the site for a residency by the Ringling Brothers and Barnum & Bailey Circus, an extravaganza of such scale that each spring the Lincoln Tunnel (which connects Manhattan to neighbouring New Jersey beneath the Hudson River) is closed to traffic in order that elephants can walk to the most iconic of New York's five boroughs.

The appearance of Anthrax, Megadeth and Slayer at 'the world's most famous arena' was a cause for celebration for those who enjoyed music unsuited to a hangover. It was, however, an occasion that would soon be robbed of its fizz.

It was Elektra's decision to book Madison Square Garden for the world première of Metallica's fifth album; if the group required evidence that their record company were willing to go to extraordinary lengths in order to clear space for them at the very top of the musical food chain, this was it. But unlike the participants in the Clash of the Titans, the quartet did not perform at the grand arena. Instead the Garden merely provided the setting to which fans were invited to gather free of charge to listen to their forthcoming collection. Although James Hetfield believed it to be 'weird' that his band's album would play Madison Square Garden before the band themselves had graced its stage, the event was precisely the kind of grand gesture one would come to associate with Metallica.

With appetites whetted by the release of the album's lead-off single 'Enter Sandman' earlier that same week, on the evening of Saturday August 3, 1991, no fewer than 10,000 people convened on 7th Avenue in order to be the first to hear the fruits of Metallica's labours. Among this number were the members of that summer's other most celebrated band: Nirvana.

At 8 p.m. the Garden's house lights faded to black. From the darkness the opening notes of 'Enter Sandman' eased their way from the public address system and began to climb to the wooden rafters of the ceiling above. Standing in the wings of the stage, his eyes scanning the arena, James Hetfield admitted that he had never felt more nervous. But as row upon row of the venue's crimson and turquoise seats were tipped back to afford those gathered in Metallica's name the space to bang their heads, pump their fists and shred the fretboard of imaginary guitars, Hetfield exchanged a smile with Lars Ulrich.

ACKNOWLEDGEMENTS

Like many a crackpot scheme, *Birth School Metallica Death* was born in a pub. This location was Big Red, London's finest rock bar, situated on the Holloway Road in Islington. As we sat at a table crowded by empty glasses, the conversation turned to the possibility of two writers – one the author of *This Is a Call*, a best-selling biography of Dave Grohl, the other a working journalist of occasional high standing – collaborating over the writing of one book. 'Capital idea!' we both agreed. But about whom should we write? The answer was not so much staring in our faces as screaming in our ears: Metallica. If you're going to climb a mountain, it may as well be Everest, no?

Realising our idea wasn't quite berserk enough, we decided to raise the stakes. 'Let's write a biography that spans two books,' was the suggestion. 'Brilliant thinking!' came the response.

So let it be written, indeed.

The first volume of *Birth School Metallica Death* – a project that at times was more deserving of the title 'Breakfast Metallica Bed' – would not exist without the invaluable help of a cast of characters, all of whom provided their services with an uncommon degree of patience, and free of charge. The authors' sincere gratitude goes to Michael Alago, Geoff Barton, Chris Bubacz, Michael Burkert, Rachel Cohen DeSario, Paul Curtis, Malcolm Dome, K. J. Doughton, Adam Dubin, Jerry Ewing, Andy Galeon, John Gallagher, Doug Goodman, Bill Hale, Martin Hooker, Gem Howard, Lisa Johnson, John Kornarens, Bobbie Lane, Joel McIver, Bob Nalbandian, Doug Piercy, Ron Quintana, Xavier Russell, Patrick Scott, Brian Slagel, Steve

'Zetro' Souza, John Strednansky, Brian Tatler, Kurdt Vanderhoof, Joey Vera and Jen Walker.

The work undertaken by the indefatigable Scarlet Borg in sourcing and compiling the photographs that feature as part of this book's landscape has been both diligent and expert. It is for these qualities and more that Scarlet has been a colleague and friend for more years than either party dares to remember.

The authors are also indebted to a body of men and women who made this book possible. Our agent Matthew Hamilton of Aitken Alexander Associates acted not only as a superb representative but also as a good friend. As a man who first saw Metallica in concert in 1984, Matthew is also not short on bragging rights. Sally Riley from the same office protected us from those who would tap their watches and mutter darkly at a time of most need. On the continent to our left, our US agent Matthew Elblonk of DeFiore & Company lobbied on our behalf with sufficient aplomb that had we had day jobs we would have been able to give them up.

The authors can count themselves fortunate that this book has been edited by two men who have not just provided sound counsel, but are also fans of Metallica. Ben Schafer at De Capo responded to the testing of his patience with a level of tolerance befitting a man who opens up his spare room to visiting punk musicians. A standing ovation goes to our British editor, Angus Cargill of Faber and Faber. A most supportive and thorough collaborator, Angus's role in the gestation period of this book stands comparison with the work undertaken with Metallica by Bob Rock. Credit and thanks must also go to James Rose, Luke Bird, Anna Pallai and all at Faber for their invaluable input.

We would also like to thank our European editors, Henrik Karisson at Forma in Sweden and Kristiina Sarasti at Like in Finland. Our sincere gratitude is extended also to Paula Turner at Palindrome and Sarah Barlow, our proofreader. Their eagle-eyed attention to detail and pin-sharp text editing spared our blushes in more than one instance.

On a personal note, Paul would like to offer heartfelt thanks (and in many cases, sincere apologies) to the Brannigan and Kato families, the fabulous Sammy Andrews, Nick Knowles, Chris McCormack and Jen Venus, Ben Mitchell, Matthew Tibbits, the staff of *Classic Rock* and *Metal Hammer* magazines, and most importantly, my wonderful, beautiful, hilarious family – Hiroko, Yuki and Tyler – who rock my world each and every day.

Ian would like to dedicate this book to my loving and supportive mother, Kathy, and to the memory of my late father, Eric, who would hopefully have regarded this collection as being 'good stuff'. The author is also gravely in debt to the friendship of Dan Silver, Lawrie Edwards, Jonathan Winwood, Giles Ward, Sean Hogan, Wendy Ainslie, Alistair Lawrence, Paul Harries, Tom Bryant, Rod Yates, Tim Sledmere, George Garner, Dave Everley and Bettina, Fergus, Florence and Freddie McCall, all of whom were kind enough to offer words of support equal to anything available from the Samaritans. Special thanks go to Sylwia Krzak, whose patience in the face of a completion date that at times appeared unwilling to come down from the horizon remained unwavering.

A special mention goes to Ashley Maile: friend, colleague, comrade and travelling companion. A gifted and much-loved photographer, Ashley died shortly after this book's completion, an event that shocked and greatly saddened both authors and which continues to do so. We consider it a privilege to have known him.

The authors first interviewed Metallica half a lifetime ago. In the twenty-one years that have elapsed, we have found ourselves in the band's company on scores of occasions. Theirs is an operation that runs with a militaristic might, but it is also one staffed by courteous and helpful people in the name of a quartet the members of which are never less than gracious. Thanks, then, go to James Hetfield, Lars Ulrich, Kirk Hammett, Robert Trujillo and Jason Newsted, as well as Kas Mercer at Mercenary Press and Sue Tropico and Peter Mensch at Q Prime Management. A tip of the hat also goes to Dave Mustaine, whose candour and articulacy helped drag several of the book's chapters out of bed.

There is a select number of bands whose music resonates with a clarity and emphasis sufficient to provide the soundtrack for an entire life. Metallica are one of those bands. This book, then, is also dedicated to any reader who has made the group a permanent fixture of each waking day.

SOURCES

All quotations are taken from the authors' interviews, except as noted below.

introduction   the ecstasy of gold

'If Radiohead does it . . .' David Fricke, 'Metallica: The Biggest Bang', *Rolling Stone*, May 31, 2012

1   no life 'til leather

'That alienated me . . .' David Fricke, 'Don't Tread On Me: Metallica's James Hetfield', *Rolling Stone*, April 15, 1993

'I am so glad . . .' Mick Wall, 'James Hetfield: My Life Story', *Metal Hammer*, June 2009

'Everybody has sung about . . .' Metal Mike Saunders, 'A Dorito and 7-Up Picnic with Black Sabbath', *Circular*, September 1972

'Sabbath was the band . . .' Dom Lawson, 'Forever Blackened', *Metal Hammer*, May 2012

'Music was a way . . .' Terry Gross, 'Fresh Air', NPR, November 9, 2004

'I liked being alone . . .' Ben Mitchell, 'James Hetfield: Iron Man', *Guitar World*, November 2009

'My ear was developed . . .' Arthur Rotfeld, *The Art of James Hetfield*, Cherry Lane Music, 1999

'It was like "Who's this guy. . .' Terry Gross, 'Fresh Air', NPR, November 9, 2004

'We watched my mom . . .' Ben Mitchell, 'James Hetfield: Iron Man', *Guitar World*, November 2009

'We had no idea . . .' Pounding Pat O'Connor, 'Shockwaves', www.hardradio.com, 1996

'He is a sort of gargoyle . . .' Mark Kram, 'The Not-so-melancholy Dane', *Sports Illustrated*, April 7, 1969

'I grew up pretty quick . . .' Ben Mitchell, unpublished Lars Ulrich interview, 2007

'My dad had a room . . .' Dave Grohl, 'Musical Memories with Lars Ulrich', *Sound City* film trailer, 2012

'I probably travelled . . .' Steffan Chirazi, 'The Conversation: Lars and Torben Ulrich', *So What!*, volume 12, no. 2, 2005

'There was a tennis . . .' Ben Mitchell, unpublished Lars Ulrich interview, 2007

'Once *Sounds* showed up . . .' Ben Mitchell, unpublished Lars Ulrich interview, 2013

'All through the Seventies . . . Ben Mitchell, unpublished Lars Ulrich interview, 2007.

'Where I grew up . . .' Howard Stern, 'The Howard Stern Show', September 13, 2011

'I'd been there . . .' Jens Jam Rasmussen, *Forkaelet med Frihed: Lars Ulrich – og hans band Metallica* (*Spoiled by Freedom: Lars Ulrich – and his band Metallica*), Lindhardt & Ringhof, 2004

'Nobody in America . . .' Ben Mitchell, unpublished Lars Ulrich interview, 2013

'I'd been in America . . .' Ben Mitchell, unpublished Lars Ulrich interview, 2013

'Because of my last name . . .' Joe Berlinger with Greg Milner, *Metallica: This Monster Lives*, Robson Books, 2005

'I'd heard the single . . .' Neil Perry, 'Yikes! It's Metalli-Head!', *Kerrang!*, July 24, 1993

'Mötorhead were obviously . . .' Ben Mitchell, unpublished Lars Ulrich interview, 2013

2 hit the lights

'He was incredibly shy . . .' Ben Mitchell, unpublished Lars
Ulrich interview, 2007

'I was a rock 'n' roll rebel . . .' Dave Mustaine, *Mustaine: A Life
in Metal*, Harper, 2011

'My first impression . . .' Steffan Chirazi, 'Ron McGovney:
The So What! Interview', *So What!*, volume 14, number 2,
2007

'We were outside a club . . .' K. J. Doughton, *Metallica
Unbound: The Unofficial Biography*, Warner Books, 1993

'In those days no-one . . .' David Fricke, 'Don't Tread On Me:
Metallica's James Hetfield', *Rolling Stone*, April 15, 1993

'We had heard . . .' Pounding Pat O'Connor, 'Shockwaves',
www.hardradio.com, 1996

'It was our first encounter . . .' K. J. Doughton, *Metallica
Unbound: The Unofficial Biography*, Warner Books, 1993

'As soon as . . .' Thomas Kupfer, *Rock Hard*, June 2009

'That night, in a . . .' Xavier Russell, *Classic Rock*, November
2006

'We heard this wild solo . . .' David Fricke, 'Don't Tread On
Me: Metallica's James Hetfield', *Rolling Stone*, April 15, 1993

'I used to say . . .' Harald Oimoen, as quoted in *To Live Is To
Die: The Life and Death of Metallica's Cliff Burton* by Joel
McIver, Jaw Bone Press, 2009

'Cliff didn't take . . .' Harald Oimoen, as quoted in *To Live Is
To Die: The Life and Death of Metallica's Cliff Burton* by Joel
McIver, Jaw Bone Press, 2009

'We said, "Okay . . ."' Harald Oimoen, as quoted in *To Live Is
To Die: The Life and Death of Metallica's Cliff Burton* by Joel
McIver, Jaw Bone Press, 2009

'That term alone . . .' Dave Mustaine, *Mustaine: A Life in Metal*,
Harper, 2011

'Cliff was frustrated . . .' Anon, 'Cliff Burton's Former
    Bandmate Sets Record Straight About "Lost' Video",
    Blabbermouth.com, February 9, 2004
'It was then . . .' Jens Jam Rasmussen, *Forkaelet med Frihed: Lars
    Ulrich - og hans band Metallica* (*Spoiled by Freedom: Lars
    Ulrich - and his band Metallica*), Lindhardt & Ringhof, 2004
'After I heard them . . .' Pounding Pat O'Connor, 'Shockwaves',
    www.hardradio.com, 1996
'What bothered me . . .' Steffan Chirazi, 'Ron McGovney: The
    So What! Interview', *So What!*, volume 14, number 2, 2007

3 jump in the fire

'The first thing that . . .' *Nine Hundred Nights*, Eagle Vision,
    2004
'If there was any . . .' Dave Mustaine, *Mustaine: A Life in Metal*,
    Harper, 2011
'We started being more comfortable . . .' Mick Wall, *Enter
    Night*, Orion, 2010
'We sent them $1500 . . .' Joel McIver, *Justice for All: The Truth
    about Metallica*, Omnibus, 2009
'On the big continental trip . . .' Ron Quintana, 'Rampage
    Radio', KUSF, 1983
'Fortunately no one was hurt . . .' Dave Mustaine, *Mustaine: A
    Life in Metal*, Harper, 2011
'By now . . .' Dave Mustaine, *Mustaine: A Life in Metal*, Harper,
    2011
'It wasn't really working . . .' Ben Mitchell, unpublished Lars
    Ulrich interview, 2007
'My dad was somewhat of an alcoholic . . .' Ben Mitchell,
    unpublished Kirk Hammett interview, 2007
'I'll never forget my sixteenth birthday . . .' Ben Mitchell,
    unpublished Kirk Hammett interview, 2007

'I was abused . . .' Rob Tannenbaum, 'Playboy Interview: Metallica', *Playboy*, April 2001

'James and I have always . . .' Ron Quintana, 'Rampage Radio', KUSF, 1983

'He fucking sucks man . . .' Steffan Chirazi, 'Friends', *So What!*, volume 13, number 3, 2006

'Fuck, what the . . .' Steffan Chirazi, 'Friends', *So What!*, volume 13, number 3, 2006

4 seek & destroy

'The 'bangers out here . . .' Trace Rayfield, 'Metallica: James Hetfield – Lars Ulrich Interview', *Whiplash*, 1983 (via YouTube)

'We just have to be patient . . .' Trace Rayfield, 'Metallica: James Hetfield – Lars Ulrich Interview', *Whiplash*, 1983 (via YouTube)

'Our so-called producer . . .' Pushead, 'Metallica', *Thrasher*, August 1986

'As a twenty-year-old kid . . .' Jaan Uhelszki, 'Metallica Week: Kirk Hammett Interview', musicradar.com, September 11, 2008

'From start to finish . . .' Jaan Uhelszki, 'Metallica Week: Kirk Hammett Interview', musicradar.com, September 11, 2008

'I'd been all over . . .' Paul Travers, 'Kill 'Em All', *Kerrang!*, January 23, 2013

'We just didn't pay our bills . . .' Paul Travers, 'Kill 'Em All', *Kerrang!*, January 23, 2013

'Oh no, oh no . . .' Steffan Chirazi, 'Friends', *So What!*, volume 13, number 3, 2006

5 fight fire with fire

'We were very depressed . . .' David Fricke, 'Don't Tread On
     Me: Metallica's James Hetfield', *Rolling Stone*, April 15, 1993
'I'm sure I wasn't . . .' David Fricke, 'Don't Tread On Me:
     Metallica's James Hetfield', *Rolling Stone*, April 15, 1993
'It was my favourite Marshall . . .' David Fricke, 'Don't Tread
     On Me: Metallica's James Hetfield', *Rolling Stone*, April 15,
     1993
'It was only later . . .' Mark Putterford and Xavier Russell,
     Metallica: A Visual Documentary, Omnibus Press, 1992
'It was my first time . . .' Mark Putterford and Xavier Russell,
     Metallica: A Visual Documentary, Omnibus Press, 1992
'We decided that maybe . . .' Bernard Doe, 'Metallica–
     Lightning Raiders', *Metal Forces*, issue 8 (1984)
'We're as happy . . .' Bernard Doe, 'Metallica – Lightning
     Raiders', *Metal Forces*, issue 8 (1984)
'When they played "Fade . . ."' Brian Lew, comment on
     'Metallica: The First Four Albums – Fade to Black', www.
     invisibleoranges.com, July 20, 2011
'I instantly felt . . .' Steffan Chirazi, 'Tribal Elders', *So What!*,
     volume 9, number 1, 2002
'While only being twenty-one . . .' Steffan Chirazi, 'Tribal
     Elders', *So What!*, volume 9, number 1, 2002
'Cliff Burnstein who signed . . .' Bernard Doe, 'Metallica –
     Lightning Raiders', *Metal Forces*, issue 8 (1984)

6 creeping death

'The whole fucking place . . .' Steffan Chirazi, 'The Road', *So
     What!*, volume 16, number 4, 2009
'My original idea . . .' Ross Halfin, *The Ultimate Metallica*,
     Chronicle Books, 2010

'We have rather overlooked . . .' Malcolm Dome, 'Lightning Strikes', *Kerrang!*, June 14, 1984

'[It was] like an invisible . . .' Anon, 'WASP Interview', www.metaldreams.net, 2008

'Girls would come on . . .' Rob Tannenbaum, 'Playboy Interview: Metallica', *Playboy*, April 2001

'They enjoyed what . . .' Rob Tannenbaum, 'Playboy Interview: Metallica', *Playboy*, April 2001

'I'm always saying . . .' Brad Tolinski and Alan Paul, 'Black Sabbath Meets Metallica: The Heaviest Interview Ever!', *Guitar World*, August 1992

'are some of my best . . .' 'MTV Icon: Metallica', MTV, 2003

7 damage, inc.

'From a musician's point . . .' Dante Bonutto, 'Creeping Sensations', *Kerrang!*, December 13, 1984

'One of the reasons . . .' Sue Cummings, 'Road Warriors', *Spin*, August 1986

'That's when it kicked . . .' Mat Snow, 'Metallica: One Louder', *Q*, September 1991

'We pulled into Corpus . . .' Mat Snow, 'Metallica: One Louder', *Q*, September 1991

'On the news . . .' Beth Nussbaum, 'Speed Metal? Punk Metal? Thrash Metal? Don't Call It Anything But Metallica', *Metal Mania*, April 1987

'We think Ozzy is great . . .' Sue Cummings, 'Road Warriors', *Spin*, August 1986

'We told the management . . .' Pushead, 'Metallica', *Thrasher*, August 1986

''You break a leg . . .' Pushead, 'Metallica', *Thrasher*, August 1986

'The mass media didn't . . .' Jörgen Holmstedt, 'No Day More', *Classic Rock*, January 2005

'Frankly, no one was . . .' Jörgen Holmstedt, 'No Day More',
    Classic Rock, January 2005

'He just sat there . . .' Jörgen Holmstedt, 'No Day More', *Classic
    Rock*, January 2005

'The first card that . . .' 'Metallica: Behind the Music', VH1, 1998

'I saw the bus . . .' David Fricke, 'Don't Tread On Me:
    Metallica's James Hetfield', *Rolling Stone*, April 15, 1993

'I recall, in my . . .' 'Metallica: Behind The Music', VH1, 1998

'My parents were very . . .' K. J. Doughton, *Metallica Unbound:
    The Unofficial Biography*, Warner Books, 1993

'We thought we . . .' K. J. Doughton, *Metallica Unbound: The
    Unofficial Biography*, Warner Books, 1993

'I may have lain . . .' Rob Tannenbaum, 'Playboy Interview:
    Metallica', *Playboy*, April 2001

'It was a little . . .' Ben Mitchell, unpublished Jason Newsted
    interview, 2007

8 blackened

'You must be . . .' Simon Young, 'Jason Newsted', *Kerrang!
    Legends: Metallica*, 2003

'It was certainly . . .' Ben Mitchell, unpublished Jason Newsted
    interview, 2007

'I remember we'd do . . .' Erica Forstadt, 'Metallica: The MTV
    Icons Interviews', www.mtv.com, 2006

'At the time . . .' J. Bennett, 'Now the World Is Gone: The
    Making of Metallica's . . . Justice for All'', *Decibel Presents
    Thrash Metal Hall of Fame Special Issue*, 2011

'a Japanese woman . . .' Ross Halfin, 'Diary of a Lensman',
    Kerrang!, December 11, 1986

'a pile of puke . . .' Ross Halfin, 'Diary of a Lensman', *Kerrang!*,
    December 11, 1986

'The term "garage" . . .' Steffan Chirazi, 'The Biggest Garage

Band in the World', *Kerrang!*, August 20, 1987

'We never had . . .' Steffan Chirazi, 'The Biggest Garage Band in the World', *Kerrang!*, August 20, 1987

'To be honest . . .' Howard Johnson, 'Cliff 'Banger', *Kerrang!*, April 30, 1988

'Well to be perfectly . . .' Howard Johnson, 'Cliff 'Banger', *Kerrang!*, April 30, 1988

'I guess my best . . .' J. Bennett, 'Now the World Is Gone: The Making of Metallica's . . .*Justice for All*', *Decibel Presents Thrash Metal Hall of Fame Special Issue*, 2011

'But it never really . . .' J. Bennett, 'Now the World Is Gone: The Making of Metallica's . . .*Justice for All*', *Decibel Presents Thrash Metal Hall of Fame Special Issue*, 2011

'We were waiting . . .' J. Bennett, 'Now the World Is Gone: The Making of Metallica's . . .*Justice for All*', *Decibel Presents Thrash Metal Hall of Fame Special Issue*, 2011

'One time in LA . . .' Ross Halfin, *The Ultimate Metallica*, Chronicle Books, 2010

'For …*Justice*…, my . . .' J. Bennett, 'Now the World Is Gone: The Making of Metallica's . . .*Justice for All*', *Decibel Presents Thrash Metal Hall of Fame Special Issue*, 2011

'It's gotten so safe . . .' Jon Pareles, 'Heavy Metal, Weighty Words', *The New York Times*, July 10, 1988

9 the frayed ends of sanity

'We came offstage . . .' Ben Mitchell, unpublished Lars Ulrich interview, 2007

'Jason Newsted might . . .' Ben Mitchell, unpublished Lars Ulrich interview, 2007

'Those guys really . . .' Ben Mitchell, unpublished Jason Newsted interview, 2007

'It was amazing . . .' Ben Mitchell, unpublished Lars Ulrich interview, 2007

'Obviously there's some . . .' Elianne Halbersberg, 'The Justice League', *Kerrang!*, April 16, 1988

'Basically, at that time . . .' *Rolling Stone*, Tom Bryant, 'Flying the Flag', *Kerrang!* Legends: 25 Years of Metallica, 2008

'We were very much . . .' *Rolling Stone*, Tom Bryant, 'Flying the Flag', *Kerrang!* Legends: 25 Years of Metallica, 2008

'after that tour . . .' K. J. Doughton, *Metallica Unbound: The Unofficial Biography*, Warner Books, 1993

'You have to keep . . .' J. Bennett, 'Now the World Is Gone: The Making of Metallica's . . .Justice for All', *Decibel Presents Thrash Metal Hall of Fame Special Issue*, 2011

'To answer [the] question . . .' J. Bennett, 'Now the World Is Gone: The Making of Metallica's . . .Justice for All', *Decibel Presents Thrash Metal Hall of Fame Special Issue*, 2011

'It wasn't [a case . . .' J. Bennett, 'Now the World Is Gone: The Making of Metallica's . . .Justice for All', *Decibel Presents Thrash Metal Hall of Fame Special Issue*, 2011

'being drunk at three . . .' J. Bennett, 'Now the World Is Gone: The Making of Metallica's . . .Justice for All', *Decibel Presents Thrash Metal Hall of Fame Special Issue*, 2011

'It's the only record . . .' *Classic Albums: Metallica*, Eagle Rock, 2001

'I call [...And Justice For All] . . .' K. J. Doughton, *Metallica Unbound: The Unofficial Biography*, Warner Books, 1993

'It's not me sitting . . .' J. Bennett, 'Now the World Is Gone: The Making of Metallica's . . .Justice for All', *Decibel Presents Thrash Metal Hall of Fame Special Issue*, 2011

'I can remember . . .' J. Bennett, 'Now the World Is Gone: The Making of Metallica's . . .Justice for All', *Decibel Presents Thrash Metal Hall of Fame Special Issue*, 2011

'some friends of mine . . .' J. Bennett, 'Now the World Is Gone: The Making of Metallica's . . .Justice for All', *Decibel Presents*

Thrash Metal Hall of Fame Special Issue, 2011

'We never said that . . .' J. Bennett, 'Now the World Is Gone:
   The Making of Metallica's . . .*Justice for All*', *Decibel Presents
   Thrash Metal Hall of Fame Special Issue*, 2011

'At the time there . . .' Chris Cocker, 'Metallica: The Frayed
   Ends of Metal', St Martin's Griffin, 1992

'It's a complicated . . .' Chris Cocker, 'Metallica: The Frayed
   Ends of Metal', St Martin's Griffin, 1992

'We managed to avoid . . .' Steffan Chirazi, 'For Whom the Bell
   Tulls (2)', *Kerrang!*, March 25, 1989

'I remember watching . . .' J. Bennett, 'Now the World Is Gone:
   The Making of Metallica's . . .*Justice for All*', *Decibel Presents
   Thrash Metal Hall of Fame Special Issue*, 2011

'It was a new . . .' K. J. Doughton, *Metallica Unbound: The
   Unofficial Biography*, Warner Books, 1993

'Looking out there . . .' K. J. Doughton, *Metallica Unbound:
   The Unofficial Biography*, Warner Books, 1993

'It's nice to be . . .' Steffan Chirazi, 'For Whom the Bell Tulls',
   Kerrang!, March 18, 1989

'The theory behind . . .' Steffan Chirazi, 'For Whom the Bell
   Tulls', *Kerrang!*, March 18, 1989

'I dunno, you sometimes . . .' Steffan Chirazi 'D'Ya Wanna
   Sandwich?', *Kerrang!*, May 26, 1990

10 nothing else matters

'There was something . . .' *A Year and a Half in the Life of
   Metallica*, Vertigo, 1992

'By the end of . . . ' Mick Wall, 'If The Guy's Name Really Is
   Bob Rock, How Bad Can He Be?', *Kerrang!,* April 6, 1991

'about halfway through . . . ' Mick Wall, 'If The Guy's Name
   Really Is Bob Rock, How Bad Can He Be?', *Kerrang!,* April
   6, 1991

'Halfway through the . . .' J. Bennett, 'Now the World Is Gone: The Making of Metallica's . . .*Justice for All*', *Decibel Presents Thrash Metal Hall of Fame Special Issue*, 2011

'I used to be . . . ' Mick Wall, 'If the Guy's Name Really Is Bob Rock, How Bad Can He Be?', *Kerrang!*, April 6, 1991

'Peter [Mensch] called up . . .' Dan Gallagher, Much Music, 1991

'We were sitting there . . .' Jon Hotten, 'The Men in Black', *Classic Rock*, March 2002

'He's saying all this . . .' Mick Wall, 'If the Guy's Name Really Is Bob Rock, How Bad Can He Be?', *Kerrang!*, April 6, 1991

'They had broken through . . .' Joe Bosso, 'Metallica's Black Album Track-by-Track', www.musicradar.com, July 31, 2011

'It's funny because . . .' Morat, 'Pretty in Pink', *Kerrang!*, August 3, 1991

'The fact of . . .' Mike Gitter, 'Metallica Rock Out!', *Kerrang!*, October 13, 1990

'I remember going . . .' Ben Mitchell, unpublished Kirk Hammett interview, 2007

'All I could . . .' Rob Tannenbaum, 'Playboy Interview: Metallica', *Playboy*, April 2001

'When I went . . .' Rob Tannenbaum, 'Playboy Interview: Metallica', *Playboy*, April 2001

'We really put . . .' Jon Hotten, 'The Men in Black', *Classic Rock*, March 2002

'The whole first three . . .' *Classic Albums: Metallica*, Eagle Rock, 2001

'Our reaction to . . .' Jon Hotten, 'The Men in Black', *Classic Rock*, March 2002

'They said, "Well isn't . . ."' Joe Bosso, 'Metallica's Black Album Track-by-Track', www.musicradar.com, July 31, 2011

'The word "Bob" strikes . . .' Jon Hotten, 'The Men in Black', *Classic Rock*, March 2002

'I went to [a vocal coach] . . . *Classic Albums: Metallica*, Eagle Rock, 2001

'I wouldn't be where . . . *Classic Albums: Metallica*, Eagle Rock, 2001

'It wasn't a fun . . .' Joe Bosso, 'Metallica's Black Album Track-by-Track', www.musicradar.com, July 31, 2011

'In retrospect, the . . .' *Classic Albums: Metallica*, Eagle Rock, 2001

picture credits

BIBLIOGRAPHY

Berlinger, Joe, with Greg Milner *Metallica: This Monster Lives*, Robson Books, 2005

Daniels, Neil *Metallica: The Early Years and the Rise of Metal*, Independent Music Press, 2012

Doughton, K. J. *Metallica Unbound: The Unofficial Biography*, Warner Books, 1993

Eglinton, Mark *James Hetfield: The Wolf at Metallica's Door*, Independent Music Press, 2010

Hale, Bill *Metallica: The Club Dayz 1982–1984*, ECW Press, 2009

Halfin, Ross *The Ultimate Metallica*, Chronicle Books, 2010

McIver, Joel *Justice for All: The Truth about Metallica*, Omnibus, 2009

McIver, Joel *To Live Is To Die: The Life and Death of Metallica's Cliff Burton*, Jawbone, 2009

Mustaine, Dave *Mustaine: A Life in Metal*, Harper, 2011

Oimoen, Harald, and Brian Lew *Murder in the Front Row*, Bazillion Points, 2011

Putterford, Mark, and Xavier Russell *Metallica: A Visual Documentary*, Omnibus, 1992

Rotfeld, Arthur *The Art of James Hetfield*, Cherry Lane Music, 1999

Rotfeld, Arthur *The Art of Kirk Hammett*, Cherry Lane Music, 1999

Various, *Guitar World Presents Metallica*, Backbeat Books, 2010

Wall, Mick *Enter Night*, Orion, 2010

The following magazines and fanzines have also been invaluable in researching *Birth School Metallica Death*: *Classic Rock, Creem, Decibel, Kerrang!, Metal Forces, Metal Hammer, Metal Mania, MOJO, NME, Q, Rolling Stone, So What! Sounds, Spin, Terrorizer, Thrasher.*

BIRTH SCHOOL METALLICA DEATH: THE INSIDE STORY, 1991–2014

The second part of Paul Brannigan and Ian Winwood's 'definitive' Metallica history.

As they embark upon the fourth decade of their career, Metallica's legacy is as unique as it is remarkable: having sold over 100 million albums their status as the biggest metal band of all time is indisputable. Following the acclaimed first volume, which chronicled the band's rise to international stardom, the authors now explore the challenges and tensions that ensued for the band.

From the phenomenal, breakthrough success of 1991's 'Black Album' to the band's reinvention with the *Load/Reload* albums; bassist Jason Newsted's shock exit in 2001 and the group's subsequent meltdown, as laid bare in the unvarnished fly-on-the-wall documentary *Some Kind Of Monster*, to the divisive *St Anger* and *Lulu* sets (recorded with Rick Rubin and in collaboration with Lou Reed respectively), they brilliantly capture this extraordinary band's epic, louder-than-life saga.

Coming in Spring 2015

INDEX